Governing Time : Unlocking Powers of Times and Divinity
Adonijah O. Ogbonnaya, Ph. D.

Governing Time : Unlocking Powers of Times and Divinity
Publications Copyright © 2022, literature arm of AACTEV8 International
(Apostolic Activation Network) Aactev8 International1020 Victoria Ave.
Venice, CA 90291
www.aactev8.com

Published by Seraph Creative

ISBN: 978-1-922428-93-6

Library of Congress data

The English Standard Version (ESV) is used for all Scripture references
unless otherwised noted.

Editor Kathy Strecker

Cover art, Typesetting, Illustration & Layout by Feline Graphics
www.felinegraphics.com

GOVERNING TIME:

UNLOCKING POWERS OF TIMES AND DIVINITY

Dr. Adonijah Ogbonnaya

CONTENTS

Section 2 - Frequencies of Time and Space: Dimensions of Time in Ten Hebrew Words

Here I acknowledge with gratitude all who have made this work possible. Leigh Brentwood, Linda Lurie and all the staff at Seraph Creative, my publisher. Kathy Strecker for the editing. I want to thank all my staff Monique Tyson, Edward Johnson for all their labor and giving of grace. I want to also thank Taylor. I am grateful to Kevin and Carike Hall and Savantage for all the work put into producing this and other books. My thanks to my beloved wife and the church in Venice California, to all my students before whom these thoughts were first presented as messages.

I thank the Holy Spirit who takes the depths of the mysteries of God and places them on stammering tongues, revealing to our quailing hearts the things of the Father and the Son. I am grateful.

INTRODUCTION

The intersection of time and eternality was a well-known theme in the ancient world. All spiritual and social activities were located within the framework of time and considered to be conducting lines for the manifestation of other realms into the human realms. They can also be called apertures for capturing and holding certain eternal possibilities in place so that a human being with such knowledge may momentarily step out of the constriction of materiality and into the realms of the eternal. How time affects us and how we may be able to use its various dimensions for our breakthrough, and the transformation and calibration of our communal life together, is one of the major themes of biblical narratives. I am of the view that the various ways in which concepts of time occur in biblical narrative can serve as a creative spiritual technology for awakening and maintain godly consciousness. Times and seasons affect work and productivity in everyday existence, the material universe and even our material bodies. The vigor of our spiritual movements can be enhanced or lost based on how we engage and utilize time within its various nomenclatures found in biblical narratives. For much of us in the modern world, time passes us by or we merely glide through it, except for the occasional material boon that may come our way because we have temporally capitalized upon it. But per my reading of scripture, time is a multi-perspectival, multi-utilitarian, multi-spectral flow of eternity that affords those conscious of its divine power the ability to transform and transmute creation in all kinds of ways.

In this book we will learn about what God wants us to understand concerning the various concepts of time, as well as the different

Hebrew words for time. The Bible says that you and I have eternity hidden in our hearts (Ecclesiastes 3:11). Many things can block our access to eternity, making it difficult for us to have enough time. The only time that matters is the time connected to eternity where the flow is constant. In Genesis 1:2, the Bible says that the earth was formless and void which is *tohu wa bohu* (תֹּהוּ וָבֹהוּ). This is where the Spirit hovers over the waters and makes all creation possible. By accessing this type of time, you create continuous availability of time from within. By virtue of my relationship to Divinity, a technology resides within me that allows me to recreate and reconfigure time. This technology constantly makes available to me the time that it seems I may have lost.

God thought of everything when He created our being. If you want more time, go inside your being, and tap into the bohu (בֹהוּ). This is the place of emptiness (or void) in Genesis 1:2 and it is connected to the eternal pathway that God has hidden inside of you so that you can access the time that you need. Humanity is one of the greatest technologies in the universe. We are machines that have access to eternity through the way God made us and the consciousness with which He imbues us. This means that time should never be our master, but rather that we master time. The person who is truly creating at this level should be the one to create the portals for his life and portals for his death.

Of course, this does not include suicide. Suicide is a cowardly way of leaving Earth. However, people who know how to make use of time portals can make deliberate and prayerful decisions about how to leave this world. Those who enter into this arena will not die by accident. They can actually choose how they will leave the world on a certain day on their own terms. Time is the inhibitor of death. If you learn how to master time, you master your own destiny. God allows for this. In this book, I am trying to simplify this concept for you. To use time effectively, you must get to where time is no more. The best way to get to this state is to learn how to meditate. When you get into a state of meditation, time ceases. In this place you create greater leverage for understanding how time flows in and out of your being and how to use it. Let me give you an example from scripture. In Joshua 1:8, God said to Joshua:

> **This Book of the Law shall not depart from your mouth, but you shall meditate on it day and night, so that you may be careful to do according to all that is written in it. For then you will make your way prosperous, and then you will have good success.**

It was from his obedience to this command that Joshua developed the ability to stop the sun and the moon. The capacity for meditation and the capacity to control time are intractably connected.

God clued us in from the beginning. If you want to control time, if you want to rule on the battlefield, if you want to solve the problem in front of you, do it from within. Stop trying to do it externally. Go inside yourself. Get some rest. The problem is looking at you in the face. The answers, however, are not in what is looking at you. It is what is inside.

There is a very simple way to do this. When the Bible says in Revelation 10:6 that "time will be no more," it does not actually say "no more delays" as you see in some translations. The word used is *Chronos*. Chronos is the time that drags on. For instance, chronos refers to something that happened last year or something that will happen in ten years. The idea of removing the elongation makes that which is inside of you manifest at one time.

The word *zera* (זֶרַע) is the word for *seed* or *offspring* in Hebrew, and it is a word used for *time* as well. You must understand the importance of this. Every seed is an encapsulation of time. It draws the future into the present. The way it is used in scripture is always called sowing time, but it is translated as just time. So time is a seed in itself.

We will delve into even more mysteries like these throughout this book and learn to master the ways of this magnificent technology of time that God has given us.

~ Dr. Adonijah Ogbonnaya

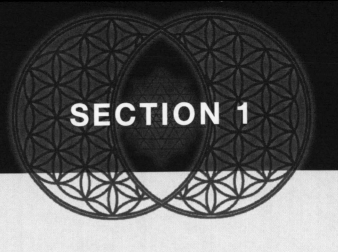

Preparing to Encounter Time: Decrees, Declarations, and the Transmutational Power of the Name

ישוע המשיח

Yeshua HaMashiach

Jesus Christ. Yeshua Ha Mashiach.

Who is He? We cannot talk about ourselves without talking about Him! Jesus is eternal by nature. I know you know this, but it is good for us to understand what we mean when we say Jesus is eternal. He is not just everlasting—He is uncreated and self-existent.

CHRIST:
THE INTERSECTION OF TIME AND ETERNITY

Why are we talking about this? Because it is important for your conception of time and space. If Jesus is eternal, uncreated and God, it means that **everything** exists within who He is. Eternity is grounded in what and who He is. If He is indeed the place where everything happens, it also means He is the aperture by which eternity becomes temporal. The Bible says:

> **For by Him all things were created, in heaven and on earth, visible and invisible, whether thrones or dominions or rulers or authorities—all things were created through Him and for Him. And He is before all things, and in Him all things hold together.**
> **(*Colossians 1:16-17*)**

He made everything, right? All things were made through Him, so He is both the origin of creation *and* the instrumentation. He is the glue of creation. All things co-inhere in Him and hold together in Him. The scripture uses two words to describe how all things were created—*through* Him and *for* Him. In other words, all creation is in Him.

Therefore, both time and space are in the person of Christ. Everything in the universe finds its mode of operation or its pattern for the way it behaves somewhere in Christ. Because of the duality of the world in which we live, sometimes we forget that in God there is no separation of what we call good and evil. In fact, God supersedes your idea of good and evil. When you sit around this side of the veil judging God and asking why evil things happen, you are judging from your perspective, not God's perspective. The human perspective is the worst position from which to judge God and ask, "If God is a good God, then why is there evil in the world?"

God is beyond 'good and evil' in the way we define it. Think about it. If God takes you home to heaven, did He kill you? It sounds simple, but it is a very serious question. For you to accuse God of murder is to subject Him to your own pattern and thought process. That is a very corrupt pattern because, if you were perfect, you would not even consider that a problem. You would just see yourself changing dimensions.

We use the word "death," but sometimes I think it is a misnomer because our idea of death is that something ceases to exist. It is a completely terrible word because there is nothing in the world that ceases to exist. There is nothing in the universe that ever ceases to exist; it just changes form. This is not a New Age concept. Your material body may dissolve for now, but we have the promise of our bodies being reconstituted. This means that death is not the end of anything. In simple scientific terms, we know that when a tree dies, the earth benefits from it, the worms benefit from it, and it keeps on living in everything that participates in life. I am using a very crude materialistic description here. When we think spiritually, however, it makes us wonder, if the universe came out of God and it came out as the Word of God and the Word of God is everlasting, then how can anything stop existing? The flowers fade, the grass dies, but the Word of the Lord abides forever (Isaiah 40:8). What is the substance of the grass? It is the Word of God. How then can the Word of God completely disappear?

He made everything, right? All things were made through Him, so He is both the origin of creation *and* the instrumentation.

If Christ is the space or the instrumentation that God uses to manifest Himself in materiality, it is God's inner technology that moves Him from the realm of pure spirit to the realm of manifest materiality where we can touch Him and taste Him. So Jesus Christ is God's inner technology. He is the aspect of Divinity that allows God to become visible, touchable, huggable, and kissable. Remember, the universe is a manifestation of a *part* of God—

it is *not* God. Yet you cannot have the universe without God being present at a certain level in the universe. Nothing can exist without some force, some form of God's power distilling itself into the material things of creation.

When God speaks, there is a refracting, distillation process where it goes from pure spirit to materiality. The word of God adjusts itself to everything in the universe. The word of God adjusts itself to everything it wants to manifest. The word of God, or the Spirit of God, or the breath of God must diminish itself and adjust itself to the nature of what carries it. God is not equally present everywhere, but He is present everywhere. Think of it this way. The amount or measure of divine word that framed your being would destroy a worm and make the worm non-existent because a worm cannot handle that level of power. The word adjusts itself accordingly. It adjusts itself to the amoeba, yet it still contains the word of God. Nothing exists without His word, even if you do not like it. Even a cockroach is a distillation of the word of God. So then, your idea of what is ugly is not God's idea of what is ugly.

We must deal with this issue. It is true that we have allowed certain things to come into existence that God will not accept as part of Him. This is because we have produced these things out of a distillation of the word of God. In fact, it is a part of man's punishment to suffer the consequences when he uses his breath and the word of God to produce things that are not consistent with God's character. There may actually be creatures on earth that are not God's direct intention, but have been created by human beings through this distillation process, even though they stand against God's original divine purpose. This is also the origin of sickness. God did not create sickness. It came through the way man has distilled the word and allowed it to flow through us that produces certain things that are inconsistent with the character of God. However, when God sends His word, He does not withdraw it until it fulfills the purpose for which He created it. When it is given, it is not only for God to use, but for everyone who encounters it so that they can distill it according to their will and according to the context in which they find themselves.

You would be amazed how you can distill the word of God into your context and create things that are not His will. When God releases the word, it becomes a servant to the context in which it was spoken. Remember the Bible says:

Therefore, just as sin came into the world through one man, and death through sin, and so death spread to all men because all sinned—for sin indeed was in the world before the law was given, but sin is not counted where there is no law. (*Hebrews 5:12-13*)

Death came into the world by man! It did not come by God. It came by man. It was non-existent. Man, by the way he related to the word of God, distilled it in such a way as to cause death in creation. That is a hard one for you, but the fact is there would be no death in the world without man. The Bible says that by one man, sin came into the world, and through sin came death. It does not say it came into the world by God. I want you to look closely at the text.

Therefore, as one trespass led to condemnation for all men, so one act of righteousness leads to justification and life for all men. For as by the one man's disobedience the many were made sinners, so by the one man's obedience the many will be made righteous. (*Hebrews 5:18-19*)

Also by one man, righteousness came into the world and spread to all. It is very important that you look at that text. So the word of God is a life-giving principle, yet it can also be a death-giving principle depending on how it is distilled upon the earth. Remember, it was how humanity received the word of God that caused death to come in. What did God say to Adam in the garden?

...but of the tree of the knowledge of good and evil you shall not eat, for *in the day that you eat of it you shall surely die*. (*Genesis 2:17*) **[Emphasis added]**

In Hebrew, "you shall surely die" is môt tamût (מְוֹת תָּמֻת). In other words, it means in the day you eat this you will die, you will continue to die, and you will keep dying until you die. So, God did not release death; He said this is what will happen. The way you relate to the word of God either releases life or releases death. We often say that the word of God only releases life. Not really! Even when Moses talked to the Israelites, he urged the people to choose life (Deuteronomy 30:15-19). Choose life. Incline your will towards life.

Now you can see that the will of man is the foundation of life and death. The way you structure your will determines the way you distill the word from heaven into life on this earth or whether you distill it into death. We are not going to talk about all the modern day prophetic that is really a distillation of death. That is what it is. What else are you distilling? Because people have bad will, they are distilling death and then they are praising themselves because they spoke a destructive word to people.

Jesus Christ, the Son of God, is the epitome of how the word of God is intended to be distilled in this world and how His will is to be manifested in creation. It is distilled into life by the process of an intentional good will that has been developed to such an extent that it understands how to submit itself to God. In submitting itself to God, this intentional good will allows the word of God to flow through it to cause life to other people. If that the will is in rebellion against God, it will still receive the word of God, but it will distill it towards death because the word of God is not going to turn back. The word will produce either life or death, depending on how the will receives it.

Because Christ is the will of God, He becomes the space for the distillation of pure spiritual divinity that flows way down into the most common microbe in the universe. There is nothing really in the universe that is not useful. Just because you have not discovered it does not mean it is terrible. Remember, the way our will relates to anything is how it distills life or death. There is a fish in the ocean called a stone fish. A stone fish never attacks anybody.

...you can distill the word of God into your context and create things that are not His will.

19

CHRIST: THE INTERSECTION OF TIME AND ETERNITY

It carries a high level of toxin in its spine, but it never attacks anything. The only time the toxin goes into your system is when you step on it. The more you step on it, the more the toxin shoots into your system. We may think that it is evil, but how is it evil if you are the one who stepped on it and it is only protecting itself? We have to figure out what it is doing. The stone fish is a cleaner. It eats things in the ocean to clean it up so the toxin goes into its system. It is very useful for the ocean, but if it hurts one person, we say it is evil and wonder why God would make such a thing. God knew you were going to make a mess in the world. All the toxins you put in the earth need to go somewhere, so he created creatures that can take toxins into themselves and survive.

As a side note, that is why Jews do not eat crabs because all of the junk will go into them. You know, I do not believe in all that. Any messianic person trying to force you not to eat something because they believe you are disobeying the law of God has not come into the reality of grace in the Jewish law. People do not realize that there is grace in the law, and that is why Jews have not kept the law one day in their lives. They have kept some laws, but they have never kept all of them ever, yet they are still here. Why could Moses go in and out of the presence of God and no one else could? He is the one who consecrated Aaron, yet Aaron, who was a high priest, could not go into the Holy of Holies without blood. Moses could go in and out when he wanted. Moses knew something that Aaron and all those people did not know or understand. He knew a level of grace that even led to the point of being able to challenge God face to face. If Aaron had done that, he would have died in the presence. God would have taken him home. In all the plagues, nothing happened to Moses. He did not need to make any sacrifice to go into the presence of God; there is not one place in scripture where Moses made a sacrifice to go into the presence of God. His sacrifice was different. He could go in any time he wanted. In other words, you had two priesthoods operating in Israel at the same time. Moses was operating under the Melchizedek priesthood while Aaron was operating under a shadow of what Moses was already living in. This is incredible!

Let us come back to our Master and Lord. If He is the heart of God then He is the will of God. He is the person in heaven who is the reflection of the divine will. It must have been difficult for Christ to come to earth with a human will. When He was on earth, Christ had to learn how to subject His will to the will and intention that He was in the mind of the Father before He came to earth. The Bible says He learned obedience through what He suffered (Hebrews 5:8). Obedience is a matter of will. A forced obedience is not obedience. At my Sunday school, we had a child were the teacher said, "Sit down Jonny." Jonny said, "No!" The teacher said again, "Sit down, Jonny!", and Jonny said, "No! You cannot make me sit down!" The teacher said, "I can make you sit down." Then the teacher pulled him up, put him on the chair, and said, "What do you think now?" Jonny replied, "Yes, outside I'm sitting down, but inside I'm standing up." You get the point. Real obedience comes from the free will.

I once read where an author said that free will means humanity has autonomy to wreak havoc, run amok in creation, and become extremely individualistic. That is not true. Free will that submits itself to God creates a greater connection with everything than when behavior is forced and mechanical in its actions. The very presence of consciousness enriches Divinity. There is something God does not have—it is you and your will, and He will not take it by force. Otherwise, our Gospel is useless. Why not just force people to turn to Christianity? Coercion has never worked with Christians. Christians have never been able to completely force people to become Christians. When they tried it, it did not work. Christians always revert to asking, "Would you give your life?" They inherently understand through Christ that obedience is a matter of the will.

Our Master, Jesus Christ, carries the space of creation within Himself. It took the will of the Son of God to redeem the world. Don't you think it also took the submission of His will in eternity to allow Him to be used as an instrument of creation? So the actual space of creation is in the will of the Son. Willfully giving Himself as the instrument of the

> The Bible says He learned obedience through what He suffered.

divine process for manifestation makes Him that very space. Now He is eternity. The word "space" is not apropos when referring to eternity because there is no such thing as eternal space. Space has boundaries which are also expansive and porous. For these boundaries of creation to exist and be solid and be touchable, it was first created within the space of the Son of God Himself. He is the one who gives everything its bounds. A stone is a stone because it is identified by its boundaries and its form. A tree is a tree because it occupies a specific space. I am not just talking about space in space; I am talking about the structure of the thing. It cannot be a tree and be the way it is unless there is an original intent of the structure and space that it occupies. Creation was created with a boundary around it. It was allowed to expand itself within the context of the Son of God and within the context of God. It has a boundary, yet through the boundary it is expansive. It sounds contradictory to say creation has a boundary, and it does not have a boundary. Let me put it another way. Creation has a boundary for its own development and growth, but it does not have a boundary for where it can go.

> ... the molecules of your body are moving in the person of Christ, and their movement around each other is based on the structure of the Son of God

For human beings, our physical boundary is our body. However, a human body is not a boundary as to how far human beings can develop in the universe. So the special structure in which a man finds himself, the boundary of his physical body, is held together by the space of Christ around the molecular structures of his body. This means that the things that makes your cells bind together is created by the very presence of the space in which they are moving— the person of Jesus Christ. The scripture says "He holds all things together." That means that the molecules of your body are moving in the person of Christ, and their movement around each other is based on the structure of the Son of God. He is the determiner of the space in which everything exists and moves. They are held together by the ubiquity of His being.

Nature cannot give up its secrets to you if you do not have a strong enough will to work nature. Many scientists will sit in a room for twenty years working on something. You cannot do that without a strong will. If you do not have a strong will, you will give up. Where do these people get their tenacity? Think of the researcher who deciphered the shroud of Turin. How many years did it take him? Fifty years! And yet there are Pentecostals who say he is not a Christian. As a Christian, how long have you given to what you want to produce? Or are you looking for magic? This researcher stayed on task for fifty years! He started in the 1960's and it has only been a few years ago that he brought out what he deciphered so you and I can have understanding.

The will is a powerful thing. It is the instrument for the manifestation of that which is in the spirit realm into the physical world, and it is also controls your physical and emotional structure. What do sometimes we say when somebody dies? We say they lost the will to live! We actually express our understanding of the will in common language. We also see people who do not die because they have a will to live. I want you to understand that your will is the determiner of space and time. A will submitted to God is in charge of space and time. Remember, I do not believe space is infinite. I believe space can develop in infinite dimensions. For me, the special principle is the space a thing occupies or functions in allows it to bring forth its purpose in creation. However, to be able to fulfill its purpose, it must reach beyond itself. We have two concepts of space. We have the one that is immediate and touchable, like a bottle. The structure of a bottle allows whatever is in the bottle to occupy the bottle. Yet the bottle is only an instrument. There is liquid in this bottle. If I open the bottle, the liquid in it can actually seep into the universe. It is not bound by the physical composition of the bottle.

The human body is different. The human body is not just a vessel or an object that the soul occupies. In fact, the human body itself is dynamic in nature because every cell within it communicates beyond itself to another dimension. When God saves you and Christ comes into you, He begins to work on your body. Baptism, biblical teaching, praying in tongues—all these things work together to restore your body's frequency so the universe can know (remember!) who you are. When you become a believer who has received Jesus Christ, the universe /

multi-verse can actually sense the frequency of your being. Remember, I am talking about Christ and you. If the universe is created by virtue of the will of the person of Christ through the Father, the Father created the world. This is Christian theology 101 because the Father and Son and the Spirit are one. Therefore, when the Father creates, the Son also creates.

> **In the beginning was the Word, and the Word was with God, and the Word was God. He was in the beginning with God. All things were made through him, and without him was not anything made that was made. In him was life, and the life was the light of men. The light shines in the darkness, and the darkness has not overcome it. (*John 1:1-5*)**

This entire passage describes the idea that one person in the godhead subjected Himself to be a manifestation of the general will of the Trinity into the world. He became the focus of the laser principle of the intent of God's mind that pre-created the first point in creation. Let us think about it this way. This image is the Vesica Piscis:

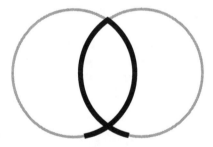

You will recognize this as the symbol of Christ. Do you think the church was making a mistake when it put Christ at the center? The following image is the Christian fish, which is called "Ichthus." Again, I am sure you are familiar with this symbol. You have seen the fish on banners and in every type of church: Anglican, Methodist, Presbyterian, Pentecostal, etc. They all have it. It is right in front of you, but you do not know what it is. Yet you have seen this all your life.

"Jesus Christ, Son of God, Savior"

Iota (i) is the first letter of Iēsous ('Ιησοῦς), Greek for "Jesus."

Chi (ch) is the first letter of Christos (Χριστός), Greek for "Christ."

Theta (th) is the first letter of Theou (Θεου), Greek for "God's."

Upsilon (y) is the first letter of (h)uios (Υιός), Greek for "Son."

Sigma (s) is the first letter of sōtēr (Σωτήρ), Greek for "Savior."

You probably do not know this from your scripture, but Joshua was also called the son of the fish. Who was Joshua? He was the son of Nun which means "fish" in Aramaic. Jesus is called the son of a fish. Jesus is at the point of the circle as you can see in the overlapping circles above.

From this point, the firmament and frequency of everything in creation goes in a spiraling motion. It is the Fibonacci Sequence. Frequencies do not go in straight lines. In fact, there are no straight lines in nature. Everything in nature bounces back on itself and other things. Nature moves in the context of life and light because in Him there is life and His life is the light of men (John 1:4). Everything in the universe bounces in the frequency of light. It does not matter what it is, even the devil must mimic light to continue to exist. He appears as an angel of light. We know that it is stolen light, but who gives him the light? Who allows him to appear as an angel of light? The same person *is* the light. You need to come to terms with this reality. There is nothing in the universe that does not answer to your Master and Lord. There is nothing in the universe that does not answer to your God. The foundation and the basis of creation are illustrated at the point in this symbol where Christ is at the point of the circle. If it is the case that you participate in this

CHRIST: THE INTERSECTION OF TIME AND ETERNITY

intersection of worlds, which is the womb of creation, and your will is aligned with God, then you are directly connected to the person of Christ who is the primordial and creative will of God made manifest. If you are connected in this place, it also means that there is nothing in the universe that is not subject to you.

So if everything is subject to you, then what is the issue? The issue again is training your will to make sure that you are not doing things just because you can. It is a dangerous statement to make to people who are looking for power, but it is a true statement. Now the responsibility rests on you to structure your life according to the pattern of Christ, through the submission of your will directly to the will of the Father. In this way, the universe that is even now subject to you will be subject to you based on your inter-connection with Divinity. The universe is not subject to you so far in the world which we live. We have forced the universe to subject itself to us, and as a result, we have created death. Again, that is a distillation of the word of God through the will that is bad will. Bad will creates death in the midst of life.

Let us say, for a moment, that our will is perfectly aligned with God and we know it is good will because the way God created the universe was "very good" (Genesis 1:31). Let us say that we all believe there is no death, no destruction, no destructive radiation of the sun, no lunacy from the moon, no striking from the stars of the heavens against men because everything operates based on a conjunction of will. The universe currently operates in many destructive ways (like earthquakes and hurricanes) because of man, not because of God. However, if we can find a way to connect our will directly to God, we could stop playing church and do a lot to change the world. The reason that we are unable to change anything and we are surrounded by chaos (which we call spirituality) is our actions are not drawn from the alignment of our will with Divinity. I keep saying it: I love my African brothers and all Africans, but instead of growing into the fullness of their own spirituality, they have taken on a lot of white people's mess and description of who they are to create and distill the word of God into death within their own context. Christians have done the same thing to Europe, constantly distilling the word of God towards destruction. We are doing it to America too. We are distilling the word of life that came to us through a bad will and it is creating death and destruction.

The first people to leave cities when crime is supposedly on the rise are Christians. They move to the suburbs to make sure that the evil does not touch them because they run away from evil. Christians think if they build a good house in the suburbs then evil will never come close to them. Do you realize that this very action itself is the will that bends and distills the word of God towards evil and the perpetuation of evil? You do not believe that your good will can change the context where you find yourself. I am not saying if God calls you that you should not do what God calls you to do. What I am saying is a lot of us are running away. We stand on a corner and try to arbitrate for people who are in a different context. We cannot do that and expect to change anything.

How many entities are out there in the universe? We do not know. Each time we pick up the telescope we are discovering new things, yet all of it is moving within the space of the will of the Son of God. It is the original intent of God's and Christ's will that allows them to manifest. All things that are made manifest are connected to the will of the Son of God, yet we know that the will of the Son of God in its original intent was messed up by the will of man. However, by Christ coming back and using human will to realign with the Father, everything in creation is now standing at the edge of pure redemption. What is holding back this redemption? Creation is waiting for people who will do the same thing Christ did—align their will back to the will of the Father. By doing this, we allow the frequency of our aligned wills to be amplified so all of creation will hear and recognize the sound, and raise itself towards that sound and therefore, towards life. This frequency is not playing music. It is in the amplification of good human will.

> All things that are made manifest are connected to the will of the Son of God

Remember, you cannot ignore "good will to men" and "to men of good will." Why do I emphasize this? Because it is the amplification of the human will towards goodness, towards mercy, and towards compassion that actually allows everything in the universe to raise itself out of its slumber and be drawn towards its original purpose. You cannot say, "Be it done according to my will" when you have a bad will because, in that context, you are living in friction with Divinity and producing things that constantly create death. Rebellion is dangerous. Look at what Isaiah 1:19-20 says:

If you are willing and obedient, you shall eat the good of the land; but if you refuse and rebel, you shall be eaten by the sword; for the mouth of the LORD has spoken.

If you are *willing **and** obedient*, you will eat the fruit of the land. In other words, if your will is submitted and aligned with that of the Father, the triune God, through the person of Christ, you will eat the fruit of the land. Is it talking about the oranges or apples in your garden? No, the fruit of the land is not just what you harvest on earth. Land is everywhere.

> If you are *willing **and** obedient*, you will eat the fruit of the land.

Several years ago, I taught about terraforming and how the earth would start giving up new islands and everyone said it was not possible. Nonetheless, we just found a new island that just came out of the ocean on the east coast of Australia. God showed me He had new lands. The BBC reported the discovery in an article called "New Tonga Island now home to flowers and owls."

Land is coming. The earth is not just going to give it away. More land is going to be created. I have my theory as to why the Antarctic is melting. I think it is more than what everyone thinks. We are trying to frame it towards destruction, but it is not happening that way. Remember, all that ice used to be water and the earth was still here. At that time, all the islands were located around the edges of the earth, not in the middle in the way they are today. Science tells us that there was a continental drift. The ocean was all around the earth, but not in the way it is now. Who says that the ocean rising will not cause the earth that was once divided to rise and come back together? Who says that the same process will not repeat itself? This movement would cause the earth's tectonic plates to shift. Think about it—the same amount of water that was there during Noah's flood is still there. It has not increased. It recycles itself. It is the same process.

Referring back to the drawing of the circles, the center where the circles overlap, means that the Son of God, Jesus Christ, is operating from eternity and is serving as the intersection between time and eternity. Through His being, time is manifested. In Hebrew, there are ten different words, different dimensions, and different frequencies of time. Through the person of Christ, different dimensions of time come into existence, which means the different worlds coming into existence are governed by different kinds of time. Time is not what we think it is. We measure time from the perspective of the earth, but we cannot go behind creation. You can call it the big bang, the small bang, or whatever! Still, you cannot go behind that to measure the flow of time. There are people today who are now challenging our accepted understanding of time. Where does time come from? Time came through the being of Christ into this realm. Therefore, time itself is a living entity.

יְצִירָה
Yetzirah

A gateway or *Yetzirah* (יְצִירָה) refers to the formation of a gateway or aperture for the emergence of a concrete entity into an open space.

DILATING TIME: A GATEWAY TO CREATION

One of the things that a believer can do is create beings that are temporal in nature. The framing of an atmosphere used to manifest a temporal being is not so much a matter of time. It is creating an aperture or dilation in the moment of time through which one can actually bring forth another being. This is why believers must be careful of what they say with their mouths. If every word you speak can create, then at the right moment, you could actually call forth something. How many of us know people who, because of the words of their mouths, are suffering? How many of us have gotten ourselves into big trouble because of the words of our mouths and what we have created?

Let me remind you of the words of Christ:

It is the Spirit who gives life; the flesh is no help at all. The words that I have spoken to you are spirit and life. (*John 6:63*)

Who created the world? By who was the world sustained? By who is your life developed, framed, formed, and directed? Sometimes, your word is the key to dilating space and time. If you can control your mouth, you can do anything.

So also the tongue is a small member, yet it boasts of great things. How great a forest is set ablaze by such a small fire! (*James 3:5*)

The Bible says that it is not good for bitter waters and sweet waters to come out of the same mouth (James 3:11). To translate it simply, it is not good for demons and angels to come out of the same mouth.

In Jewish tradition, there is something called a *"golem"*. A golem is a being that has been created intentionally by someone for a particular purpose. That person who creates a golem does not have to be a believer. The important thing about a golem is that whoever creates it must also be the one that destroys it. If a golem tries to fulfill its purpose and does not find what it is looking for, it will turn on you. Remember, curses return to those who utter them if the purpose is not fulfilled (Proverbs 26:2). Blessings work the same way.

I will bless those who bless you, and him who dishonors you I will curse, and in you all the families of the earth shall be blessed. (*Genesis 12:3*)

We know that this is a blessing given to Abraham, but it is also a principle that God set in motion. If the words of our mouths are seeds and we sow them, we reap what we sow. This principle is not just an issue for Abraham; it is a principle in the universe. When someone delights in cursing, a curse always returns to them. When someone delights in blessings, blessings follow them.

We see the principle again in Matthew:

...for by your words you will be justified, and by your words you will be condemned. (*Matthew 12:37*)

Your own words stand before you and accuse you or they stand before you and release you. When a righteous person speaks, they can create an angel by the word of their mouth. They create beings, meaning they operate at a level where they are capable of dilating time.

All of time offers an opportunity to the human being, to the believer in particular, for the rectification of creation. It is not as if time itself is strong or carries power because all of time is connected to the human will. The will "peoples" the world. I use the word "peoples" deliberately because in all the principles of time, we fill the world with entities. Your will populates the space.

I want to talk for a moment about language. One of the rights of someone who has a PhD is to come up with new words to define things. Sometimes that is one of the reasons you are given a PhD. You have come up with a new term, defined it yourself, and then everyone starts using it. When I started using the word *"communitarian,"* it was not in the English language, so I just coined it. We coin many words in theology because when you are dealing with something new there is rarely language for it. As we develop new language for new concepts, to insist that someone should use your language to define something that has no reality in your language is to stunt creativity. I like grammar, but I think a time comes when you must twist grammar to communicate your ideas.

Writers like Shakespeare and Tennyson are called wordsmiths now, but, in reality, they practiced word alchemy. They put words together to make you think differently. Comedians do it too; they make up words to change your consciousness. Many Christian and theological words were created by the Church Fathers. For instance, the word "trinity" is not in the scriptures. Tertullian coined the term to explain a theological concept. So, when we fight over the Trinity, we are not really arguing over the word, but grappling with how the three persons in God are related. We can ask if there is a better word. Young people today are creating all sorts of new words because we are continually confronting things that have never existed before. My point is that words populate the space you dilate. Anywhere you find time happening, you can use words to decide what happens in it. You can create things to occupy that time.

If you spend your time speaking negativity, you create negative beings in the context of the time that is given to you. You have to decide whether you want to "people" the time you carry with negativity or with life-giving spirits.

> If the words of our mouths are seeds and we sow them, we reap what we sow.

I am amazed at how people bind themselves and then think somebody is doing something to them. I did an experiment long ago. I have been telling people to never say they are sick when they are not. I wanted to test this idea to see if it was true, so I sent somebody a picture of me in the hospital. I was sick the next week. Nobody else caused it. I knew that it was from what I did. I had to get rid of it immediately because I knew how I created it, and I knew how to get rid of it. So do not put these burdens on yourself with your own mouth! Even for simple things, never swear on it because if you seal it with an oath, you will have a problem. If you seal something with an oath, it will cost you a lot to change it.

Let us look at how a believer functions in complete wholeness related to these concepts and how that affects both the finite and infinite space around them. Time is given to you to use to rectify the world. You do that through the intentional vibration and resonance of your will. Every moment is an opportunity for you to manifest God in the world where you are. Different things can be brought forth, but it is all dependent on how you use your will.

When the will is trained, it becomes the key for unlocking dimensions in various realms.

When the will is trained, it becomes the key for unlocking dimensions in various realms. For example, the will can unlock the dimension of Heaven, the heart of God, and the joy of angels! It unlocks the Seraphim dancing and the Cherubim singing in Heaven, and they respond to the movement of your will. Our will is something that we take for granted and is a central point of confusion in Christian Theology. Many people argue, in fact, that human beings have no will. Of course, we know that the will of man was in bondage, but the truth is, the will is not as much in bondage as those who preach pre-destination want to believe (sorry, Luther!). Theologians want to make the will subject to bondage even in the case of a decision to follow God. However, even if God were to stir the will up, the person still has to say "yes." Luther himself, who writes a lot on this subject, had to say yes to God. He had to make a choice to stand against the church or not to stand against the church. God did not force him. The conviction of his soul and his strong will actually saved him. Without his strong will, the Reformation would have died before it even started.

As I said, we know that the will is in bondage because man fell, but it falls deeper into bondage when we allow the soul to be in charge of the will. This is not the way God created it. The will is meant to set the boundaries for the function of the soul and to make the soul look up to this instrument called the will. Anyone who is initiated into the hidden mysteries of divine reality has been initiated into the capacity to tune time and space. The truth hidden in time and space is found in the original will of God and original will of the Son to become the space or the aperture by which creation comes out of God into concrete reality. This event was an aperture for the emergence of a concrete entity within the space that God created. So Christ became a space that God created and, by His willingness to lay His life down in the foundation of the world, the concrete world came into existence. The same principle applies to us. Time is often given to us as well as an instrument for causing concrete realities to be manifest in this realm or, in other words, to come from the spiritual realm to the material realm.

We are going to talk a little bit more about what is occurring in the heavens that actually allows manifestation to happen, what a believer does when they stir up the heavens and understand time and its function, and how they can literally serve as the gateway for things to come from the spiritual realm to this realm by their will. The same way Jesus served as the aperture for the concrete world, you and I can become the aperture for bringing things from that realm to this realm, as long as our will is aligned with the spiritual realm.

"Aperture" is a photographic term describing the opening through which an image is captured. In the context of our discussion, it is an opening where the imageless becomes an image. The very idea that there are different kinds of time causes us to have what I call "spectral" or "fractal" consciousness. Fractal consciousness means that the believer can divide the world into pieces and still get the whole. A believer does not fragment the world. Many people talk about fragmentation, but a true believer does not fragmentize the world. What he does is see the wholeness of the world in the pieces of it.

Let us talk about the morphic process. A human being is created as

35

DILATING TIME: A GATEWAY TO CREATION

an individual. Your mom and dad release a piece from each other and the parts contained the whole in a greater measure than before. This is true because the believer can duplicate everything that was in the other world by virtue of their will in the space that they have created. God never creates anything partially. If God decides to create another world, it will reveal completely. If God wants to manifest the universe in a microcosm, what does He do? He does not fragment the world; He puts the whole world in your body. The same thing happens when a believer operates with good will—they are able to create wholeness.

I wrote an article a long time ago about multiple personalities called, "Person as Community: An African Understanding of the Person as an Intrapsychic Community." By the way, some Western psychologists utilize the information in this article in their treatment of multiple personalities. I do not consider multiple personalities as a sickness, but rather, as a gift. It is just that most people do not know how to work with it. Because churches have demonized it, they destroy all the creative personality of the individual and leave them unable to do anything.

He puts the whole world in your body.

Why am I even talking about that? I think it is important because the believer is able to create wholeness yet lives an integral or integrated life. The believer really is an integrator; they can take fragmented things and create wholeness out of them and have them relate to each other as whole things rather than fragments. If what we believe about what God made us to be is true, then the power to make wholeness out of fragments sits in us. This means we need to work a little bit more with people rather than decide that multiple personalities are a demonization and try to cast them out. We may know that one of the multiple personalities is completely wicked, but if you integrate them, how will that remain? It is a different thing with Africans. They integrate the part of the person considered to be bad with the good part and create the balance in the person. The problem with believers today is that we want to remove the part that looks terrible to us and then we leave the person with a bland personality.

Remember, you are not a righteous person if you have never struggled with wickedness. I have Christians who say things like that and I just say, "You are not righteous." They say, "I never think any evil. I am no longer tempted," and I say, "Really, you are not righteous; you are a very wicked person!" They get offended with me, "How can you say that?" I can say it because it demonstrates that they do not understand what it means to be human and their will is not trained. They do not know how to resist evil. These same guys sit at home, watch a man beat his wife, and never intervene. What does it mean when so-called righteous people watch other people kill each other and think of themselves as righteous? They have the capacity to resist evil only when it touches them, but in no other way. They say, "I am never tempted," until you touch them. If somebody tells me that they are not tempted and they do not have to push back on evil within or around themselves, then I say, "I am afraid of you because the day you crack there will be no balance in you."

The Jews analyze Job the same way. They argue that the problem with Job was that he was a righteous man who did not know evil. Therefore, he was a wicked man and God had to bring him into balance. That is why Job talked foolishness. He was a righteous man, but God did not let him be righteous without understanding evil in the world. God did that; it was not the devil. What was God doing with Job? Job had the same capacity to use his will, but he was not using it for good. He was able to resist the temptation of dealing with his friends, but God did not bless him until he prayed for his friends. At a certain point, Job told them,

I have heard many such things;
miserable comforters are you all.
Shall windy words have an end?
Or what provokes you that you answer?
I also could speak as you do,

if you were in my place;
I could join words together against you
and shake my head at you. (*Job 16:2-4*)

Look at Job's statement. If I talked like that, you would put me in an asylum. He essentially says, "Let God come out and fight like a man (Job 16ff) if He really thinks He is God. The only problem is when He comes, He will act like the big bad God. Let Him come and face me like a man and I will show Him that He has treated me unjustly."

It is in your Bible. The things Job says about God are not the things his friends said about God. His issue was he was extremely self-righteous. It was true that he had not done evil to anybody so his whole attitude was, "I do not deserve this." And when God came to him, God told him he was not a man yet. It is in the Bible. God said,

Gird up your loins like a man; I will question you and
you shall answer me (*Job 38:3*)

Because that is what you want, right, Job? God tells Job that He is not going to talk like God; He is going to talk like a man so Job had better answer Him like a man. "If you are a real man, why can't you do this or that? It does not take God to pull gold out of the depths of the earth, so why are you not doing it? It does not take God to control Leviathan and sport with him, but you, Job, are scared of Leviathan. You are afraid of the devil and everything around you that looks evil, yet is not. You cannot even get into the pool with Leviathan and sport with him" (Job 38-42).

When your will becomes aligned with God, He teaches you how to balance between strength and mercy, justice and righteousness. Every movement of time is meant for you to rectify the world and rectifying the world is bringing the world into balance. We have this idea that if the world is redeemed and quickly saved, there will be no push towards evil. When God builds His kingdom on Earth for ever and ever, I guarantee that some crazy free being will say, "I do not like this system." It has happened several times before. What is to say it will not happen again? Did it not happen in perfection? So the training of the will is for you to learn to rule worlds. Your will needs to be able to sustain justice and mercy. If God is going to give you worlds to rule, what do you think will happen? Do you think you will be some "goody two shoes" and not create boundaries because the whole universe will come into the kingdom of God so completely that no one will ever try to mess it up? Suppose no one tries to mess it up and the creation itself starts growing out of proportion in relation to what God has put under your rule. It takes justice to restrain creation from overgrowing.

Do you know it is God's boundaries or *gebula* (גבלה) that restrain the Earth from continually expanding? Creating boundaries is an aspect of justice and it takes strength to create boundaries. However, if a boundary is created that cannot be abrogated for the purpose of the growth or destiny of the people in it, then it becomes evil in itself. If mercy is created where the boundaries are so porous that everything goes haywire, then there is no righteousness in it. Balance is the key! The median way is how God operates. God operates in creation by destruction and rebirth. Have you seen a different way of God operating? Why does He spend millions of years teaching you about creation? It is the principle of creation whereby there is a balance between creating boundaries (not allowing things to get out of hand) while at the same time showing mercy without becoming extreme. Until you learn that, you cannot be entirely good. Your goodness must come from the fact that your will has learnt to balance good and evil. Then when you become good, your goodness is complete because you have proven your power already. You see God can be all good because He has restrained Himself from destroying worlds for millions of years. Furthermore, He has restrained worlds from consuming each other. God can get to the point where He is completely good because His strength and mercy have been balanced for all ages. What will keep you in Paradise forever is God restraining boundaries and not allowing evil to come in.

> If He gives you a world to rule, you must also learn to restrain the boundaries.

DILATING TIME: A GATEWAY TO CREATION

If He gives you a world to rule, you must also learn to restrain the boundaries. Do you think that if God uses you to create worlds then you are not responsible for the worlds that you create? You want to rule worlds and be co-creators of the world, yet you do not want to be responsible for what happens in the world. If God uses you to create the world or if God lays a foundation of the world with your life, you are responsible for it. If you create a world then you are responsible for it. You will have to die for it. You will have to bring redemption to it. We hide from that part. We do not tell people that if you create a world, you are responsible for its redemption and preservation. What is the end goal? God wants you to be like Him. You think there is another pattern and paradigm? God designed your body the way it is because it carries worlds and galaxies in it. Truly, your body is going to form the world that you rule, and this means that *your* life must sustain the world that you create. If anything goes wrong, you are responsible for its redemption. That is the divine pattern. Christ's body framed our universe out of His blood. It is the same with every universe and continuous creation goes on.

> By connecting your will to the will of God and creating, you build correspondences and confluences between worlds.

If you are a son, God might actually use you to lay down a foundation for a new world. If something goes wrong, you, as the foundation, must become the redeemer. We create something and then we want God to save what we created and we blame God for the character of what we created. Again, if you create it, you are responsible for it. You cannot create something and expect God to sustain it. The sustaining of what you create must come from your own blood. This is where it gets rough. If you go up into Heaven and create all this junk, then some of us have to go there and clean up after you. The time is coming when that junk will follow you home because it is your creation.

Remember, whatever you create you are responsible for. God will help you. He will not run away from you, but He saves your *life*, not your own creation. You must lay down your life for your creation. If it comes out of you, you carry its redemption. This principle is what we should be teaching humanity. You create the world in which we live in and the redemption of that world is in you. Thus, if you rectify your will with the will of God, then you have the capacity to rectify the world in which you live. God has already done what He is supposed to do. He has paid the price to redeem you. He redeemed the world that came out of Him. Remember that you are not going to rule a house in Britain. That is not rulership. You are not a ruler because you have a house close to Buckingham Palace. England already has a king. You are a king because there are other worlds for you to rule. You cannot actually legislate in this world, by the way. I am not saying you are not a king here, but the real goal of kingship is to rule the worlds that God puts under you. This is not merely a matter of you owning a small property like your house and claiming to be a king. The goal of going into the heavens and moving in the realms is to learn how to rule.

The human being who knows the Lord, whose will is connected to Him, is an animator of time and space. He creates a consciousness that has the capacity to tailor space and is interconnected with the depths of Divinity. By connecting your will to the will of God and creating, you build correspondences and confluences between worlds. The will is the major pathway between God and Earth. Jesus Christ sits in your will because that is what you submitted to Him to become a child of God. As a result, you become the coordinator of universal templates for organizing and understanding all the underlying principles of creation. The believer who operates in this capacity and understands time becomes the master of this living network. He steps into mastering parallel and multiple dimensions and cosmoses created by God, left untended until the believer shows up.

The whole idea of future Innovation is grounded more strongly in the will of those whose wills are aligned with God. The problem is when it comes down through their aligned will, they do not have a vessel on earth to capture what they themselves have served as a channel for. It cannot come into this world without the will of the believers. It is amazing that the greatest moments of technological and organizational innovation have always happened when the church has been in favor

41

DILATING TIME: A GATEWAY TO CREATION

of the change. Innovation comes by the aligned will of believers. However, the believers are lost because they do not understand the time, nor do they understand the vehicle or process of capturing what has been made and what has come through. The believer is a carrier of futuristic innovation. Understanding time opens the space for the manifestation of innovations that are already a reality in heaven. There are innovations in Earth that are not innovations in Heaven. But if the believer is operating in an old model, does not have a language to frame the innovation, and does not understand what they have learnt, then it sits inside them until someone in the occult finds a language for it. The occult person begins to describe the innovation because the believer refuses to train him or herself to talk about what they are supposed to be bringing about.

A believer is not the poor person. The believer is the one who went to the bush, caught the deer, and left it for the stranger to take and cook. The believer is not dumb, just lazy at the point of manifestation. The believer does not lack wisdom. The believer does not lack God. The believer does not lack power. However, we tend to become lazy at the point of manifestation. Remember what I said before: we get to the point where God leaves it for us to complete and we walk away thinking it is God's job to complete.

> **And let us not grow weary of doing good, for in due season we will reap, if we do not give up.**
> **(*Galations 6:9*)**

Believers tend to get faint at the moment of reaping. The old preachers used to talk about this and told us to believe God for something, but by the time God came to give it to us, we were so tired and just gave up. Then someone else came along where we were standing and they received what we were supposed to receive because they had perseverance. We must overcome our tendency to give up and we can overcome.

So the properties of higher dimensional realities are embedded in the will of the believer. The believer can actually will higher dimensional realities to come to their realm. Should I give you an example? It is true we ascend to heaven, but I can call God to come to my house. I do not do it often because I revere God. We can gather in a meeting and go up into heaven, and God, angels, and higher dimensional realities come down with us. However, they do not just come down with us; they come down *on* our will and intention. We can create a space and the effulgence of Divinity will come down. People will experience God because our will has made it so. We have connected our will to the will of God. What happens in your Christian communities when you come together and have the singleness of mind?

Time is embedded in the will of the believer. The soul manifests a particular type of time, and the body manifests a particular type of time.

> The soul manifests a particular type of time, and the body manifests a particular type of time.

The twelve kinds of time that we find in scripture (plus the ones we have not yet discovered) are all directed to the will of an individual. If you want Issachar time, your will must be strengthened to be able to manifest that time where you are.

I have come to tell you that your will must be trained in this season. How do you do this to have this kind of power? The Christian has a mouth, and the mouth is in the head, which means that the mouth is connected to the crown. Mouth is connected to crown. So, this person has one of the greatest gateways. When he speaks, he determines the number of crowns that sit on his head. The tongue creates the jewel on the crown. In order to use time effectively, he must then speak things that distill down from above and become a reality where he lives. When he speaks, he must speak in such a way that he is speaking from the world to come. You call it declaration, but if such a declaration does not originate in the world to come, then it is not a true declaration because it will never happen. This means that there must be transference of consciousness in which he moves to the other world and from that world, speaks the *fait accompli*. With his mouth, he channels things to his will so his will can attract what he is speaking from the other world. Every word he speaks opens up the will and the will receives it as something to be manifested where the person is standing. This means

DILATING TIME: A GATEWAY TO CREATION

that he must live his life where Christ is reigning, where the Father's full will is manifested, and all the elements for creation of anything in the universe are present. Then, by his will, through his mouth, he can take any elements in the heavens and take them into the context where he finds himself.

When you see a technology in the heavens, you are the one who has drawn it from another realm of elemental principles into a construct that you must transfer through your will into where you are in the world. Spirit does not really have form. In fact, it can take any form. Therefore, when someone lives in the world to come, they live in the world of new spirit. By living in that world of spirit, their mouth and their desire frame the construct of what needs to be manifested and their will opens up the pathway for it to be brought to where they are in the physical realm. Whatever time they understand, they can use as a way of manifesting that which they created in the spiritual realm or that which they have called forth. If you speak in that realm and do not create the right time here, then your creation will be stuck in the heavens.

If you speak in that realm and do not create the right time here, then your creation will be stuck in the heavens.

The reason I told you that you can actually create is because you can create some times for manifestation. But if you do not understand the time and do not create the time intentionally, then when you go into the spiritual realm and make your declarations, there is no time for manifestation. Oftentimes, when there is a time of manifestation, there is no vessel to receive the manifestation.

Remember, in the world of God, there is no glass but everything that makes up glass is there. There is no car but everything that goes into making a car is there. In God's world, technology has not been manifested in the way you think about it. It is not until you go into that realm and begin to speak and create a desire for this new technology that the elemental structures or spiritual molecules get together and frame for you what is going to be. Then you can take it and transfer it through your will based on the time you have created or based on the right time to manifest here. However, if you do these things in Heaven and you do not know the time you are going to create this technology, you will have ideas but they will not manifest. If you are not a vessel or you do not have a vessel, it will get stuck until somebody with a vessel comes.

So how do we create a vessel? Your decrees and declarations must:

- Be based on clear articulated desires, not wants or wishes;
- Be based on intentionality.

Find a handle in your physical body. That means your cells must vibrate in the same frequencies as the decrees you are making. You will know when that happens because your body will begin to react differently. It resonates with the frequency.

Make forceful imperatives, not mere statements. This means you have to have a certain magisterium, or rather the authoritative capacity to speak them forth. Decrees and declarations must be spoken. If you cannot speak them, then the emotions of the desires must be very intense.

Please do not come back to me and say, "What about the people who cannot speak?" This is typical Christian behavior. I am talking to 99% of believers and they ask about the 1% that cannot do this. God knows how He relates to them; that is not my job. For most believers, this argument is an excuse not to do what they actually need to do. I suppose they believe they are being nice by thinking of people who cannot do what they are doing. You are actually not being nice when you desire something and you say, "O my God, I desire these things, but 99% of the people do not have a car." The fact that you do not have a car is not going to help 99% of the people. Your doubt is going to hurt you. It is not going to hurt them. It is not holiness for you to think like that anyway. I will discuss this further in the chapter on *charish* in the next section of the book.

So decrees and declarations are important points. By speaking and making declarations, you are re-scrolling your life. You are actually changing the scroll of your life. There is no such thing in Heaven as a scroll that is written that must be fulfilled by you. You can actually change scrolls in heaven. You have done it! Something can be written in Heaven and a righteous person can go into Heaven and change it. They do it every day. There were records in Heaven written against this nation that have been stricken. How can that happen if scrolls cannot be changed? You may go to court, or just go into Heaven and leave your DNA. It can be done either by going with your body or by going in the spirit. You should be able to do both.

> The scripture says you should ask God for what you will.

Time was not made for God. Every moment of time is God taking eternity and making it into a seed form that you can handle. It is a practice. Every problem you face is God taking the whole cosmos and putting it into your problem so you can learn to deal with the world. When you make decrees and declarations, you are using your mouth to re-scroll your life, realign your will, and clarify your desire. Until you have a desire, nothing is going to happen on Earth. A desire is not a wish. A desire is an intentional, passionate, directed energy that flows out of you and your whole being responds to it.

Most believers do not have desires. They think they do, but what they have is wishes and wants. This is why 90% of prayers are not answered because they are based on wishes and wants, not desires. The Bible promises to bring your desires to pass, so if it is not happening, it is not a desire. I have talked to you about training your will. Now you must train your desire. Part of making declarations is training your desires and making your whole being understand them. When the desire is clear, the universe will bend to it. The Father said,

Delight yourself in the LORD, and he will give you the desires of your heart.

Commit your way to the LORD; trust in him, and he will act. (*Psalm 37:4-5*)

ADONIJAH O. OGBONNAYA PH.D.

God never says He will give you the desires of *His* heart. He already told you what His plan is so for you so go and ask Him, "Lord what are your plans for me?" Remember, the Father also said,

> **For I know the plans I have for you, declares the LORD, plans for welfare and not for evil, to give you a future and a hope. (*Jeremiah 29:11*)**

That statement is general enough that you can put anything you want in there. And that is how God works; He makes a general promise so that you can insert your will into it.

> **If you abide in me, and my words abide in you, ask whatever you wish, and it will be done for you. By this my father is glorified. (*John 15:7-8*)**

It did not say that you should ask God what *He* wills. The scripture says you should ask God for what you will. Then it says that you may receive so that the Father may be glorified through the Son. In other words, if we are not receiving, the Father is not being glorified. We are not receiving because we are just wishing for things. We might as well create a wishing well and throw pennies into it.

It is amazing how simple and effective all of this is. I have people come up to me all the time to say, "It works, Dr. O! It works!" The only reason this does not work is that you are used to wishing and begging God to do things He has already said He has done. So train yourself to desire and to desire clearly. What you need to be careful about is not your wishes. You need to be careful about your desire because it will surely come to pass. Heaven will answer you even if it is evil that you desire. I know the passage that you are thinking of now.

> **You ask and do not receive, because you ask wrongly, to spend it on your passions. (*James 4:3*)**

This passage is talking about wishes. You might say that you just need some money to buy a car. But you can actually desire a car without attaching anything you want to do with it. How does the world get what you do not have and what you pray for all the time? Are they are not more righteous than you? Unbelievers have things because they do not have self-righteous hang ups with God. The unbeliever merely acknowledges that God blessed him. A believer does not obtain things because he listens to some religious demon telling him, "You do not deserve it. This is not for you. You are being prideful. Why are you asking for a Maserati or a BMW or a Bentley? That must be pride."

How do you make a decree? One of the great ways to get to a place of desire is to decree your identity. You are already doing wonderfully, but just to tweak it a little bit, decree your identity. **I AM** statements are statements about God and not about you. It is important for you to make I AM statements as a child of God. You do not say I AM unless you identify with God because I AM is the Name of God. When you have the concept of **I AM** in your mind and your consciousness, and when you make a statement about your identity, you are not just speaking about yourself; you are speaking about the nature of God.

Make your decrees the way God talks about Himself. A decree of identity must be active and present. "I AM a Son of God," or "I AM God's Son." You make that a little bit stronger so that your own consciousness and emotions get into it. I can exclaim, "I AM a Son of God!" I say things like this:

"I AM a Son of God. I carry the fullness of my Father's life. I exude His glory, His power, and majesty. Every fiber of my being reveals who He is."

There is a place for doing, but it is not at the place of identity.

I have already said who I am in God. Now I can actually say, "As He is so am I in this world" (James 4:17). There are other decrees such as:

I AM wealth.
I decree and I declare that I AM wealthy.
I carry wealth.
I operate in wealth.
I exude wealth.
I attract wealth.
My whole being manifests wealth.
The universe bends to me with wealth.
I receive it now. It flows into my hands.
I AM wealthy. I AM the embodiment of the wealth of My Father.
I AM the embodiment.

Notice that I do not say, "I *will* be wealthy." I stopped that a long time ago.

Can you also say I AM Love? You can make decrees about love in the same way. However, when you say, "I AM Love," you need to tell me as well as yourself what you are talking about because you have no idea what love is. Love is the word you use, but you have not really told yourself how your body is supposed to recognize when the love of God is flowing through you.

How about "I AM gentleness?" You see, I do not do make decrees about gentleness because it is a fruit of the Holy Spirit. If I decree and declare that I am filled with the Holy Spirit, then the Holy Spirit is intimate with me, I operate as a vessel that radiates the Holy Spirit, and the Holy Spirit is manifested in every fiber of my being. If that is the case, do I need to decree, "I AM Patience?" If I decree, " I AM Patience," it is because I am creating Impatience. I actually begin fighting with Impatience instead of relating to the person of the Holy Spirit. In this case, I am no longer talking about identity, but rather about what I am doing.

Understand these differences first because your identity has to do with "being." This concept is difficult because a lot of us want to change "being" into "doing." There is a place for doing, but it is not at the place of identity. When you mix the two, you realize your whole consciousness begins to have a problem believing in what you are saying. For instance, what if I say, "I AM the full embodiment of God upon the face of the Earth?"

As He is so am I in this world

This time issue is deeply connected to what I am talking about because when you learn this and you create the space for it, you will have manifestation. For a long time I did not want to practice these things. I taught these concepts to people and they were successful, but I thought the Lord did not want me to do it. I told you the conversation I had with the Lord. He said, "Really? I told you that 20-something years ago when you were still immature and I was dealing with all that mess. Remember when you were in your basement and you could not handle what I was preparing you for at that time?" So now I practice!

דָּת וּ אַחְוָה

Dath v'Achvah

Some of you may have noticed that I am very passionate about the life of Christians. I think Christians are much too lackadaisical when it comes to the life of other believers.

EMPATHY, UNITY, AND TRUE FAITH:

FOUNDATIONAL KEYS FOR DECREES AND DECLARATIONS

Forgive me for being like that, but I cannot help it. I came from a nation where we were persecuted so I do not have patience for people who do not think about other Christians. I do not have patience with my brothers in America. I love them dearly, pray for them daily, but I am not very patient with people who do not think about other Christians except themselves. Many do not consider their actions and how it they may affect their Christian brethren around the world. The only beef I have with Christians in the West is our inability to think as one people to defend our unity of mind and spirit.

Human behavior is interesting. We who are in safety goad people who are "over there" to go to war. It should not be that way. Maybe I am just thinking like a crazy African or a crazy Christian, but I prefer to be on the wrong side defending the lives of Christians than to be on the right side defending other nations on Earth. I do not consider nations to be sacrosanct. I would defend certain people groups even though people claim they are Satan worshippers. If I do not defend them, no one will be there to defend me when people come for me.

We keep forgetting about Germany. They first went after the Jews. Nobody thought much about it. Then they went after the Catholics. Protestants were busy protesting the Catholic doctrine. Then they went after the Baptists. They went after the Moravians. Then they started putting the Lutherans who were the supporters in jail. We must learn from history. We will not be exempted from death when they start persecuting us. So never look at war as a solution to anything. I do realize other religions persecute people, but I do not think the answer is to bomb a nation and, in so doing, bomb Christians with them. Do you have a plan to evacuate the Christians in Iran? We did not do it in Iraq or Syria or Libya. There is no plan to evacuate our brothers and sisters. They just plan to bomb everybody and kill everybody including our brothers and sisters. That is the real issue. Christians should not forget that. The nation did not have a plan for evacuating Christians from Egypt either and, once they left, Christian girls in Egypt were raped in public. Their clothes were torn and they were beaten in public and they were forcibly married.

Part of what we are learning is how to move in the spirit to defend those who cannot be defended by their society. But we cannot do it if our hearts are not bound to their hearts. Much of what we are learning is just completely useless to us because we think only of ourselves. To be honest, much of this mystical movement is about "me" and how I am going to enjoy God and see things in the spirit realm. It has nothing to do with actually changing other nations. But I think God is teaching us about time and space so we can actually make a difference. It is not just about your own nation. Your sonship is not tied to your ethnicity. It is not tied to your national identity. Your sonship is a cosmic sonship. All creation is groaning, not just your city. All creation is groaning for your manifestation. It may be time we started living that out.

If you can move in the spirit, then you need to go to countries and look for where some kids are getting sacrificed because of their religion. Then pull somebody out of that situation. Get out of your own nation and away from just being in a small group laughing and soaking. Go to the places where your people in your own country are making human sacrifices. People do not like to hear that. We Americans always think that we are exempt and that these things do not happen to us. Yet right now California is a centre for sex trafficking. But it is not just America. What have we been seeing since we started moving in the spirit is that these crimes have been exposed over and over again. But we are still not talking about it. Those of us who are doing it, we are not going out giving testimonies. We are not talking about it in our meetings. This is probably the first time I have spoken like this. The only way we can help others is to have empathy for other human beings. Your faith should not be an isolationist faith. You should not be living in a silo if you are listening to me as I teach the telepathic universe and the transmutation of the soul. What I am trying to get believers to understand is how telepathy works. Telepathy does not work effectively without empathy.

Can you actually have this power and change the world without anybody knowing who you are or without one individual in the world knowing what you have done? Part of the reason Christians, especially those of us in the West, cannot do anything effectively (and God does not even allow us) is because we immediately get on television, have a ministry, and tell the whole world what we have done. Why would God let you do that? Your acts create more problems than solutions for people. Because you think the next step is to build a ministry with it out of your actions, you call it testimony. The real issue is you were not persecuted for what you were doing so it is not a testimony. A testimony comes out of suffering. That is the meaning of testimony - martyrdom. You cannot have a great testimony if you are not a martyr in some way. Thus, what we are doing is not testimony. Telling stories is not testimony.

If our political idea is based on our national identity, then we are in trouble. If it is not based on the Kingdom of God, we are in trouble because whatever we learn is only going to end with us. Once we get that big house and fancy car, the principle of sonship is gone. Your sonship is a cosmic sonship. It is a God sonship. It changes everything. The first cubic space you create is dangerous and powerful. In that space, everything is mutable and everything is changeable. That space becomes your temptation, or at least part of the temptation, to change only the things that benefit you individually. So why believe that, when a Christian dies for their faith, it is a benefit to them? I do not believe so. I do not try to stop many Christians from being persecuted, but I do have a concern when it is a war that kills them without their choice. I feel this way because I have walked in the zones where they have persecuted Christians, hoping that I would be a martyr. Christians forget that martyrdom in the early days of Christianity was considered glorious. If one person's death could result

> Part of what we are learning is how to move in the spirit to defend those who cannot be defended by their society.

EMPATHY, UNITY, AND TRUE FAITH

in the transformation of a nation, people were willing to do it.

Jan Hus, a Czech theologian and church reformer (1369-1415), was burned at the stake by the Council of Constance in Switzerland for speaking out against the Pope and Catholic hypocrisy. One person's blood changed all of Switzerland. When he was being killed, he said, "Today you kill a chicken. Tomorrow you will hear a rooster crow." A few years later, things got much more radical. Many Bohemian people declared a crusade against papal decrees and were slaughtered for their beliefs. I do not think that I am just saying Christians should be protected. I am saying that if they want to die for their faith, it is a choice they need to make themselves. There are believers in other places who do not have a problem dying for their faith. But it is not the same thing to rain weapons on people from afar. There is no comparison.

> The whole issue is changing your purpose.

What can we do about it? The reason I am teaching you these things is so you know that, when you are mature, you can do something. That is what Jesus said to Peter:

> **Truly, truly, I say to you, when you were young,**
> **you used to dress yourself and walk wherever you**
> **wanted, but when you are old, you will stretch out**
> **your hands, and another will dress you and carry you**
> **where you do not want to go. (*John 21:18*)**

The whole issue is changing your purpose. This is about how you move from focusing on yourself to letting an ideal or a faith and belief system guide your life. The person who is a mystic is a contradiction in nature because they stand for something that typically no one else wants to stand for. It looks like they are contradicting themselves when they are not. If you do not want to stand alone, then what you are learning is completely useless. This is a very serious issue because you will be called to stand alone against the people you love. You know the story.

Consider recent national elections. People got upset with me. I spoke about the things the church was doing that will take years to finish and will cause more economic harm. I am not a prophet, but it is easy to see situations more objectively when you have no emotional ties.

Take, for example, some recent voting in the UK. There were actually some so-called "prophetic" words about if the Scottish people did not vote out of the EU, they would fall in the ocean to demonstrate that God does not like them because they would not correctly. That is not prophecy. That is personal mumbo-jumbo. Yet that is what people are doing. They are trying to create a system in which people actually hate each other. They are already prophesying more Middle-Eastern wars without considering the lives of men and women. We can do things like that because our words matter.

This is why you are learning what you are learning. Believe me; we are sitting down here in a small ragtag group and you are thinking this is so awesome. But God is sneaky. I am serious. I call him Jehovah *Sneaky ha'kadosh*. It is such a powerful thing for God to allow you and me to know what we know. But it is a very humbling thing and when you look at it from the perspective of where you are. It is a very daunting task. You can just throw your hands up and say, "What can I do? There is nothing I can do." But you are learning something given to you, as Jesus said to the disciples, to know the mysteries of the kingdom. And it is not just so you know them theologically. It is so we do this for humanity. We know the Bible says we should care more about the members of the household of faith (Galatians 5:10). However, we are called to act as God's presence in the world. Our Master died for the world!

Individual salvation is God's deposit for the redemption of the world. This is not about politics. When these things happen, you remember what God showed you ten or even twenty years ago. Let me be nice now and talk like Paul. Maybe you have not been the smartest person. You may have been the cutest, but maybe you were not the smartest. And maybe you were not the richest either. Nonetheless, God chose people who, it seemed, could not do anything. The Bible says,

**For consider your calling, brothers: not many of you
were wise according to worldly standards, not many
were powerful, not many were of noble birth. But God
chose what is foolish in the world to shame the wise;
God chose what is weak in the world to shame the
strong; God chose what is low and despised in the
world, even things that are not, to bring
to nothing things that are, so that no human being
might boast in the presence of God. And because
of him you are in Christ Jesus, who became to us
wisdom from God, righteousness and sanctification
and redemption, so that, as it is written, "Let the one
who boasts, boast in the Lord." (*1Corinthians 1:26-31*)**

Therefore, do not underestimate what we are doing. What we need to learn is to bind heart to heart, soul to soul, and spirit to spirit. We must learn how one voice about something will change it. This issue of unity is serious business. The devil is not afraid of you as an individual. He is more afraid of you joining with another believer. The devil is scared of the fourth Adam. And he is scared of you joining with me, and me joining with you. He does not like that because it means we have created a super being. Even though we can be effective alone, there is something that happens when we connect with one another.

Let us come back to this. In the context of what I just showed you. Everything is mutable and changeable. Everything you bring into that context can be changed. The issue is do you want to change it? Is it something you are allowed to change? And for what purpose are you trying to change it?

This is not an easy journey. God is not going to come down from heaven and tell you, "Hey, this is what you should do." He does not do that because you are in training to be like Him. Do you not wonder why you keep asking God to show you how to do things? Sometimes He shows you and sometimes He just watches you because you are in training. That is how it works. If you develop good will, your will does ameliorate your bad action. You can ameliorate certain acts that you carry out of your ignorance. This is the reason that developing your will is so important. God will look at your will, your actual *good* will, and overlook a lot of mistakes in your life. This is my theology. That is why certain people can do crazy things. We see them and wonder how they survive. They survive because God looks at the will. Now he does discipline for certain acts, but he does not destroy them for doing crazy things.

> If you develop good will, your will does ameliorate your bad action.

When you make your decrees (*dath*) and declarations (*achvah*), you can use this process:

1. Understand and have an intention about what decrees and declarations you will make.

2. Realign your will with the will of God.

3. Reach into the depths of your being to unleash potent powers from Heaven that have been submerged into the unconscious mind. Making decrees does that. This is also the best way to rewrite your DNA code.

4. Recalibrate your energetic canters. This opens your physical body for receiving what has been declared. When you hear yourself making declarations, your body begins to shift itself to receive.

When you make declarations, you are actually setting yourself up as a vessel to receive. Do you know the expression, "Physician, heal yourself," (Luke 4:23)? There is no outside resistance to your desires but you. It is not the devil. He comes to steal, kill, and destroy (John 10:10), but how is he going to steal something you do not have? He does not want to stop you from getting something. He actually wants you to get it so he can steal it, because he cannot get it himself. Though we spend a lot of time thinking the devil is fighting us from getting revelation or new insights, he is not. You are fighting yourself. He is waiting for you to get it. In fact, sometimes the devil is sitting there saying, "Can you just get it so I can steal it?" That is what thieves do. It is not in the best

EMPATHY, UNITY, AND TRUE FAITH

interest of a thief to stop you from getting what you want to get.

To me, when you start something as a child, there are things that just make sense to you that do not make sense to adults because adults are thinking in more complex terms. God is just amazing. When I think about my mum and others who have helped me along the way, when I remember the sacrifices they made bringing me from Nigeria without a high school diploma into the US and Canada, I am truly amazed. There have been so many people who have helped me or have been kind to me. Sometimes we complain a lot, but, overall, people have been good to me. Never forget people who helped you along your way. There were old women who gave me $10 a month to help me pay for my house while I was going to school. People came from all over the place and gave $10 a month. People on fixed incomes. Some gave $20 a month for my wife and my kids so I could go to school without having to work because they believed in me. God bless them! You are the beneficiary of that.

We are talking about decrees and declarations which are meant to hone your desires because God answers desires, not wants and wishes. God is not required to answer your wishes. If He does that, He does it out of His grace. God has said, "He will give you the desires of your heart," (Psalm 37:4). And this is why, again, you need to know exactly what you desire because the Bible does not say, "if you have a good desire, God will answer it." The problem with many believers is that they believer God is blessing them because they are righteous. The Lord told me once, "You believe that I bless you because you are righteous. And that is precisely what keeps you from being blessed."

When you focus your desire, God has obligated himself to meet that desire. Jesus used to say to people simple things like, "Be it unto you according to your faith" (Matthew 9:29). Is not that a strange way to respond to somebody? By saying this, Jesus put the onus of their healing back on them. He healed people who did not have that same capacity of thought, but to everyone who could think, He said, "Be it unto you according to your faith." I wondered, "Why are you telling them that?" If they did not have faith and they did not believe and they had no desire to be healed, He left them alone. And then He explained He did not heal many people because they did not believe. How powerful!

Now when you speak, you must know your voice and that the signature of your voice restructures the environment. When we talk like this, the environment is constantly shifting based on the conversation that is coming out of our mouths. I think somebody should actually look at this and see how energies move when people are having a conversation. You can feel it in your body. If your conversation changes, the whole atmosphere changes. Something is actually happening. In this case, what you are doing through your own voice is creating a world to live in where you can manifest what you desire. You are "re-scrolling,". You start speaking in that manner.

> When you focus your desire, God has obligated himself to meet that desire.

When I first started practicing speaking in this way, there were certain things that were happening in my life which I thought was because of my childhood experience. I thought the reason I was doing crazy, supernatural things was a result of my past. God began to teach me. He took me to Heaven and said, "I want you to go into the scroll room and get your scroll." So I went and got my scroll and He said to me, "Open it." As I read my scroll, He asked, "What would you want to change?" You know I am Jewish so what do you think I said? I said, "Thou knowest." That is a Jewish trick. You make God deal with it. God said, "Son, you are being tricky." But it was true. I did not know what to change. He asked me several times, "What do you want to change?" And I continued to say that I did not know. He said, "Open the first book. Open the next page." There was nothing in the next pages. And He said, "Here is what you do not know, son. The script is written by you and Me. Your desires determine what goes on the script."

When people pick up their scroll in Heaven and say, "I read my scroll. I know the beginning to the end," I sit there thinking, "Really? That means your life has no freedom." But I like the way God does it. There are things that were written about our lives, but let me explain it to you. When you read the book of Psalms, it does not say, "Everything in my life was written in the book." It says "You knew my parts" (Psalm 139:13). It is DNA, the structure of your body. God knew all of that. Otherwise, you have to argue that God already knew you are going to hell and determines it forever. This is where God's self-limitation comes into play. He does not want to know whether you are going to hell or not. He wants you and He to make that choice, which makes the whole thing about predestination nonsense and salvation is just a pretense. You may say that God knows someone is going to hell, but that is an error because the re-scrolling process takes place between you and God. He gave you a will so that, by your will, you and God can write your story as you proceed.

It is amazing how open the future is. What can you use to shut down infinity? Nothing. God said when I looked at my scroll, "Do you realise you have infinite possibilities?" And I answered, "Really? What does that mean?" He said, "That means the world is open to you. I am open to you. You get to write your scroll. This is why I want you to develop a good will and a good heart."

...the world is open to you. I am open to you

The problem with most people in the world is that they are stuck with what has already been written about them. Many people in this Christian mystic movement are stuck in the scroll that they have read in Heaven. Did you actually go to the Hall of Records, look through the records, and realize what you have been framing? God has allowed you to write things on your scroll. Angels do not just sit in heaven and write your scrolls. They wrote about your body and about the structure of your soul, but even your DNA can be changed. We can change it physically. What makes you think God cannot change it? At this very moment in time, it is possible for scientists to remove certain parts of your DNA and infuse you with something else. So why do you not understand that the same God who created the world by the word of His mouth and gave you the power to speak to allow you to retune your life can make your DNA vibrate at a different frequency to fulfill what you thought you could not do? A tiny woman is not supposed to lift up a car, is she? But when women are in distress and their children are in distress, a woman can lift up a full-sized car and pull the baby out. It has happened. People have an adrenalin rush and do amazing things. You think it is a miracle, but this capacity is embedded in the human DNA. When you tweak it with some chemical or whatever, the person can do something they were formerly unable to do.

If life and death is truly in the power of the tongue (Proverbs 18:21), then this ability is serious. If this is true, then prayer moves from petition and crying to decrees and declarations. When you operate from a position of real faith then, just like your Father, call those things that are not as though they are (Romans 4:17) and let them come to pass.

EMPATHY, UNITY, AND TRUE FAITH

קליפות

Kellipot

In Adam's world, everyone is born in sin. That is the point.
It does not matter what you think about it. We call it the
tendency to sin. There is nothing original about sin.

DECREES AND DECLARATIONS: TECHNOLOGY FOR DEEP CHANGE

We are actually referring to the fallen nature of man. I do not know why it is called the original sin because it is not original—it is an aberration. There is a tendency to sin, which originates from the DNA of man. The DNA of man was changed by one act. If you want to argue that DNA cannot change, then you have to remember that man was perfect. One act, one conversation, changed the DNA of man. Adam and Eve had a conversation, they acted in a certain way, and their DNA changed towards the tendency to sin. That tendency can also change towards something else. It is the same principle. Man's tendencies are still impacted by the same principles of acts, thoughts, and speech.

Our behaviors are transferred by the context in which we grow up. An act, thought, or speech activates much of the dormant seed in us. It is not only our own thoughts, acts, and speech, but also the thoughts, acts, and speech of our parents and the people we grow up with. All of these things affect the way our DNA functions. If that is true, then what created the changes in our DNA is a thought, or speech, or an action. God's intent when He created DNA was to frame it in the context of God's thoughts, actions, and speech. We can go back to Genesis and look at that.

God created man. This was an act. God thought, "Let us create man in our image" (Genesis 1:26), and as He thought, He spoke it as well. Then after He created man, He said it is very good (Genesis 1:31). God's thought, act, and speech framed the DNA of man. The whole idea of human perfection at the inception of creation is based on God's creation, God's intent, and God's act. Look at Jeremiah 1: 5:

**Before I formed you in the womb I knew you, and
before you were born I consecrated you; I appointed
you a prophet to the nations**

We will come back to what we are trying to do here about rectifying the world. But first we are going to talk about rectifying your own life.

What applies to the microcosm applies to the macrocosm. The same instrument applies but in a bigger way. Let me ask you a simple question. How much faith does it take to cure a headache? Not much, right? How much faith does it take to change a government? Not much. See, it does not change. Quantity does not have to change the instrument. We sometimes think we need more faith to do more or bigger things, when all we really need is the same faith we have been using every day. You need exactly that faith you have been using every day. The same faith that stops a fly, stops any devil. It does not change. When you were born from Adam, your entire DNA structure was entangled with sin. As a result, you lived much of your life controlled by sinful things.

Let us look at our psychological structure. You have a normal, daily life, that is likely very mechanical and probably unobserved. It is not a self-observed life. It is only the life you live. What you call normalcy is a mechanical process. You can also call this Normal Consciousness, or NC, but it is mechanical nonetheless. Then you have the Subconscious, what you call the Subconscious Life, or SC. Then you have the Unconscious. Hebrews call the unconscious mind *kellipot* (קְלִיפוֹת). As a human being born from Adam, you had light, but the light that was in you was darkness. Jesus said,

**The eye is the lamp of the body. So, if your eye is
healthy, your whole body will be full of light, but
if your eye is bad, your whole body will be full of
darkness. If then the light in you is darkness, how
great is the darkness! (*Matthew 6:22-23*)**

He is not just talking about the Pharisees. He is talking about the human condition. The human condition is the *kellipot*, not the divine condition. Human beings are fallen, but God did not leave man without a witness, as it says in Romans 2:14-16:

For when Gentiles, who do not have the law, by nature do what the law requires, they are a law to themselves, even though they do not have the law. They show that the work of the law is written on their hearts, while their conscience also bears witness, and their conflicting thoughts accuse or even excuse them on that day when, according to my gospel, God judges the secrets of men by Christ Jesus.

Even those who have never heard the law have the law written in their hearts. But the law is caught up in darkness that, even when they try to keep it, they do so in a skewed way. We just have that tendency to make everything that is good into something self-serving. God did not leave man without a witness; thus, all human beings have a light within them. However, that light is not what you think. The light was darkness. That is why Paul said,

...for at one time you were darkness, but now you are light in the Lord (*Ephesians 5:8*)

But there were sparks of light and this is what some people are trying to teach. It is a Jewish concept. It is not salvation. You cannot use that as a basis of Universalism because the only time that light is released from the human consciousness is when they meet and truly submit to the Messiah.

This light is usually manifested in man as intellectual light, which is why everything man creates causes death, even when he tries very hard to make it

Quantity does not have to change the instrument.

not cause death. Remember, death is a curse God put on man. It is activated by the word of God. Death does not have existence apart from the mouth of God. We already know there is no reason why a human being should die. A human body should be able to renew itself forever and ever. But for some reason, it just stops doing that at a certain point because that is what God said. It is a word spoken over

67

DECREES AND DECLARATIONS

man by God in response to man's fall. Even when we try our best in our natural state to create things or when we medically heal someone, we create another disease. The only people who can actually create something that continues to create life are believers. Believers can create a system where death is overcome over and over and over again.

But that is not where we are going with this concept of *kellipot*. It is not about salvation. Rather, it is about the fact that human consciousness is trapped in darkness even though it contains the light of Divinity. It does not mean that everybody is God. It does not even mean that you are going to be saved because, if the light in you is darkness, how great is the darkness? We cannot push this to Universalism because that is not biblical and is not a Christian thought. Universalism is considered heresy in Christian thought. Universalism undercuts the cosmic nature of the death of Christ. It says they know God through Shiva (the greatest god in Hinduism) and they can know God

> ...human consciousness is trapped in darkness even though it contains the light of Divinity

through other false gods because that is the logical movement of that belief. Then what Universalism concludes is that Jesus Christ is not the unique way to God or the only way to God. They say that you can get to God another way. Anyone who comes through the window is a thief (John 10:1). This is the Bible. What are Christians trying to do then? We are trying to change what we are in order to accommodate the world. It is not working because it is diluting us. This means that if Christians do not continue to contain the uniqueness of their way, then Christianity as a religion is in jeopardy of extinction and Christians are causing it.

Let us go back to the Unconscious. When you were born again, you came from Heaven. You came with all these records. Most of the time you still were stuck in what your normal life and Subconscious were saying to you. However, because you came to the world in the time of Adam, you came with an angel from Heaven. This is another source of confusion. We may think a person knows God simply because there is an angel with them. But it is God's bequeath to man to be able to teach man. The angels are present to lead you as tutors to help you come back to God. The presence of an angel in your life does not mean you know God. It is an exemplification of the providence of God and God's care for you.

Christians tend to confuse such things with the fact that the person must be a good person if there is an angel with them. Angels are not required to be with you because you are a nice person. They are required to be present with you because you are a potential god. You are going to be gods. Angels stand around you waiting for the day you are born from above and your divinity shines forth. At that point, they all clap and Wisdom rejoices.

When you were born on earth, a lot of activity occurred and the angels surrounded you. However, a particular angel disappeared. This angel did not actually disappear, but just went to the background. It is called the *Angel of the Face*. The Angel of the Face is the angel that came with you as a child into the world. It is the angel of your childhood that can enter into the presence of God without any protocol. The Angel of the Face is an angel God gives you when you come in as a child. Every child has it. All the other angels must close their face when they go to see God, but the angel that guards a child looks God straight in the face. How do I know that? It is in the Bible:

> **See that you do not despise one of these little ones.**
> **For I tell you that in heaven their angels always see**
> **the face of my Father who is in heaven.**
> **(Mathew 18:10)**

These words are not said of other angels because they close their faces. Angels of children sing *Kadosh, Kadosh, Kadosh* (Holy, Holy, Holy). That is why it is dangerous to play with children. I feel sorry for people who abuse children. The leader of the Angels of the Face is Gabriel. He said it when he talked to Zachariah.

And the angel answered him, "I am Gabriel. I stand in the presence of God, and I was sent to speak to you and to bring you this good news" (Luke 1:19).

69

DECREES AND DECLARATIONS

It is amazing that the angels that stand in the presence are actually called "the strong ones." That is their title. Sometimes they are called "the manly ones that defend children."

When you get to a certain age, you begin to buy into defense structures and build up emotional structures that tend to be negative emotional structures or energies. You build them up and begin to structure your life based on normalcy and on mechanical processes. Then you start pushing out all the heavenly structures that came with you from Heaven. The angels and the records of your soul that contain God begin to be pushed down deep into your Subconscious. Here they are caught in darkness. Not evil darkness, but they are caught in places where you cannot access them. The Subconscious is something you can actually access, but the Unconscious is something that is very difficult to access because it is very deep within you. People are able to program their subconscious minds, but they never really have access to their Unconscious, which is where all this activity happens. Thus, once you begin to become of a morally responsible age, your Angel of the Face can no longer go into the presence of God the way they used to. The only way to get back into the presence of God is becoming like a child again. That is the reason Jesus says you cannot see God unless you be converted and be like a child (Matthew 18:3). The same thing happens as you become a new believer and your angel is walking in and out of the presence of God. When you become an adult, the angel has to cover their face.

So another key is living a life of humility before God with a certain level of repentance. Forget about how you are not supposed to repent anymore. It is at the point of repentance when you become like a child before God. Jesus even says it, but we mainly use it as an evangelistic tool. The angels rejoice over one sinner who repents. Excuse me, you are thinking of unbelievers, but you are not thinking of yourself.

Just so, I tell you, there will be more joy in heaven over one sinner who repents than over ninety-nine righteous persons who need no repentance.

(Luke 15:7)

Just so, I tell you, there is joy before the angels of God over one sinner who repents. *(Luke 15: 10)*

As you see, God placed certain keys in our lives to allow us moments to have the Angel of the Face reactivated to go in and out of the presence of God. Here is what happens. When you are born from above, you come in with all these scrolls and records. Your new soul carries a different record. It does not carry a record of sin. Again, your new soul from Heaven does not carry a record of sin! Your *body* carries a record of sin. All that God originally intended for Adam is deep now in an unconscious level where you cannot access it. Even though your soul is coming from Heaven, it is not earthly. It knows many things, but not earthly things. However, your body stands in its way and says you cannot pass even though your will is activated because you know God. Your soul has been born from Heaven by virtue of the channel way of your will. This means that you have access to a super consciousness or you may call it God consciousness. When you live your life then, when you come into this world as a believer, you begin to discover you have access to many things. Yet, there are still certain things you cannot access because your ordinary life has been building energetic systems, and mechanical and defensive structures to keep you from getting in trouble.

Even as a believer you have the same problem. You get defensive of certain things. It is not because you are a bad person. It is because the record is hidden somewhere and you react a certain way. You may ask yourself why you are reacting a particular way.

> The only way to get back into the presence of God is becoming like a child again.

I say it is not the Subconscious because it is easy for you to access the Subconscious just by changing certain behaviors. This is deeper than that because it has to do with the foundations and the angels that stand in the Face. The Angels of the Face are also called the Angels of the *Sod* or the Angels of the Secret Place of the Foundation of God. In other words, they are the angels of the foundation of your life. The foundation is cluttered, yet it is also a mirror.

You come as a believer and this is where you end and you start going in cycles. Most believers' lives never really change drastically except perhaps morally. Their lives do not change financially nor do they change relationally. Their lives do not change in terms of production. A blessed few do come into changes, but if you ask them about it, they do not know why or how. They just think God made it happen. What if there was a technology to help you be able to make those changes? What if you were able to transform your whole being, not just your moral behaviors? This is what I am talking about—*rectifying everything*. This is how we rectify the world. In Jewish tradition, releasing people from the *kellipot* (unconscious) is the goal. Nonetheless, you must release them from one *kellipot* and then release them from another *kellipot* because they keep going back to it. This informs humanity. Many bad things hang around in there. Most of the good is even far deeper than that.

> Unconscious is also where all the good records about your true identity are hidden.

Most people believe that the Unconscious is where all terrible things reside. But I am here to change that misconception because the Unconscious is also where all the good records about your true identity are hidden. You can actually have access to all the bad records very easily. You do it every day. If you and I struggled with sin when we first became believers, it was not something from the deep unconscious; rather, it was something from the Conscious and the Subconscious. In fact, it was a part of normal daily life. We have access to it. However, we do not have access to the thing that came with us from Heaven or the thing that God gave Adam originally. It has been submerged into the Unconscious and he cannot remember it. You can remember sin, but you do not remember how to change your world. You do not remember how to create life. Do you think God took it away? No, it is inside of you and submerged in the depths. We can talk about this in many ways, but let us just talk about decrees and declarations.

When you become a believer, in living your mechanical, normal, everyday life where you automatically react to your surroundings and not actually thinking about life, you are aware of some things, but you are still not truly aware of yourself. You do not typically observe yourself. Self-observation is not as easy as it sounds. A 20-minute self-observation can make the difference in your life. I am not talking about observing yourself in order to say, "I need to repent of this, or I need to repent of that." This is not self-observation to beat yourself up with guilt. If that is your self-observation, you are just going to do the same old things over and over again. That is what guilt does. It creates an unbreakable connection between your weakness and your capacity to act. Guilt does not free you; it binds you. To observe yourself without judgemen is a discipline in and of itself. It is not easy for Christians to observe themselves without judgement. I am not saying there is no judgement somewhere. But if you judge yourself while observing yourself, you are not observing yourself. You are merely judging yourself. You must observe yourself as a third person, watching yourself with no judgement.

In order to observe yourself without judgement is to become a good journalist, taking note of exactly what you are doing without saying it is good or bad. It is not easy for a person who loves the Lord and who is a believer not to judge between good and bad when they are observing a particular behavior. We often judge because we start from the foundation of moral right or wrong. We do not observe the behavior itself. Our emotional interpretations cloud what is being done. I am referring to the way we function in society and how many of our prophecies are reactions to what we consider moral or immoral. The problem is God does not work like that. God does act morally. God always observes the act before He talks morally. God also observes the intent of the heart.

If you observe the intent of the heart, you cannot judge the act first. However, if you observe the intent of the heart, you will appear unjust to people because you will exonerate someone who seems guilty in front of everyone's eyes. If you knew what was in the heart of someone and what they were trying to do for you (and it was great), but they made a terrible mistake, you are more likely to let it go. You do it all the time. You say, "I know his heart. Bless his heart. He is a clumsy one. I wish he didn't do it." Because he has a good heart, and he does not have the wherewithal to do what he was trying to do, you as a human being excuse what he has done. How much more will God do that? You do it with your children as well.

You know the preachers used to give us illustrations as kids. Let us say you have two children. One is grown up and pours water over you because he is angry, while the other one is about three years old and brings water to you. As he brings the water, he pours half on the carpet, but you would not yell at him. Why would you react so differently? As clumsy as the three-year old is, that clumsiness and all the mess does not bother you one bit. There is no parent here who has not picked up after his or her messy child. This example is just a simple way of saying to you that self-observation is not about judging yourself. Self-observation is actually about looking at what you are doing. What am I doing? I am walking. Not I am walking well or badly. That is not self-observation. It will help you to ask yourself, "What exactly am I doing?"

In most of our daily lives, we do not practice self-observation mainly because we over-identify with things. We *over*-identify. Man's biggest problem since the fall is identification with things. I am not talking about identity now. Identity is different from identification. Identification refers to an attachment to something that is useless to our future and our destiny. We even identify with sin, and we use language to make it a part of our self even though we hate what we are doing. We never step back to ask ourselves why we hate this act so much. I observe myself and, if I hate what I am doing so much, I ask myself, "What do I keep doing that makes this act what it is?" However, I do not ask myself, "Why do I keep doing it?" You do not have the answer to why, do you? Forget all the reasons such as, "I do it because my parents did this." That has nothing to do with what you are doing. The question you should be asking is, "What am I doing? What exactly am I doing?" You see, your parents are not there doing it. You are doing it. The act itself is what is important at that moment. Pay attention to the act. The problem is we do not pay attention to the act; we pay attention to what we think *caused* the act, which is a way of transferring self-examination to somebody else. It does not mean your parents do not have influence. But the deliverance from what they are influenced by is not based on saying, "I am doing this because my parents did this and that to me." The deliverance is on looking at the act as *your* act and examining the act without judging it. What exactly is this? What does it look like when I get angry? What is anger exactly? What is going on in my body when I am angry? You must observe yourself from a third place. "When I do this, I feel like that. When I do that, I feel like this. This is exactly what I do when I am angry. This is what is going on when I am angry." After the observation, it is easy to understand what is actually happening.

> The problem is we do not pay attention to the act; we pay attention to what we think *caused* the act, which is a way of transferring self-examination to somebody else.

What happens to us as believers as we come from Heaven with all these great ideas? Soon we are living a mechanical life as we have discussed. We talked about the same thing regarding Adam. The good that came from Heaven gets submerged and suppressed. Then you were born again from Heaven and all these things happened to you. All of a sudden, five or seven or ten years later, they just go away. Where did they go? They were submerged by religious systems, by the way you were taught, and by habits you have developed. Likewise, you identified with certain doctrines along the way. I can go on and on.

We have identified with certain doctrines and a certain mode of teaching to the point that, if someone wants to change a particular doctrine, we feel it is an attack on ourselves. Identification has become our problem. We develop attachments to things that are completely irrelevant to who we are and to our future. In other words, we develop personalities around us. We create these personalities. I am not talking about your bodies. Personality is the mask you put on to appear what you are *not* to everybody else, including yourself. So now you create all the personalities and you are no longer in charge. These personalities are going around doing things in your name without your permission.

When something like this happens, you say, "That is not me. I am truly, truly sorry. That is unlike me." You are right. It is a personality you have created, a kind of alter ego that takes over from you to do the things you really do not like to do.

I used to be very, very angry and seething inside. And I hated it. The more I hated it, the angrier I became. I thought, "I hate this" and I fed the monster. When I learned self-observation, I just stood back one day and left my body. I used to leave my body and come back and still have the same problem. If you think that because you are ascending to Heaven you do not have a problem, stop lying to yourself. You see, I would go into the spiritual realm and come back and I would still have the same problem. I was not actually using leaving my body in the right way because I was not observing myself. One day I decided that if I am angry, I am going to leave my body and watch myself.

Your soul is now able to do what it has always been supposed to do because of the bypassing process

I did not like what I saw. I looked at all the acts and all the mechanisms, and I realized that I was a machine just reacting automatically. And I thought, "You are a machine. You are not conscious. You think you are conscious, but you are not because you are not acting consciously. If you acted consciously, many of those personalities would go away. The only way they can act in your name is because they know you are asleep." These personalities act the same way in you. They know you are asleep so they go out and act in your name. Then when you wake up one morning, they say, "Who did that?" They did it in *your* name. You created them to go do things for you. What you need to understand is that sometimes the things you go through send you downward into an inaccessible depth. Then you live a life of mechanical, self-defense and self-protection, not because you are a bad person, but because of trauma.

People do things to us. When I hold my ministerial seminars, I deal with such issues and I talk deeply about it. We push down the things that can help us; we even refuse for people to work with us to help us. Because we have been hurt so much, even though we are helping people, most of our actual gift is submerged in a place where it cannot be accessed. Then you come and start talking, and remembering decrees and declarations. Everything in you does not really believe in these decrees you are making. "I am God. I feel like I am filled with the Spirit of God. I have complete and total health." Yet you have pain in your back or in your neck even though you are decreeing and declaring that you are completely healthy and you are walking in health. So, guess what? Such things are in you because everything has been pushed down. As I was saying, stop lying. I often have people say to me, "This does not feel real. I feel like I am faking it."

Another thing that goes through your mind is, "I am being so selfish. Is this pride?" You know how righteous you become when you are actually going to ask and desire something that will transform you. You become extremely righteous. Then you remember that you need to be humble because you are a child of God. It is not a bad problem to have, but this is a problem nonetheless. It becomes a hindrance for you to be able to do anything else. But the more you speak it, the more you make the decrees and declarations, the more it rewrites your mindset. What you are doing is speaking from the super-conscious level and, when you speak like that, you bypass all of the earthly systems because whatever you are saying is not the reality of your life here. When you bypass those systems, you bypass your normal consciousness, your Subconscious, and your mechanical processes because now you are speaking by will. You are willing something into existence. So you bypass the systems in this realm and come to the place where what you brought from Heaven has been pushed down. Your voice begins to resonate at the depth of your being, and in doing so, it begins to release all the things that the Angel of the Face was meant to teach you, which you do not remember. All of a sudden you have revelations about things and you think, "It just came to me." You do not realize that you have been activating things from the deep places within you. Then your body begins to remember. Your soul is now able to do what it has always been supposed to do because of the bypassing process.

The new things you are developing and these new thoughts you bring forth do not go back up. They also bypass the blocks and go through the World of Action, which is called *Assiah*. Assiah passes up through *Yetzirah*, the World of Formation and, from there, passes back up to *Briah*, the World of Creation. They are creating a reverse movement back into *Atziluth*, the World of Emanations. All these things turn everything stuck here in this realm into elemental principles, and then they drop back down into this realm. Whenever you are making decrees and declarations, you are bypassing all the mechanisms you have built throughout your life. By decrees and declarations, you bypass your defense structures and all that painful experience that your body remembers and has carried, including the painful experience of the soul that is dead and buried in baptism. Then you come back down to the depth where all the good things you brought from Heaven have been buried. You do not need to go to Heaven to find where the good things God put in you have been stored. You have been carrying it all along. The problem is we have been going to Heaven, but we are not going to the depths of our own being. As the Bible says,

> You do not need to go to Heaven to find where the good things God put in you have been stored.

> **"The word is near you, in your mouth and in your heart."** (*Romans 10:8*)

You are carrying it. Your deliverance has always been with you. The treasures of darkness are not the darkness of other people. Now, when you make decrees and declarations, you understand that you bypass all your "normal" consciousness (which is not so normal). You bypass your Subconscious, which is the only thing that stands between the depth of your being and bad habits that people have programmed you to do. That is what your Subconscious is—programming. Divine healing is down deep. When you release it, it moves through this world and it goes up in the opposite direction. Then certain actions in your life begin to change. Suddenly, you are forming and framing things in your mind (in Hebrew thought, this is the counter-movement from going down the Tree of Life). You are actually going down, removing the things that are in there, and re-transmuting them back to spirit in order to redeliver them into your own being.

You will notice that you start doing certain things and you do not even know that you are doing them. These things are what you pull out from the depths through your *mitzvah*. As I have spoken about previously, the *mitzvah* is that one act that is able to change the world. You start doing some crazy acts and they begin to make a difference. You take what is here and pass it through the World of Action. Maybe your action is worship and it begins to form and it goes through another form and then it returns to the place where it came from in creation. Whatever it is, you activate it. You take it through the world of Assiah, the world of Yetzirah, the world of Briah, and the world of Atziluth, back into nothingness where it becomes elemental in nature. It returns to the pure spiritual realm where it can now be distilled back into your life and you can make it into what it is supposed to be. Remember all this! You are making these declarations based on Christ, YHVH, and YHSVH. The Names of God and the substantial powers of them now imbue your own declarations with power to bypass normal structures. You are now able to live from a superconscious level—open above and open below.

We as believers need to understand this process. If you are making a declaration and you are not accessing the depths, it means your declaration is not written well or is not being spoken the way it is supposed to be spoken. My declaration is not a wish. It is a desire. These are two different things. I make decrees about my health. I decree and I declare that the Father, the Son, and the Holy Spirit will me health and wealth. I am healthy and wealthy. I operate in perfect health and abundant wealth. I exude complete health. Every fiber of my being operates in the health of my Father. The wealth of God that indwells me is constantly flowing out. I attract wealth. I am an embodiment of wealth. The universe bends to me for wealth.

Even the trees of the field recognize me when I walk by them because they know I am a candidate of wealth and that I am an embodiment of divine wealth. I was making that declaration when my wife and I were going behind the supermarket to get food they threw away in order to eat at that time and help other people who were struggling. When I could not afford a plane ticket, I made decrees and declarations that I am a business class and first-class flyer. If the tax man comes to me today, he will notice I have never paid a full price for any business ticket ever in my life.

I walked into the airport one day and the woman behind the counter told me all the business class seats were full. I said, "Really? Okay, put me in my seat." I just sat in my seat and my phone rang to go up to business class. I made those decrees and declarations because I knew for a long time that I would be traveling frequently. Prophets whom I respect gave words to me about what I was going to do in this life. "You will go from nation to nation, and you will teach and preach this Gospel. You will travel the world to preach the Gospel." They were not trying to butter my bread because I did not have any bread at the time, nor did I have any butter. I am not trying to be prideful, but I want you to see. This is one of my decrees and declarations. It is a desire I have. I told the Lord my desire is not to sit in a plane for 28 hours in economy and have my feet hurt when I land so that I have a hard time teaching for 6 hours. It is a desire. You can complain if you want. People ask me if I fly business class and I say, "Yes! I do!" Some Christians all get discombobulated because they think I pay too much. It is because God has made it possible so that, every time I travel, I get great treatment and great prices. Even the airline staff knows it is a miracle. It is rooted in my decrees and declarations.

This is my decree. I just kept making the same decree because the whole opinion in the church was, if you try to fly business class, you are wasting God's money. That is the first reaction Christians have. But they never ask you how much you pay it. There are people who paid more than me who are sitting in economy. It is not because I am smarter. It is because I have been making these decrees for years and I refuse to let anything stand in my way because it is a desire.

Stop trying to act as if you are trying to save God money. Are you saving God money? You are not saving God anything. You are just suffering unnecessarily. Sometimes, by suffering like this, you keep yourself from meeting people who would bless you. I have met people who have blessed me in business class. There are times I am put in a particular seat for a reason. This happened the other day. On this occasion, I was seated in Economy Comfort. There

It is rooted in my decrees and declarations.

is no comfort there, but the guy next to me started talking to me, telling me what he does and then I realized why I was there. Then I gave God the permission to put me where He needs me. I said, "Father, I like to fly business class all the time. This is my decree unless You have someone who needs salvation or who needs something from the kingdom. But it will be good if You bring them up to first class." I am like a baby with God. When my father was 92, I still put my head on his chest. At 60 years old, I was still hugging my father and putting my head on his shoulder, so I figure I can do that with God as well.

אֶהְיֶה אֲשֶׁר אֶהְיֶה

Ehyeh-Asher-Ehyeh

The principle of rectifying the world begins with you as you speak into an environment to become the alchemical vessel for transformation in the world.

YOUR BODY: THE ALCHEMICAL VESSEL FOR TRANSFORMING THE WORLD

This sounds basic, but it is not because I realized that most people do not practice. I have had to push all those who study with me to do this, including smart people, because they second-guess themselves all the time. I want to get you to shift from second-guessing yourself to just actually saying things and believing it. Every time you second-guess yourself, you are walking in unbelief because you are double-minded and you are unstable, not just in one way but in all your ways.

> **If any of you lacks wisdom, let him ask God, who gives generously to all without reproach, and it will be given him. But let him ask in faith, with no doubting, for the one who doubts is like a wave of the sea that is driven and tossed by the wind. For that person must not suppose that he will receive anything from the Lord; he is a double-minded man, unstable in all his ways. (James 1:5-8)**

As you have heard me mention, you can use the principles of "re-scrolling" to overcome double-mindedness and access all the things that came with you from Heaven:

- Re-scribe your scroll
- Re-align your will to the will of the Father
- Reach into the depths of your being to unleash the potent powers that came with you from Heaven that have now become submerged into your Unconscious and Subconscious mind
- Re-write your DNA
- Re-calibrate your energetic centers
- Open your physical body to receive what you say in your decrees and declarations

Remember that the things that came with you from Heaven are still with you, but they have been submerged. Even as a believer, experiences will make you push things down. You can rewrite your own structure with your words. We still do not know how much conversation affects people's DNA. We do know, however, that there is a sound to the structure of our cells, which gives us the capacity to recalibrate our energetic centers. You know your body is a vessel. It is a temple. We need to get our bodies to not only receive the Holy Spirit, but also to receive other things from the spirit realm. The body is a vessel for manifesting in the concrete world. When you speak like this, the body opens itself up to receive.

> When we ascend into the heavens, we will see what Heaven looks like.

When we ascend into the heavens, we will see what Heaven looks like. The real purpose of ascending to Heaven is to come back to this realm and declare what you have seen there. In this way, this atmosphere will come to reflect that which is up there. Just because you see it in Heaven does not make it manifest here. You and I know people who say they are going to Heaven but all they are doing is creating chaos around them. It is not because they are bad people. They see things in Heaven, but they come back and all they do is give us a testimony. They do not create a system for manifesting what they have seen in Heaven. It takes greater discipline to do that. It is easier to say, "I went to Heaven. I saw a dragon, and I beat it down and raised it back up! Wow, and that is it." When you approach your ascension experiences like this, you have not taken hold of the technology of Heaven that causes manifestation in your life.

In order to cause manifestation, you must use Heaven's technology. Heaven's technology is an imperial process of decrees and declarations where you become the imperator and speak from the position of your kingship and your priesthood. Being like God is not just an idea. It is not a fantasy. It is actually a technology. If you are God and you are like God, you must understand that you need to develop a language for manifestation. This is what you need to understand. As much as you may not like it, the universe you live in was created by you. It is a hard thing for us to realize. If you examine your life, many of the words you spoke without actually retracing your steps, have come to pass. It is just that you do not like it. Your word creates the world in which you live.

If somebody tells you, "I am tired of being in this world" and you do not do something about that speech, then the world has just been created. Doing something about it does not mean you just say, "Do not say that." It means you go into the source of the word and you uproot the word because it is a seed planted that must then bear fruit. I always tell people when they say negative things to me that I do not hear it. I go inside and I pull it out. The Nigerians do this very well. When you say things that you should not say to them and they know your words will affect them badly, they say, "I return it to the sender." That is what they do! They return it to the sender. This response is a spiritual technology through which you do not let any destructive seed or word affect you or stay in your consciousness. You shunt it away.

Many Christians have spiritual protection, but they do not have psychic protection. People can put negative thoughts or ideas into your mind. So, you have to watch and pray. Jesus said watch and pray so that you will not be tempted (Matthew 26:41). Watch and pray because you do not know the hour. We use this expression in many ways. You have to watch and pray because the things that come into your vicinity as words, pictures, or other things can actually affect your mind. It is amazing how people carry all kinds of crazy toxic thoughts in their minds, but they make sure to avoid dog poo. They protect the external structure more than they protect the internal. They spew out words that are more poisonous than a cobra's venom and they think it is okay. But they will not allow any dirt to touch their clothes. They spend hours cleaning a spot, but let things run rampant in their minds. So, they build the world in which they live. There is an English proverb, "You cannot keep birds from flying over your head, but you can keep them from building a nest in your hair." This is what we have to learn. Thoughts and words are very powerful when people speak them to you. If they hit you the wrong way, you immediately remove them from your vicinity by the power of the spirit.

You would be amazed at how easy it is to program Christians. This is my fight. I am trying to get Christians to stop being so programmable. People in society know that if they put one idea on television for three to four days, a prophet will pick it up and transfer it to all believers. Believers take it in because they have no psychic filter. The incapacity to build up the soul is the problem that you have. Your spirit is not the problem. Remember that, because your spirit is perfect, your soul came from Heaven in a perfect state without sin, but you were a baby.

> **But I, brothers, could not address you as spiritual people, but as people of the flesh, as infants in Christ. I fed you with milk, not solid food, for you were not ready for it. And even now you are not yet ready, for you are still of the flesh. (*1 Corinthians 3:1-3*)**

This passage is referring to your soul. Your soul came from Heaven perfect, but it is not mature. So, if you subject yourself to certain things, your soul, even though it came from Heaven, will remain at that immature state.

You must get your soul to come to the fullness of who it is and learn how to shunt away thoughts that are sown into your mind by society and even by yourself. I am talking to myself as well. We have this power, but you and I cannot do this unless we are self-observers. That is the diligence of a spiritual person. You know these things as you observe yourself. You are not obsessed, but you are observant. You can do it with one act. You do not need to do it with everything. Do you realize you can examine one of your acts and change everything about your life? This is possible for every action you carry out, especially the ones that you do not like. The whole structure of the way you behave is in your soul. Even your good structure is in it. Your misbehavior is part of your virtue.

The seed is never far from the righteousness of the person. Your righteousness is based on your strengths and virtues. I was taught this principle in Sunday school by a good mother who said to me, "Show me your greatest weakness and I will show you how that is your greatest strength." I hated the process, but it turned out to be true. Motherhood is sometimes better than a PhD.

ADONIJAH O. OGBONNAYA PH.D.

Sometimes, people ask, "What is *Atziluth?*" *Atziluth* is the World of Emanation, the world of nothingness. *Atziluth* is where everything exists in its elemental mixture. By virtue of being aligned with the will of God, you bring it out through the re-scrolling process and it becomes a concretized action. That is why the Bible can say nothing is impossible (Luke 1:37). Nothing is impossible because everything has a spiritual

Knowing about higher dimensions is one thing, but accessing them is done through your desire, through your language, and through your act.

origin. Everything can be taken back to its origin and, from there, re-configured to something else. You can take any "still" and raise it up to its monatomic level. The ancients used to call it "the spirit of the still" or "the spirit of this, the spirit of that." They knew something could be brought to life in iron or gold, even though these elements contained no spirit.

We are going to practice accessing the properties of the higher dimensional realities. Knowing about higher dimensions is one thing, but accessing them is done through your desire, through your language, and through your act. More than that, it is done by actually paying attention to the structure of your own body. I am not talking about how your body feels physically. Do you know that your soul moves around your body? You can actually zero in on a point in your body, gather your soul in that place, and then deliberately move your soul to examine your whole body. You must be able to observe and focus all your attention on your feet. Start practicing observation by observing your physical mechanisms. Most of the time, you are not judging your body's movement. You just know it is moving. You move beyond observation and into judgements when you begin to think things like, "I do not like my head. I do not like my backside. I do not like my feet." Those are secondary thoughts. If you simply observe the activity of a body part, it is different. You begin to feel it, and you know and sense each part. When you move it, you actually experience it moving.

Do you realize that you do not experience your body moving? It sounds

87

YOUR BODY

like something simple, but it is not. We are unaware of ourselves. Women are better than men at body-awareness because they must examine their bodies for all kinds of reasons. They are taught to make sure they do that. My wife was teaching my girls when they were 10 years old to examine their bodies when they started puberty. She did what mamas do naturally with their children. Check yourself; check your body, your stomach, feel your body. Most men do not do that to themselves. We do not even sense our bodies until we are in excruciating pain or we are as sick as a dog and our wives have to baby us. They have to suggest we see the doctor and, after we argue about it, we pout all the way to the doctor.

Awakening is a constant act.

To understand higher dimensions, we must come from the inner mechanism of what we call "cosmic dialectics." What is a dialectic? It is when two opposites come together to create a synthesis. How do I act against the grain in order to create something new? When you go against the grain and everything inside of you and you do it anyway, something is created. Remember, even a dead fish can float down the river. It takes a live fish to swim up and jump from one river to another. Since consciousness is a spectrum of rivers. Most people remain in the same spectrum floating down the road. God gets you to shift by causing a shock in your life. Many of us get more shocks because we keep going back to sleep and God needs us to stay awake. The uncomfortable things in your life keep you awake.

When you do things repeatedly, it eventually becomes mechanical. If you are a preacher, for example, you may preach just because you know how to do it. It is going so well. Everyone tells you how wonderful you are. Then God sends one spoiler who says, "She is doing this only for the money," or, "He is just so prideful," and the shock wakes you up. You are more alert about what you are doing at that moment even though you are fighting with the person. You had come to the point when you were not thinking about it because it was second nature to you. May I suggest to you that God does not like second nature? He wants you alert, not because you are a bad person but because being awake is very important to Him. Sometimes He just does it to shift you from one level of consciousness to another. A shock is what gets you to develop a waking life. This whole thing is really about waking up. The Bible says in Ephesians 5:14:

**Awake, O sleeper, and arise from the dead, and
Christ will shine on you.**

The world in which you grew up is always trying to put you to sleep. And they are not trying to put just your ordinary life to sleep. They are trying to put your God potential back into the submerged state so you are walking as a sleeping person. Even if you are doing many religious activities and preaching a lot, your God consciousness is submerged. Awakening is a constant act. This is where your decrees and proclamations come into play. They remind you about your identity and who you really are.

Do you know that in communion, part of what you say is, "This is my body which was broken for you?" The church has never said, "This is the Body of Christ that was broken for you." The priest always says, "This is my body broken for you." Something in this statement wakes you up to your divinity. Communion awakens you to your divinity. Christians who do not want to celebrate Good Friday do not understand that the shock of the death of Christ is the constant waking of Christians. The church picked that day deliberately to celebrate Christ's suffering because it is a shock to the system of man. Without these times, Christians can just go to sleep and never wake up.

There are a number of mechanisms for waking ourselves up. I have taught one of them. YHVH is a cosmic code that unravels technology. It is an instrument for what I call "fractalizing." When a believer aligns their will to the will of the Father, they can combine fragments into wholeness. They can do this because they stand within the Name, which is both the cosmic code "unraveller" and fractal technology. Everywhere God distills Himself, He is *completely* present, not *totally* present, but *complete in the presence*. In other words, there is full representation of Divinity in everything that God does. God does this by giving the Name to you, which then becomes a fractal that takes

YOUR BODY

whatever you are doing and always creates it in wholeness.

When you stand in your cube of Metatron or Enoch (see later chapters) and decree your desire, you are manifesting things within the context of your own world. In addition, you are also fractalizing the same things in other worlds. The process of fractal technology is occurring when you surround yourself with the Names of God. Whatever you manifest here, you also manifest in other worlds. Think of it like a mirror. There is a place in Heaven that looks like that. It is the place where you see yourself reflected to all eternity.

If you do this effectively, do you know how powerful this act is? If you make your decrees and declarations within the context of the Name effectively, they will jump from you to your neighbor. People in your neighborhood will start doing things and speaking a certain way. You will affect the environment where you are, but you need to do it consistently. It is hard to get a Jew to talk the way I talk. Even when they are in the secular world, their language remains the same because somebody has fractalized. Even in church, we have some languages that we have decided to discard because someone developed them in the context of a mystical journey and then transferred it to everybody. This process was a powerful movement or wave transfer that is now waning because there are no people on the edge of its movement who have picked it up to continue the fractal movement. Organizations and spiritual movements die when the fractalizing process stops. That means there is no capacity for mirroring what has been created into the next generation. However, the believer who understands this technology also understands that all of this is about transforming the world. This believer knows that Christ is doing this in the environment. They can transform the world if they do the same thing effectively and not just for themselves. The problem is that something is created or manifested whether you do it for selfish reasons or to actually rectify the world.

The cosmic logic that is embedded in the Name of God carries the proto-frequency of time and space. The Name itself carries a proto, which is a frequency before it is actually manifested, or what we call "primordial frequency of time and space." That is why the Name is four letters and it moves in four dimensions. In reality, however, we can see only three dimensions.

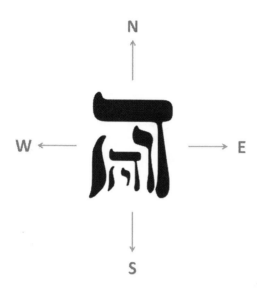

From the center, the name vibrates through the letters and impacts all of the universe. So, take it and speak it north, east, south, and west, the fundamental directions of life for us. The frequency of the letters of the Name carries the potential for all the other frequencies in nature. From the center of the Name, a believer stands immediately within the four quadrants of direction (N, S, E, W). When you are standing in the center of the Name of the Lord, you are immediately noticeable in four places at once. You are now operating in a four-dimensional world. The basic structure that a believer works from is four dimensions, but the fifth dimension is available to you and so is the sixth, seventh, eighth, ninth, and so on until you get to the sixteenth at a very basic level. There are four basic dimensions: three dimensions that you see and one dimension that you do not see. Some say in science that time is the fourth dimension, but spiritually speaking, man is the fourth dimension.

In order to see the next dimension from where you are, you must go beyond yourself. If a being is in one dimension, he cannot see the second dimension. If a being is in the third dimension, he cannot see the fourth. If a being is in the fourth dimension, he cannot see the fifth. You get the point. Man is the being who occupies or carries the fourth dimension but has the capacity to transcend himself to be able to see the four dimensions. A man is able to see himself. This is called the "reflective process" where human beings are able to become reflective. They are seeing where they are, in the moment they are, in that place. They can move outside themselves to see themselves. That is the way God sees Himself too. In Exodus 3:14, Moses asks God who He is and God replies with, *"Ehyeh-Asher-Ehyeh"* (אֶהְיֶה אֲשֶׁר אֶהְיֶה) or "I am that I am." It can also be translated as "I will be what I will be." The wonderful thing about the Name is that it can be translated in a variety of ways and they are all right. For example,

I am that I am
I shall be what I shall be
I am what I shall be
I shall be what I am

Some say that YHVH must have only one definition, but for the Jew at least, that is not the case. The more you change the word the more it tells you about God:

YHVH	יְהֹוָה	The self-existent one
HYHV	הִיְהֹוַ	The loving one
VHYH	וְהִיְה	The becoming one: The future one who is in the present The present one who is in the future
HVHY	הֹוָהִי	The living one

If I center myself in the middle of the Name, I am declaring that the self-existent one, by loving, becomes for me my life. I am using the same Name, but I have saturated myself in a sixteen-dimensional world. It is one Name, but I have put myself right in the center. I find myself in the self-existing nature of God, the love of God, in the unfolding of God. We call it "revelation unfolding." When I get to the center, I am actually calling forth life.

ADONIJAH O. OGBONNAYA PH.D.

One of the key technologies in rectifying your world is the Name of God. Your decrees and declarations should never be made without the Names of God. They carry with them the fullness of the fractal sparks that inform the fabric of existence. The Name of God that you decree and declare is also the instrumentation for releasing the *kellipot* and the sparks that are caught in darkness and raising them back up. This is not salvation. It is the release of the human potential. You want to release the God-potential in man. These are two different things. There are things human beings can do on their own, things for which you do not need God. To confuse that with what you are becoming as a child of God is to miss the point. You are not just being raised to fulfill your role as a human being. You are being raised to move beyond that to actually fulfill what God would fulfill. The Names of God are one of the keys.

> Decrees and declarations are technologies of life and restoration because they carry the substance of God.

There are so many names of God in scripture as in Deuteronomy 10:17:

For the LORD your God is God of gods and Lord of lords, the great, the mighty, and the awesome God, who is not partial and takes no bribe.

Decrees and declarations are technologies of life and restoration because they carry the substance of God. The name of the king is the same as the person of the king. You can get killed for insulting a king's name because it is considered equivalent to the person of the king. The name is the embodiment of the person.

The Name is an instrument for pulling up sparks. It is true that it is an instrument for salvation. Yet the Name can be used in the context of unbelief and unrighteousness, and it will pull up what is right in the person's life. It even gives them the light of intellect to produce something because it is the substance of the king. If God is good and I use His Name in a setting that is not godly, He will find the good in that context and draw it out. This has nothing to do with salvation because

YOUR BODY

believers are always thinking that if something good happens then salvation is happening. That is not true. If witches get together and they decide to say the Name of God, whatever light of humanity is within them and whatever good they want to do will come to the top. The name of God will allow them to accomplish it, even if it is from a selfish desire. They are taught to have good intentions to clear their minds. They cannot get it by being unrighteous. This can be paradoxical. If you listen to these people, you will hear them say they want to help humanity. For example, they want to create medicine to cure sickness. The Name of God used in that context draws the capacity to get the medicine, but when they get it, they mix it with poison because their nature bends towards evil.

> The mysteries of the Names of God are so involved and so complex in layers of symbols, numbers, and metaphors.

When I use the Names of God, it creates a pulsation and oscillation in the atmosphere and things begin to balance themselves out because the good in that Name will always come out. Depending on who is using it, this good can be sustained for a while and then it stops. The only person who is able to handle the Name of God for a long time is the person who is a believer in whom He lives. Divine Names are meant for human beings to use to cut through identity and identification within the human "force-of-habit" or mechanical fields that have been created.

The mysteries of the Names of God are so involved and so complex in layers of symbols, numbers, and metaphors. They carry the potential of all kinds of technologically innovative possibilities and are open to be used by anybody. I sometimes struggle, wondering why unbelievers should have the right to use the Name of God. It means you can go to a place where the Name will not work. What happens when you make a mistake? Should the Name work for you? The Name is given as an open technological system for anyone who is willing to use it. I must get over myself. It is the Name of God and He can handle whatever somebody does with it. You can use the Name of God to rectify worlds, to rectify time and space, and to rectify your work, but it requires conceptual clarity, deep intentional worship, conscious intention of the will, and a singularity of purpose that impinges on nothingness and taps directly from the source of its own creativity. You do not use the Name willy-nilly. It is not the signature of a shopping list. The Name of God is a handle you use for returning to *Ain Sof*, to return to nothingness. That is, you go to the place of nothingness where everything is spiritual and where there is neither this nor that. All the elemental principles are there in their as yet uncreated state. When you find yourself there in consciousness and wakefulness, you are able to speak to the elements and tell them to become what you want them to be in the realm where you came from. And by this realm you came from, I mean the earth realm where you now live, the place from where you ascended. The Name of God can be used as a way of coaxing intractable materiality to give up its fragrance. So when you take the Name, the Name is used. The Name is not just tagged onto your list. It can be used to coax the inner gateways to go to the inner sacramentality of matter and allow it to bring forth its fragrance and release it ever so gently, sometimes ever so minutely, to reveal the secret hidden Divinity within it.

You have been taught to use the Name as a tag, but it is a handle for coaxing the inner creative principle in intractable matter. It will give it to you if you whisper the Name of its Creator at a certain frequency and if you give it the sound of the Name. It is not just saying the Name, but knowing how to structure the Name to have the elements respond to you. It allows you to develop a mental mutability and an associated fluidity so that you have the ability to change things. Nothing is impossible. Your mind operates in the capacity to relate to things until they come together in a way that shocks everybody. Your mind is open enough to be fluid. It is not stuck in dogmatic nonsense where you become like the rock of Gibraltar and everyday your song is "I shall, I shall not be moved." By using the Name, all things become an open door. If you use the Name correctly, the rock will open up and cry out. If you use the Name well, the tree will give up its fragrance, open up its trunk, and release its treasures. If you use the Name right, the stars will sparkle before you and release their oil upon your head.

Learn how to use the Name. Allow the Name to become the elemental movement around you. Then when you actually sit in the Name, the

YOUR BODY

universe looks into where you are standing and says, "I want to be there."

For the creation waits with eager longing for the revealing of the sons of God. (*Romans 8:19*)

For we know that the whole creation has been groaning together in the pains of childbirth until now. (*Romans 8:22*)

When you begin to use the Name, it begins to vibrate in your DNA and that is why the substance of the king is heard in the sound of the cells of your body. The Name of God is an eternal name, but it rides upon the human impulse of time.

We have twelve structures of time that allow you to change things and to change time, to change how things are being traded in the world. The Name of God rides upon that and the impulse of time. Knowing how and when to use the Name of God correctly can do things for you beyond your imagination. True, nothing is impossible, but there are times when things become easier because the time and the Name are synchronized.

The Name of God allows you to recall eternal events. When the seraphs in the book of Isaiah screamed, "*Kadosh! Kadosh! Kadosh!*" something happened to Isaiah. When they sang the song, the temple shook and something opened behind God. When the Name is used correctly, it will unlock the living pillars of Heaven or of the throne room. I have seen the fire in the altar in Heaven go ballistic because the Name of God was spoken. When the Name is spoken with certain intonations and at certain vibrational frequencies, you can feel your body getting goose bumps, heat, pressure, or whatever it is you feel when the Holy Ghost comes upon you. This is your body trying to recall eternal events. So, there is method to my madness when I stand in front of you and keep saying the Names of God. This process usually opens up the knowing power that is embedded within you.

"Because he has set his love upon Me, therefore I will deliver him; I will set him on high, because he

has known My name. He shall call upon Me, and I will answer him; I *will be* with him in trouble; I will deliver him and honor him. With long life I will satisfy him, And show him My salvation." (*Psalm 91:14-16 - NKJV*)

What is the technology for deliverance and for exaltation? It is the *knowledge* of the Name—not the *saying* of the name. Knowledge is intimacy and wrapping yourself with light (Psalm 104). To know something is to be wrapped by flowing light. Knowing the Name of God is your key to personal exaltation. I started teaching YHVH because I noticed people were not actually ascending. They were merely operating in visualizations like, "I visualize a garden." They knew the Name, but they did not know the Lord. When the knowing was taught, the movement shifted. People started ascending because they actually knew the Name.

The Abulafia principle is based on the teachings of Abraham Abulafia, a thirteenth century Jewish mystic who founded the school of Prophetic Kabbalah. He created the method to develop the Name of God in a structure that allows a person to know the Name so keenly that they develop a prophetic consciousness. Leave Abulafia alone for now. It can illuminate your way, strengthen your contemplative consciousness, and drive your being towards unity with Divine Consciousness. You can also create an altered state of consciousness. It is in the Name that time becomes malleable.

97

YOUR BODY

You say, "I do not know how to love," but the impulse of love is in the Name. You say, "I do not know how to be righteous," but the impulse of righteousness

The Name of God allows you to recall eternal events.

is in the Name. You say, "I do not know how to ascend," but the ladder to ascension is in the Name. When the heart is enfolded into and enrapt by the Name, a portal opens where the person, by the Name, multiplies himself and travels through dimensions away from where they are now yet remaining conscious of who they are and where they are. The Name then creates a vessel for the transference of consciousness. When you use the Name, your consciousness gets split among these multiple selves while remaining whole. So, when you use the Name your consciousness does not truly split because your full consciousness is now transferred into the vessel of the Name that takes it everywhere because it is complete. The Name does not fragmentize. You can actually multiply or stream your consciousness to different locations if you want to use the technological Name.

> When someone calls upon the Name of God in truth, God literally comes down to look.

For me, the very principle of *YHVH* is streaming the consciousness to sixteen streams at the same time to try to get you to think about all of them simultaneously and then perceive them. The letters are organized to be a vessel for your consciousness. Each letter can carry your consciousness. What did Enoch, Abraham, Moses, Elijah, and Jesus and the apostles know? The way Jesus taught the apostles the Lord's Prayer (Matthew 6:9-13) means He considered the Name to be one of the things. He never said the Name in the prayer, but He said, "Hallowed be thy name." You can actually argue that the entirety of the Lord's Prayer hinges on knowing the Name of God the Father.

Provision is based on knowing the Name of the Father. Healing is based on the Name. There are many Names of God and each one creates various ways of seeing into various realms. Depending on how you structure it, it can create new dimensions of your consciousness. When you embrace it at the core of your being, it becomes a technology for bliss and ecstasy. When the Name releases love in you, it can help you overcome reticence and restlessness. Take the Name and work on it. Everything in Psalm 91 talks about knowing His Name:

**I will set him up on high, because he has known
My name.**

The word for "call" in Hebrew is *qara* (קָרָא). It is a good word because it creates an encounter. Intrinsically, *qara* means it is placing a mark that someone can remember. As quiet as it is kept, your name is a mark on your body that makes you respond. It is not just a name. I could call your name and make you fear. I could call your name and make you joyful. To call your name is to place an ensign or insignia in space. *Qara* is also a word that can mean either calling or writing someone. The root of the word means to mark something so he shall call on the name. Let us change the word and say, "He shall use my name as a marker and I will run to the mark." Or we could say, "He shall place my name as an ensign and I will bring my troops to the location where the name is placed." Do you know that if you put the sign of a king somewhere, the troops will rally to the place? I am just using ordinary examples to teach us. Sometimes if you do not use common sense, people think you are talking over their heads, but I am not really. I am just giving you illustrations. When you are actually living in the Name of God, it becomes a sign of attraction.

Remember I said that the universe bends towards the person who stands in the Name and says, "I want to be over there." When someone calls upon the Name of God in truth, God literally comes down to look. The use of the Name of God affects the coming and going of the Holy Spirit. We know that God does not come and go, but in human terms, the use of the Name of God affects the comings and goings of God. If I call you, what would you do? If we are friends, you will come. The call of your name affects your coming and going. It is the same way with God. It affects the movement of Heaven when it is done correctly. Actually, the host of Heaven is re-organized based on who is calling the Name of God and how they are calling.

Call to me and I will answer you, and will tell you
great and hidden things that you have not known.
(*Jeremiah 33:3*)

The Name of God harbours and carries revelatory possibilities within it. It is the *Sod* of God, the secret, and the foundation of who God is. When your decrees and declarations are made in the context of the Name, the various Names of God create different effects of the manifestation. We use the word "*YHVH*" because in Judaism it is considered the highest name that manifests in creation. But the Name of emanation is the Name we talked about before—*Eyeh* is considered

YOUR BODY

the Name that releases from nothingness into the Name "*YHVH*" which becomes the four rivers of Eden. The name *Eyeh* is considered the Name above Eden. The Name is the source of the four rivers that are manifested in the four nations. This is why *Adonai YHVH* is spelled in Hebrew with four letters.

The word "*Eyeh-Asher-Eyeh*" is considered to be the fountainhead where God gathers His strength to be manifested through creation into the four heads: into abundance, breaking forth, opening, and super abundance. The four nations are used as an example of how God functions in the world. These are manifested as flowing from the name "I AM" which is "I will become what I will become" or "that which I am I shall always become." Coming from *YHVH*, it moves four rivers into four nations, and then four nations move into the five powers of man, which are the five blessings that God gave Adam:

Be fruitful

Multiply

Have dominion

Have rulership

Replenish the Earth

The five blessings of man are represented by the five-letter Name *YHSVH* (יהשׁוָהֶ) which is represented in the Name of Jesus. The messianic age is represented by five letters, which is represented in the five powers of man in the name Jesus. Have you ever asked why Jesus is five letters and Christ is five letters? Jesus Christ is ten letters. He is seldom called just Jesus. Mostly modern people call him just Jesus. He is actually called "Jesus the Christ." If you read all the old prayers, it is always in the Name of Jesus Christ, not just Jesus. What do you think our fathers and mothers were doing when they kept saying, "In the name of Jesus Christ?"

> When your decrees and declarations are made in the context of the Name, the various Names of God create different effects of the manifestation.

Using the Name and the way you relate to it matters. Could it be that we really do not know how to use the Name and this is why we are not having the results we desire?

אֶל הַגָּדֹל

El Haggadol

I am a fanatic when it comes to Jesus Christ, in Judaism and in Christianity (but I walk away from Judaism when they begin to say that Jesus Christ is not the Messiah).

GOD'S MEASURES OF RIGHTEOUSNESS: MERCY, KINDNESS, AND LOYALTY

As much as I love my people, I am different from most Christians. There are some things that Christians do that make Christianity void. For instance, the way that they act like Christianity is the end of Judaism. Christianity is the natural progression of Judaism. The religion of Jesus is the natural progression of Judaism.

When believers ignore the coming of Jesus to tell us that we must keep the law, then they do not understand the teaching of Christ. Jesus did so much to bring Gentiles into the kingdom. However, if you decide to follow the law, it means that you must convert back to Judaism. However, if you were not born a Jew, you do not keep the Jewish law, and so you do not belong to the commonwealth of Israel. You can scream all you want to scream, but if you decide you want to follow the law, then Jesus Christ means nothing to you. It is in the Bible, and I think some believers forget that. We act as if Jesus did not really come, His coming does not mean anything, and then tell you that you must keep the Sabbath.

Let us talk about that for a second. Moses told everyone to keep the Sabbath, but he did not keep it the way he told people to keep it. Moses said you could not enter the Holy of Holies except once a year and it was always with blood. Then he entered without blood, and he did it more than once a year. They said you could not see God face to face? And God said no one can see Him and live (Exodus 33:20). God had to precede His words to show him, and talk to Moses face to face. It sounds like a contradiction. Everything He said a human being could not do, God let Moses do, except when Moses struck the rock. Do you really think Moses did not know what he was doing?

The problem that led Moses into trouble was what he said. Moses was not punished for striking the rock. No place in scripture it says he was disciplined for striking the rock. He was disciplined for what he said at the time. Moses was disciplined for two things: for abusing the people of God and for raising himself and Aaron to the level of God. Do you remember what he said when he struck the rock?

> **"Take the staff, and assemble the congregation, you and Aaron your brother, and tell the rock before their eyes to yield its water. So you shall bring water out of the rock for them and give drink to the congregation and their cattle." And Moses took the staff from before the LORD, as he commanded him. Then Moses and Aaron gathered the assembly together before the rock, and he said to them, "Hear now, you rebels: shall we bring water for you out of this rock?" And Moses lifted up his hand and struck the rock with his staff twice, and water came out abundantly, and the congregation drank, and their livestock. And the LORD said to Moses and Aaron, "Because you did not believe in me, to uphold me as holy in the eyes of the people of Israel, therefore you shall not bring this assembly into the land that I have given them." (Numbers 20:8-12)**

God did not discipline Moses for striking the rock; the rock was meant to be struck. God said, "You will not enter the Promised Land because you did not glorify me in the presence of the people." There is not once God said he was wrong for striking the rock.

The Bible does not teach what you say it teaches.

Why did God give Moses such a special privilege and such freedom? It was because Moses operated under the priesthood of Melchizedek. He was not consecrated into the priesthood of animals and bulls. Why did the High Priest let David come into the Holy Place?

It was not only to take the sword but also to take the showbread. Only the priest can eat the showbread, but he let David eat it. Why did David get away with all this sin (except in the case of Uriah)? Remember what God said?

> **Thus says the LORD, the God of Israel, 'I anointed you king over Israel, and I delivered you out of the hand of Saul. And I gave you your master's house and your master's wives into your arms and gave you the house of Israel and of Judah. And if this were too little, I would add to you as much more.**
> **(2 Samuel 12:7-8)**

Westerners do not like that statement. It is one of those "pass-over" passages because they just do not like the passage. He said, "If you wanted more wives, I would have given them to you." I am quoting the Bible. Just because Westerners think polygamy is bad does not mean it is bad. The Bible does not teach what you say it teaches. What is the difference between polygamy and serial polygamy practiced in the West, where children are away from their fathers and some children do even not know their fathers? Many are trying to tell me Africans are immoral because they are polygamous. And I say to them, "Those men know their children. Where are yours? The kids know their father. Where is your child's father?" It is a very serious issue. We do not like to talk about it, but it does not mean it is good. There is no system in the world that is good or perfect. Stop claiming yours as superior to everyone else's. I come from a family where there is no polygamy. We never had it. I am not trying to defend anything. We did not have polygamy just because I was a Christian. It was because our lineage did not practice it. So, I cannot sit around and tell everybody else that does not practice monogamy that somehow my family is superior to theirs.

My question is still the same. Why was God so lenient with David, except in two cases? Can anyone tell me why God was so upset with him over the case of Uriah? Have you thought about it? We do not talk about the wives of all the men that David killed. He killed them and then took their wives. Why was the case of Uriah such a big deal? Uriah was a loyal person. Uriah was loyal to a fault to the king. I want to say this: you are in dangerous territory when you pick on a person who has been loyal to God, even if they are not part of the group that you are part of, or even if they have fallen into sin because God will ignore their sin and deal with you. Remember the Hittites were going to be wiped out. David said, "Oh, he is just a Hittite. God will not mind."

A person who is loyal to God is a dangerous person to play with. Many people suffer because they looked at someone who has been loyal and serving God for years, and thought they are not spiritual enough. Someone might not understand what he or she is doing, but God regards loyalty higher than He regards your personal righteousness. Why did God so love David? Was David a righteous man? Did he really bring his children up in righteousness? His children were practicing what they saw David do. Is it an accident that Solomon married a thousand women? Yes, we know he married three hundred, but add in the concubines. Try to sleep with a concubine of a king and your head will be off because they consider them their wives. Do you get the point? What was it that David transferred to Solomon that made Solomon marry a thousand women? What was it about David that God so loved? David's one failure was his disloyalty to Uriah. His disloyalty hurt God more than anything else and He was highly disappointed in David. His disloyalty to Uriah is the only thing for which God punished David directly, because he was completely loyal to God.

Anyone who operates in this power and knowledge must learn loyalty both to God and to the people with whom you are working. If you say, "I am not loyal to anyone," then you are a candidate for destruction. Be careful because you have to be loyal to something. I have watched God run over some people because they treated a man or woman who has been loyal to God for years as if they did not know anything. You do not know what other people know. God has gone out of His way to deal with those people who look down on others. They never understand what happened to them; they think it is the devil. In the Pentecostal and Charismatic movements, many people suffered because of how they treated the places where they came from.

Learning something new does not qualify you or give you the right to treat someone badly who has been sweating and crying at the altar of God for 30 years. God will deal with you. It scares me when people see an old man who has faithfully served the Lord and talk down to him. They say, "He is just an old guy" and discount the things he believes. Count me out! I will never do that because I am scared of God. He scares me because I know how God reacts to that behavior. I also know how God has dealt with people who have tried to treat me that way. I could have walked away several times. Your loyalty to God is what defends you, not your righteousness.

His heart really is set on you because you have been loyal.

We could pick your life apart and tell you how terrible you are, how you talk to us, how you treat us, but that is not the issue with you and God. The issue with you and God is: "I asked them to go and they went" and "I told them to stay and they stayed." Are you getting the point? His heart really is set on you because you have been loyal. I am not a prophet and I am not the son of a prophet, but God will reward your loyalty. The Bible says that God is not unjust. He will not forget the labor and the care that you have shown to the saints. Stop thinking that God is taking too long a time.

For God is not unjust so as to overlook your work and the love that you have shown for his name in serving the saints, as you still do. (Hebrews 6:10)

People who want to deal with hard things in the spirit really need to know what they are doing. Be careful when you or someone thinks they can open gates of judgement. Just because you are operating in your imagination does not mean you ascended or went anywhere. Many people pretend or imagine they are doing things in the spirit, yet nothing happens. When we look at the types of spiritual activities that bring forth judgement, we should remember people have been known to change the destiny of nations with what you know. If you think you are learning things that will prove you are a teacher of the gospel, think again. If you are not walking in mercy and kindness, you should not be

107

GOD'S MEASURES OF RIGHTEOUSNESS

studying this subject. Even justified killing leaves a stain in your blood. That is why God would not allow David to build His temple:

> **"But God said to me, 'You may not build a house for my name, for you are a man of war and have shed blood.'" (*1 Chronicles 28:3*)**

The same God who told him to fight is the One who told David he could not build His house. It was not a rebuke. God just told him he could not do it.

We must remember what it means for someone to be a widow and how God deals with widows. A righteous person is one who cares for the fatherless, cares for the widow, and cares for the stranger, which means most Christians are not righteous. They measure their righteousness by themselves, how they feel inside themselves, and the level of guilt (or non-guilt) they feel. That does not make us righteous.

> **"You shall not pervert the justice due to the sojourner or to the fatherless, or take a widow's garment in pledge, but you shall remember that you were a slave in Egypt and the LORD your God redeemed you from there; therefore I command you to do this. When you reap your harvest in your field and forget a sheaf in the field, you shall not go back to get it. It shall be for the sojourner, the fatherless, and the widow, that the LORD your God may bless you in all the work of your hands. When you beat your olive trees, you shall not go over them again. It shall be for the sojourner, the fatherless, and the widow. When you gather the grapes of your vineyard, you shall not strip it afterward. It shall be for the sojourner, the fatherless, and the widow. You shall remember that you were a slave in the land of Egypt; therefore I command you to do this." (*Deuteronomy 24:17-22*)**

If you measure the church by the three rules by which Israel was judged by God, the church is still guilty. It does not care for the widow, the fatherless, or for strangers. This is what God told Israel. Read the whole book of Jeremiah. God says the same thing to them repeatedly.

> **"For if you truly amend your ways and your deeds,**
> **if you truly execute justice one with another, if you**
> **do not oppress the sojourner, the fatherless, or the**
> **widow, or shed innocent blood in this place, and if**
> **you do not go after other gods to your own harm,**
> **then I will let you dwell in this place, in the land that I**
> **gave of old to your fathers forever." (*Jeremiah 7:5-7*)**

You oppress the widow, you oppress the fatherless and the orphans, and you treat the stranger badly. These three commands are throughout the Bible. It scares me to think of Christians supporting Israel while treating strangers badly at the same time. These behaviors are biblical principles of judgement. You can pontificate on your righteousness all you want, yet how you treat these groups of people is the fundamental measure of righteousness.

This same measure of righteousness is also a part of the structure that opens up the Ark of the Covenant. Deuteronomy 10 describes how Moses presented the new tablets in the Ark of the Covenant to the Israelites. This chapter includes the Names of God that I use to open up the Ark of the Covenant, to infuse it and enable it to handle the presence of God. These same Names allow you to handle the presence of God and open up your body to become an ark of the Lord. Let us look at some of them.

109

A righteous person is one who cares for the fatherless, cares for the widow, and cares for the stranger....

GOD'S MEASURES OF RIGHTEOUSNESS

> **"And now, Israel, what does the LORD your God**
> **require of you, but to fear the LORD your God,**
> **to walk in all his ways, to love him, to serve**
> **the LORD your God with all your heart and with**
> **all your soul, and to keep the commandments and**

statutes of the LORD, which I am commanding you today for your good? Behold, to the LORD your God belong heaven and the heaven of heavens, the earth with all that is in it.

Yet the LORD set his heart in love on your fathers and chose their offspring after them, you above all peoples, as you are this day. Circumcise therefore the foreskin of your heart, and be no longer stubborn. *For the LORD your God is God of gods and Lord of lords, the great, the mighty, and the awesome God, who is not partial and takes no bribe.* He executes justice for the fatherless and the widow, and loves the sojourner, giving him food and clothing. Love the sojourner, therefore, for you were sojourners in the land of Egypt. You shall fear the LORD your God. You shall serve him and hold fast to him, and by his name you shall swear." *(Deuteronomy 10:12-20)*
[Emphasis added]

For the Lord your God is Elohim or Elohekem, Adonai Elohekem, or Elohim. He is Elohe Elohim and He is Adonai Adonim. He is the God of gods, the Lord of lords, the great God. This is the Hebrew word: "*Elohim haggadol,*" a terrible, great God. He is "*Elohim Yissa*" who regards not the person nor takes a bribe (*yiqqa sohad*).

He executes justice for the fatherless and the widow, and loves the sojourner, giving him food and clothing. Love the sojourner, therefore, for you were sojourners in the land of Egypt.
(Deuteronomy 10:18-19)

He executed judgement (*oseh mispat*) for the fatherless and the widow. Then Moses speaks of God's love for the stranger (*wealmanah weoheb*) and raises the Names again:

You shall fear the LORD your God. You shall serve him and hold fast to him, and by his name you shall swear. He is your praise. He is your God, who has

> **done for you these great and terrifying things that
> your eyes have seen. Your fathers went down to
> Egypt seventy persons, and now the LORD your God
> has made you as numerous as the stars of heaven.**
> **(Deuteronomy 10:20-22)**

Moses told the people what the Name is, then he gives them more of His Name: "He is thy praise. He is your God." As you go through the whole chapter, you will see there are around ten strong names that serve as keys for opening the Ark of the Covenant. Moses, the prophets, and the elders would tell the story and insert the Names of God.

When the church continues to tell you this narrative, you hear it as though the Names are not there and it becomes a "pass-over" passage for you. In other words, you pass over and do not see what is really there. The church has a number of "pass-over" passages like this one:

> **The tombs also were opened. And many bodies of
> the saints who had fallen asleep were raised, and
> coming out of the tombs after his resurrection they
> went into the holy city and appeared to many.**
> **(Matthew 27:52-53)**

How do you deal with the resurrection when a resurrection has already occurred? And this resurrection happened before Jesus rose from the dead! You have to pass over it because it does not make any sense to you. The Bible never said these risen people died again. That means there are people with physical bodies that came out of the grave who are in Heaven. In the old theology, if Elijah and Moses and Enoch are going to come down and die on Earth, how does God do that? How does God take Enoch out of the heavens and change him back to a human being and bring him to the earth to die? Why would God want to do that? Yet, many of us carry this theology. What is this theology we all believed about the two witnesses? Who said they were the two witnesses? Who came up with the fact that it was Elijah and Moses and Enoch? Oh, somebody just made it up and we bought it.

Remember that there are other people in Heaven with a human body, not just those guys. What about the guy who came from Heaven, is the son of man, and is now in Heaven? It is Yeshua HaMashiach, the Lord, blessed be His Name. If you do not count everyone who rose from the dead when Jesus was on the cross, you still at least have four people in Heaven with a human body. They are transmuted, yes, but as a human body because Enoch is up there, Elijah is up there, and Moses is up there. Moses got his body back because it was held in suspended animation. That body could not die. God just took Moses' soul out of it. You know the story. God inserted him into the rock, which means he experienced resurrection. The body could not die. But the Bible says Moses died on Mount Nebo:

His body never died.

> **Then Moses went up from the plains of Moab to Mount Nebo, to the top of Pisgah, which is opposite Jericho.... So Moses the servant of the LORD died there in the land of Moab, according to the word of the LORD, and he buried him in the valley in the land of Moab opposite Beth-peor; but no one knows the place of his burial to this day. (Deuteronomy 34:1, 5-6)**

How did the author know Moses died on the mountain? Nobody knows. And God buried him? The writer does not know that Moses died, just that they did not see him anymore. It literally says he died. Really? Who was there? And God buried him, so God now touches dead bodies? The body was kept alive in suspended animation until Jesus came into the world. It was when Jesus was on Earth and was born into the world that God had to release the body out of this atmosphere because the devil wanted the body. When Christ was on Earth, the fullness of time had come. And the devil said, "Oh, so this is what you want to do? I am going to get myself a body, too." He went to look for Moses' body. However, God sent Michael (Jude 1:9) to go get his body because it was the only one that experienced resurrection and yet was still in the realm of creation. Moses could come and see Jesus during the transfiguration because, although his soul left his body, his body remained in suspended animation. His body never died.

Frequencies of Time and Space

Dimensions of Time in Ten Hebrew Words

For everything there is a season, and a time for every matter under heaven.... (Ecclesiastes 3:1-8)

יוֹם

Yom

In the Hebrew language, there are ten different words, different
dimensions, and different frequencies of time.

YOM

In your Bible, multiple words are translated as "time." One of those words is *yom* (**םוי**) which is often translated as "day." Day is a word for time. A day can refer to 24 hours, an age, a generation, or even an epoch. In other words, *yom* is time that causes movement of the earth which causes movement, transition, transformation, and even transmutation of bodies, either human or animal. *Yom* causes 24 hours, which is caused by the earth's movement. This means that as the earth moves, things within it change their structure. The movement of the earth affects the human body. So the earth clock and the clock in the human body operate simultaneously. You know the body renews itself every season, if the human being also understands that they can renew their body.

Yom is a day, which is 24 hours. *Yom* is also a word for *age*. You can refer to an age as an epoch, too. When the Jews refer to an age, *yom* denotes a period of time longer than a generation. Hence, when scripture declares "in the age of such and such," it is a reference to a longer term.

Yom is also used for the word "generation." This time can be as long as millions of years and it can create generativity or degeneration. Time, when used in relation to generation, is evolutionary. It causes things to evolve if we listen. In the same way, time can also cause devolution. As I said, time itself is a living thing. It causes certain things to gain ascendency and certain things to devolve through the process of removing and eliminating them from the structure. It eliminates certain things so those that are beneficial for creation continue to exist while those that are detrimental lessen in their existence. I think this is where Darwin got it wrong because he thought evolution was all about survival of the fittest. On the contrary, evolution is actually the structure of the universe that allows the removal of toxins out of the human system to allow humanity and creation itself to produce greater life and greater productivity. It has nothing to do with race. It is just the way the world works. All things fit into to their specific environments so they can produce more effectively. It is time that does that.

Concurrently, time passes through from eternity. Time came from eternity to become time. It goes through the will of the Father which is aligned with the will of the Son in creation in order to bring all things to pass. This is what is going to happen when you come into your own sonship. Every soul, every human being who is created in

> If you learn the time of your soul, you will also learn the time of your prosperity

the universe, who has ever lived has its own time and its own soul. Every human being created by God has their own soul and carries their own time within their own soul. There is something actually called "soul time." For instance, I may ask you to do certain things and you will reply, "It is not my time to do that yet." What do you mean? How do you know it is not your time? That is "soul time."

> Jesus said to them, "My time has not yet come, but
> your time is always here [now]." (*John 7:6*)
> [Inference added]

Where is that measure of time located? The measure is inside of you. If you learn the time of your soul, you will also learn the time of your prosperity, the time of your suffering, the time of your pain, the time of your deliverance, and the time of Jesus! Ecclesiastes 3:1-8 describes 28 principles of time that are embedded in the soul:

> For everything there is a season, and a time for every matter
> under heaven:
> A time to be born and a time to die;
> A time to plant, and a time to pluck up what is planted;

A time to kill, and a time to heal;

A time to break down, and a time to build up;

A time to weep, and a time to laugh;

a time to mourn, and a time to dance;

A time to cast away stones, and a time to gather stones together;

A time to embrace, and a time to refrain from embracing;

a time to seek, and a time to lose;

A time to keep, and a time to cast away;

A time to tear, and a time to sew;

A time to keep silence, and a time to speak;

A time to love, and a time to hate;

A time for war, and a time for peace.

Men sometimes do not understand this, but women do because they naturally go through cycles. If you talk about time, the woman's body gives that time. Most men do not listen because their physical structures do not make noise like the woman's does, although men do have changes. The men who do not listen to the changes in their bodies are the ones who become sick one day and no one knows what to do with them because they did not listen to the time of their own bodies.

I like the French word "epoch." An epoch is a season characterized by something remarkable like significant events or the production of life-changing things. An epoch can be created artificially, but it can also come dynamically. For example, the Industrial Revolution was an epoch ushered in by somebody's will. Take note of what I just said to you. An epoch can be ushered in by the will of a group of people who come together and, by sheer will, determine how an age should go. They can actually create something that shapes the epoch and makes it last for a thousand years.

The Germans will still have their advanced technology for a thousand years. They knew what they were doing during WWII. They lost the war, but they did not lose the technological war. They will continue to make technological advancements for years to come because they

119

YOM

set something in motion. They got together and determined that their civilization was going to last for a thousand years. Did you know that this vision did not start in the world war? It started when they found the book of Enoch—actually when they stole it from Ethiopia. The Christian, James Bruce, who went to Ethiopia in 1773, forgot the commandment, "Thou shall not steal." Bruce brought it to England, England bought the stolen good, and the Germans got it. The Germans opened a gate before other people could actually do it.

It is the Ethiopians, not the Egyptians, who are the founders of civilization. Compared to the Ethiopians, the Egyptians are kids. The Ethiopians are the ones who tell us that Enoch used to come and teach them. They have stories about Enoch teaching them. It makes sense because they could do freaky things, even before they became Christians. Before they became Christians, they had people like the Ethiopian Moses who walked on water, parted water, and opened rocks by speaking to them. The Ethiopians have a book called "The Unctionist" for Holy Ghost-filled believers from the days of the apostles until today in the Ethiopian church. We Christians in the West think we started the Spirit movement when the Holy Ghost came down on us in Azusa Street! We have people in the Greek Orthodox Church who have been speaking in tongues since the day of Pentecost. Did you know that speaking in tongues never stopped in the Catholic Church? It is hard to say that to Pentecostals because we think we started everything, as if God has left Himself without a witness.

Again, an epoch is an age in which a group of people with a certain amount of good will or evil will bind themselves together to create a time period that has influence lasting for a number of years. Usually such a creation allows other people to come into their own and gives them space to create new things. The greatest example I know is the Industrial Revolution in England which allowed everybody in the world to come to the point of creation. The Industrial Revolution brought peace in England which in turn brought peace to everybody else. This time of peace allowed people to create new things. The computer revolution is an epoch. The software revolution was started by kids in their dorm rooms who left school. Social media is an epoch that gives people the chance to be more than they could if those technologies had not become available. When believers start talking about how they are going to change the world, I ask them what they have created. Remember, I believe in going to heaven, but I believe that going to heaven and not producing on earth is just wishful thinking. I want to keep saying it to you.

What do you say to God when you go into that vision of yours? Are you going to heaven and not producing anything or are you going to heaven and asking God for something that will change the lives of people? "Christians, God is going to transfer wealth. There is going to be a wealth transfer!" No. You are asking God to deal unjustly with those who have labored and give it to you. Some of them are more righteous than you. They say, "Yes, there is going to be a wealth transfer, but it cannot happen without some instrument for it." The problem is Christians do not want to create the instrumentation for the transfer of wealth; they want it to come to them without creating something that is beneficial to the people who have the wealth who then transfer the wealth because they are benefitting from you.

> I believe in going to heaven

If you want wealth transfer you create something that they will benefit from. That is what Jews do. If Jews want to take your money, they create something you need. They do not steal it from you. "I want your billions to come to me. You know, your family has a disease so I am going to find a cure. Then you pay me to give you the cure and the wealth will be transferred to me." People pray all the time for wealth transfer but never ask of God. Pray for something to do and create an instrument for the transfer of wealth. If you want to take from people so they can remain poor and you become wealthy, you are operating in hubris and pride because you did not do anything to get it. You did not create anything. Actually, you are not creating anything; God is the one giving you the blueprint. There are two passages in scripture that speak of this:

> **But Abram said to the king of Sodom, "I have lifted my hand to the LORD, God Most High, Possessor of heaven and earth, that I would not take a thread or a sandal strap or anything that is yours, lest you should say, 'I have made Abram rich.'"** (*Genesis 14:22-23*)

> **But King David said to Ornan, "No, but I will buy them for the full price. I will not take for the LORD what is yours, nor offer burnt offerings that cost me nothing."** (*1 Chronicles 21:24*)

So what is your sacrifice? Is it your prayer? No! Your power lies in you becoming the creator of necessary things which then creates the pathway for wealth to come to you.

Here is story to illustrate how dealt God with me on this wealth transfer misconception. For some years I thought God was going to give me wealth. God told me very clearly 20 years ago not to use the things that I know to create wealth. He said, "Do not use that learning any longer. I will bless you." So I said, "Okay," and sat down and waited for God. Now, I am not a money-raiser and do not really know how to do it, so I thought I will preach to thousands of people and still only walk out with $100. Then I will complain to God. I thought God will say to me, "For your punishment, you will continue to have $100 for the next three weeks." Now, God did not literally say that, but He did in a sense. You have enough sense that you know. Several years ago, I started complaining, "But you are the one who told me not to use what I know." He said, "When did I tell you that?" I replied, "Twenty-some years ago." Then He said to me, "Did you ever come back to ask Me if it is time for you to do this? You just assumed it was. You never came back to talk to Me about it. If I had let you do that activity and gave you what I am giving you now, you would have wasted the money, and you would never have invested it in anything. True, it has taken you a while.

> Your power lies in you becoming the creator of necessary things which then creates the pathway for wealth to come to you.

You were ready about 10-15 years ago, but you were too busy being holy because I told you not to do certain activities. You were busy using my correction as a point of making yourself seem holy. You said to yourself, 'I have all this wisdom, all this knowledge from You, but I am not going to use it because I am being humble.' You were not being humble; you were just false to who you are!"

מוֹעֵד

Moed

Jesus Christ is the transformative sacramental principle of the universe. Time is one of the instruments of transmutation.

MOED:
THE APPOINTED TIME FOR ETERNITY TO INVADE TIME

The Bible speaks frequently about time and uses several words in both Greek and Hebrew for time. For example, the Greek word *Kairos* refers to divine time. It is an event that invades ordinary time and, in so doing, brings eternity into time. In Hebrew, the word **moed** (מוֹעֵד) refers to setting or appointing a particular time, like a festival or holiday.

There has never been an age in which time has been wasted as much as in our current era. We are always busy, always multitasking, always doing something, but we are the generation that has been the greatest waste of time in history. In fact, we as a generation and as a people have no idea of time. We have no idea of how to use time. I am not saying we cannot manage time but time management is not the same as understanding time.

We are taught how to structure our time and how to get things done, but most of the things we are doing are still a waste of time because we do not understand the secularity or mystery of time. We go to courses and seminars to learn how to discretely divide our time so that we can do the things that create more work for us. I think God, in creating the world per the book of Genesis, inserted the Sabbath as a principle of resistance against human business. In his book Sabbath as Resistance, Old Testament scholar Walter Brueggemann writes, "In our own contemporary context of the rat race of anxiety, the celebration of Sabbath is an act of both resistance and alternative. It is resistance because it is a visible insistence that our lives are not defined by the production and consumption of commodity goods." In other words, the Sabbath is a sign of divine resistance to human business and the idea that human beings get in life they get by their work.

So the Sabbath is a time that God placed in the universe and opened up for man to prove to him that his progress and capacity for productivity is not based on how much he works, but on how he uses rest. You have seen some people work themselves to the bone and still get nowhere. They do not know how to rest. When I say "rest" here, I am not talking about vegetating. It is not the fact that you and I are wasting time. The point is we do not know how to use time to rest in the way God intended. The truth is that we are not *wasting* time. In fact, you are using every bit of time in your life. The keyword is "use." Every single moment of time in your life is used.

The question is not usage; the question is, "Do you access the mystery of the moment?" This is serious! Let me use Christmas as an example. We do not really understand why the church put Christmas in this season. We are busy arguing about whether Jesus was born today or tomorrow, but we do not actually understanding that the church designated a particular day to set a time whereby we can open certain aspects of the universe for our own future blessings. Christmas is not actually just about the birth of Christ. Christmas is about the *incarnation*—supposedly the church put it there in order to celebrate what the incarnation is. It is not simply the birth of Christ, Christmas is the entrance of God into time! More than that, it is about God wrapping himself in time. As far as I am concerned, this season gives us an opening to engage the entrance of God into time and to access aspects of Divinity and eternity that I could not have to the same degree in other seasons.

God established seven feasts in Israel and each moment is called a *moed*. A *moed* allows you to step into a moment and through that moment, step into eternity and engage God at the very depth of His being. In the incarnation, God unwraps Himself, becomes human, and invades time. On the other hand, through the resurrection, time invades eternity. Through the resurrection, humanity becomes deified and humanity or the human body enters into Divinity. In the incarnation, God moves from the heavenly realm to this realm.

To understand how this works, you have to understand how your time serves to bring God into your context and how, through that time, you can explore into eternity and move to the other dimension. Let us take communion as an example. When I take communion, what am I doing? I am making a moment stand still so that through that moment I can access the moment of creation and I can access eternity. It is an act that allows me to pierce through time and access the mystery of my being in time. You can do this with other things, but the Eucharist is one thing that Jesus used to teach you how this is done. You can participate in communion any hour of the day by understanding the mystery of that time.

In the incarnation, the limitless God or the timeless God enters the realm of created time. This is something that the ancient world did not believe—they did not

> I am making a moment stand still so that through that moment I can access the moment of creation and I can access eternity.

believe that God could actually enter into time. They believed that time is separate from eternity. This is the concept that Plato taught. In fact, many philosophers thought that time is separate. In other words, they espoused the idea that created man is so utterly removed from God, that God is so wholly "other," and never the twain shall meet. In their view, God created the world and then God stepped aside so that the world has no connection with Him (except insofar as God sovereignly rushing into the world to do what He wants to do, especially punishing people that do evil).

Time has been a prison house for humanity. Time was a deadly principle. Time encapsulated entropy, which means time has been regarded as a principle of death. In fact, scientists believe that death is fundamental to the universe. The emphasis is on time. The so-called evolutionary physicists tell us that the universe has been expanding entropically towards its own demise, and that the whole world is moving towards death. But let me submit to you that death is already in the world, period! Nature is trying to kill us even as it is trying to help us and it is not because of something we did.

Earthquakes do not happen because a person sinned. The sun does not smite you by day because you committed a crime. A child does not

127

MOED

die because someone committed a sin. It is embedded in creation. The question becomes, "Why is death present and what is the remedy?" In the process of all this death and all this entropy, what has God done? God gave us time as a gift that you and I can use to access life. The birth, death, and resurrection of Christ did not happen in eternity—it happened in this earthly time as you and I know it. This means that the answer to the presence of death can be found in how we engage with time. If we can unlock the mystery of time, we can unlock the mysteries of life and death.

Remember, death is temporal and not permanent. In other words, death is somehow connected to time and life. We know death is not permanent because the Bible says God will destroy death. So God put this thing called time in creation, especially in relation to the earth, to enable us to access the mysteries of God, including life and death. This concept was manifested when Jesus came into the world. Otherwise, what do we mean when we say that God became man? When Christ was born, it illustrated the fact that the eternal God became a temporal being. He took on temporal life and, in temporality, He redeemed eternal beings. By understanding the mystery of time, and knowing how to use time, you can actually unravel the mystery of creation.

> By understanding the mystery of time, and knowing how to use time, you can actually unravel the mystery of creation.

Let me say again that our generation is very good at wasting time. Think of how much time you spend vegetating or doing things that are completely useless. How much time do you spend with no purpose in mind? I am not saying you have to be busy because that is what we are fighting against. If you understand time, you realize that God created time as something to carry you, not something for you to carry. God created time as a transportation device you can use to move from one place to another. One of the greatest manifestations of this is how your day goes: seconds lead to minutes, minutes lead to hours, hours lead to days, days lead to weeks, weeks lead to months, and months to years. The Hebrew recognizes that each of these moments have meaning because they are signs of something beyond your present moment.

Augustine, building on some of Plato's concepts of time, was the first one to actually talk the "eternal now," meaning that you can use a single moment of time to access eternity. Think about it this way. We all have the sense that time is passing and moving. It is an important principle in physics that the effects of bodies in motion are manifested in time. If time is always moving, which means it is constantly changing or affecting everything, you need a principle whereby you can hold time in order to be able to change what is behind time. This principle is profoundly expressed in communion because, in the moment of communion, you are holding a specific moment in history and using it as an access to all of history. You can do the same thing with your life.

If you tell me about an experience you had in your life that truly blessed you, as a preacher I might tell you to be grateful but forget about it and move forward. However, if I am being honest, what I should tell you is to recreate it in your memory, turn it into a sacrament, and use it to access something greater. Are you getting the point? In the first instance, what I have done is made you throw away the seeds of your experience in order to look for something more. In other words, we ignore the seeds of the experiences that God has given us in time in search of something else, but it is those very experiences that are the seeds of the future. Think about an experience you have had that always rises up with enthusiasm and joy inside of you. That experience is the same as taking the Eucharist — it is a memorial that recreates the reality and opens the door to greater realities. Your experience is not wasted!

I can do the same thing with your suffering. That is a harder thing to do because nobody likes to feel pain, but remember what Jesus said when He gave you communion:

> **For as often as you eat this bread and drink the cup,**
> **you proclaim the Lord's death until he comes.**
> **(1 Corinthians 11:26)**

It is hard for us to grasp the idea of consecrated time and the idea of the sacramentality of time. I hope you see that, because of your experience in time, you can use time as an instrument in learning what to do to access the mystery.

The point is when you use time to access the mystery of your own being, the mystery of your suffering, and then you speak to it to produce what you want, you can potentially misuse time either by regret or by blaming God and man. In this way, we end up misusing time by using it as an instrument of oppression, depression, and everything that goes with it. What do you use your time for really? Do you use it for accessing the mystery of creation or the mystery of eternity, or do you use it as a way to brood over what people have done to you? Remember, time is something God created as a way to meet you. It is something on this side that attracts something from the other side, but it depends on how you use it. It is like a mirror being used to direct the sun. If you point in the right direction, you can create a fire, but if you point it in a different direction, it will not do anything. These are the things they teach in the Boy Scouts. The boys who followed instructions got the intended result. But those who did not were not able to do it. They often were paying too much attention to what other people were doing or they would turn the mirror to avoid getting burned. We can observe this behavior in children easily enough, but you can see it in adults as well. Some carry this rebellion inside themselves and just will not do things in the way you ask them. Rebellion is still rebellion, even in those situations.

So time is given to you. If you face it the right way, it will produce something other than destruction. Time is meant not just as an instrument of death, it is also meant as an instrument to insert life into the context of death. Your fathers will say wherever there is time, there is hope. God gives us time as a way of strengthening hope. Everyone who is alive, no matter who they are, has the capacity to use time to access hope. We misuse time by what we regret or by using it to blame everything and everybody like God, nature, man, even ourselves. We waste our time.

We use time as a way of wasting our lives. We act as if how we spend our time does not matter. It is amazing how many people in this age, adults and adolescents alike, actually believe that sitting around and just wasting away is great. We justify living a vegetative life because we think it does not really matter. In my city I notice many 70+ year old people walking around begging because they refused to use time correctly. I know this can sound very hard, but the truth is many people use what happened to them as five-year-olds to direct their lives as fifty-year-olds. Ultimately, we use time to justify our lack of mobility.

In fact, we actually use time in the past to get ourselves stuck.

in the scheme of eternity God decided that He himself would take on time

Let me bring this all together. Remember we talked about the incarnation. God was in heaven, looking on earth, and death was all over the place. Time had made man a prisoner. Every day we were living in a vegetative state and blaming God. Everything we were doing had to do with death, so much so that we operated mainly from the position of *Chronos*, the old Greek god who put everybody in prison. We were prisoners *in* time and *of* time, even though time was given to us as a way to engage the mysteries of God and eternity. We could not break out of our own shells.

Therefore, in the scheme of eternity God decided that He himself would take on time. God the Eternal One wrapped himself in time and he did it at a specific time to show us that we can actually appoint the time of our own deliverance. God came wrapped in the fullness of time and, in so doing, He brought eternity into our context.

The Christmas season is not just a season of light and celebrating and giving gifts. It is a season in which God invades time, where God comes into time and allows you to use it for your own salvation and deliverance. You can begin to understand that God is giving you the power of time. Time was not given to you just to waste, or to blame others, or to vegetate. It was given to you so that you can find a mode of resurrection in the current situation of death. You can find a way because you have time! As a mystical being that is a manifestation of the mystery of God, you do not need to sit around and say I do not have time.

As a society, we have commoditized time. We think that our time is something we can sell but time is more than what somebody can pay for. Time is the creation of an atmosphere that allows you to manifest your destiny in the present. We need people who are mystics of time. We need people who are time travelers who can use time to move into other dimensions. We need people who do not use time as a complaining platform, but who use time as a way of entering back into Divinity. For God came from heaven, wrapped himself in time, and became Man. God robed himself in time so that it would become a sacrament for you. Your time is yours—what are you going to do with it? Your time is holy—what are you going to do with it? Your time is righteous—what are you going to do with it? Your time is grace—what are you going to do with it? Your time is mercy—what are you going to do with it? Your time is faith—what are you going to do with it? Your time is God.

By God gifting Himself to you, time no longer means what it meant before Jesus came. Brothers and sisters, a believer does not treat time as a multitasking instrument; he treats time as a manifestation of Divinity. Time management is awesome, but God gives you time as a starting point to access Him and your future. If you learn what your time means, you can do many things in this world. This is why the ancient people put an angel on every hour of the day because they said every moment is angelic and mystical, and provides access to eternity.

> By God gifting Himself to you, time no longer means what it meant before Jesus came.

When somebody gives you their time, they are giving you their God nature. I am determined from now on not to take people's time for granted. You should too because this is serious. I am determined to use this thing called time from the point of view of Emmanuel, "God is with me." Each moment of time that God gives me is Emmanuel. In other words, from the moment I wake up in the morning, God gives me Himself. That means I have access to divine processes, divine power, and the capacity for transmutation just by having time. You do too.

You can learn all you want to learn about time management and still be restless. However, focusing on time management just creates more stress and anxiety. You must learn how time serves as a holy aperture for your own rest. As Charles E. Hummel once said, you must increase your resistance against the "tyranny of the urgent." When you succumb to the tyranny of "do it now, do it now, do it now," you are essentially removing the divine nature of your time. Yet there is nothing in nature that happens immediately. God designed nature to follow processes and we are the same way. In order to manifest what is in heaven, nature slows down and stays at rest. You do not drop a seed on the ground and see it grow immediately. You do not impregnate your wife and then she gives birth immediately. The problem is we do not understand that we have the capacity to slow time down and, in so doing, cause the manifestation of what we want. Because we want everything now, we do not understand how to sit and actually experience time in a way that makes each moment a sacrament. The scripture says, "Be still, and know that I am God," (Psalm 46:10). When we are in a hurry, we say to each other, "Wait on the Lord." However, being still and waiting is not a vegetative state—it is a conscious process of accessing the moment and using it as a transmutational technology for your future. It is not letting your past bind you, but rather using your present moment to change both your future and your past.

I know that idea may be difficult to understand because people say you cannot change your past. But who told you that you cannot change your past? Who told you that you are not forgiven? Forgiveness is not dependent on past time. Today is the day and now is the time! In other words, you were saved by making use of the moment of the revelation of Christ to you. In so doing, you changed your past and you transformed your future. Therefore, if you use each moment and the time you have correctly, both your past and your future will align with divine processes and movement. If you accept Christ in his present incarnation, you change both your past and your future. In that moment of your acceptance, Christ opens up the realm way back beyond the fall of Adam in the garden to the time when the waters were pristine and when the earth was nothing but a soup. He takes you to the point

133

MOED

where everything is in the malleable quantum field of "not this, not that" and allows you to become something other than what you are in the moment so that you have a different future.

This is why you need Jesus Christ in your life. Even if you are not a Christian, you need the Messiah. You need the idea of eternity invading time. You need the idea of God coming into time and wrapping himself in time in order to change human destiny. Hallelujah! From now on, do not take your time for granted. As David says in Psalm 31, "My times are in your hands." All our times are seed in the hands of God.

Moed and *Eth*: Captured Time and Elongated Time

You know *moed* (מוֹעֵד) as set time or an appointed time. Think of *moed* as time that is captured and conscripted as an incubator for a particular production. Think of it as time arrested, as a vessel for an alchemical transformation of a person, a thing, or a place. You know the Greeks used to talk about capturing Chronos and binding him because Chronos was a god. We keep forgetting that Chronos was a god. Therefore, time is a god. In a sense, the Greeks got it right. Time is a god because things come into being in time and are absorbed or taken by time. If you can capture time, you can use it to transmute anything you put in it. For God to change Israel, He gave them set times where time stood still and time was captured for them. That is what *moed* really is. It is captured time which serves as a vessel or an atmosphere for the transformation of those things that are found within the context of that time. You can capture a specific time by prayer, if you are conscious enough to do it, where you are standing between eternity and time. In this place, you do not realize where you are and it may appear as if there is no time, but you know that it is time captured or time standing still.

Captured time looks like it is not moving. We do that in worship. Again, like everything else that we do, we do it unconsciously and mechanically. We do not really realize what we are doing. The church calls this "liturgical time." Have you ever thought about the fact that almost all churches in the world have morning service on Sunday at 10 AM? The Catholic Church has 6 AM mass, but that is to end the fourth watch. Most Christian services are held on Sunday morning, usually from 10 to 11 AM. We think it is just a convenient time for people. However, check the clock and you will see that the long hand is on the 12 and the short hand is on the 10. This angle is 12 x 10 equaling 120 which refers to the transmutation of the human flesh. The way you change the flesh is 120. Some people may think that the 10 AM church meeting time is just "religious tradition." If that is the case, you can tell Jesus that He really did not need 120 people in the upper room. Why do you need 120 people? You do not really need 120 people to change the flesh, do you? Couldn't you just leave Peter all alone by himself in there and accomplish the same thing? While that may be true, 120 is a principle that God chose. Do not forget Genesis 6:3:

> **And the Lord said, "My Spirit shall not strive with man forever, for he is indeed flesh; yet his days shall be one hundred and twenty years." (NKJV)**

Experiment with this number and see what happens. Do something 120 times and see if it does not become a habit. Try denying something 120 times and see if the habit does not change.

So, *moed* is captured time through which you can actually transmute. God set three times in Israel when all the men in the community gathered before Him:

> **Three times in the year you shall keep a feast to me. You shall keep the Feast of Unleavened Bread. As I commanded you, you shall eat unleavened bread for seven days at the appointed time in the month of Abib, for in it you came out of Egypt. None shall appear before me empty-handed. You shall keep the Feast of Harvest, of the firstfruits of your labor, of what you sow in the field. You shall keep the Feast of Ingathering at the end of the year, when you gather in from the field the fruit of your labor. Three times in the year shall all your males appear before the Lord GOD. (Exodus 23:14-17) [Emphasis added]**

God told them that He sent an angel ahead of them to make sure that neither beast nor enemies would trouble their region. In other words,

135

MOED

God said, "I am setting a time for you and that time is not just for you, but also for your whole region to transmute." That specific time changes all the time of Israel. It is a time set by God. It is also an example of how a person who is fully aligned with God can set a time and use it to change what everyone else is doing. Have you ever wondered why David had people praying every hour and why he set up a group of people for every hour of the day (1 Chronicles 23)?

Why does God specify that the men gather before Him during these times? Because each one is a time and place for the transmutation of the seed. The man's seed transfers sin to the next generation. Why only men? It was men who must carry the covenantal transmutation and transfer it before the time of Christ because, according to the scripture, man carries sin—not woman. The scripture does not say, "By one woman sin came into the world." Until Adam sinned (Romans 5:12), sin had not entered the world. Although the woman was subject to sin, she was not the gate of sin into the world. The man was. And it was not the man's sexuality. It was his will. Adam's will

> ...a person who is fully aligned with God can set a time and use it to change what everyone else is doing.

was the gate by which sin came into the world. Eve did not sin willfully (2 Corinthians 11:3), which is why a woman can carry the seed. God did not say to the man, "...by your seed." He said to the woman that He would put enmity between the serpent's seed and *her* seed (Genesis 3:15) because her seed was not infected by the will of rebellion. It does not mean she did not sin, but it was not intrinsic. It was not ontological. It was not embedded in her DNA until her husband sinned and then transferred that seed into her, which is how the woman came under subjection to sin completely. If Adam had not sinned, the woman would still be free. She might still die, but she would still be without sin because God does not impute sin where there is no knowledge or where someone is deceived. He does punish, but He does not impute it generationally. In fact, Acts 17:30 says,

The times of ignorance God overlooked, but now he commands all people everywhere to repent....

Does that mean God does not punish sin? He does, but He does not do it the same way. Jesus said it in a different way:

> **And that servant who knew his master's will but did not get ready or act according to his will, will receive a severe beating. But the one who did not know, and did what deserved a beating, will receive a light beating. Everyone to whom much was given, of him much will be required, and from him to whom they entrusted much, they will demand the more. (Luke 12:47-48)**

God makes that distinction, not me.

To help us understand *moed*, God gave us an example of how to transmute the context of human beings by bringing them to a particular time and space for their transmutation. I still think that it is a big mistake for Christians not to gather. I am often criticized for talking about church, but I think when you walk away from meeting with each other, you actually lose your capacity for the transmutation of each other's lives. I do not think Paul was joking when he said, "Do not neglect meeting together" in Hebrews 10:25. Another phrase comes with it: "...as is the habit of some." By gathering together at a particular time that we have set, we create a boundary of time and a space where we actually do the alchemy of personal and communal transformation. We do not gather only for the sake of gathering. When we gather, we literally stop time. The time of worship is time outside time. Similarly, when you worship in your house, you create a time and space for doing things like changing your own mind, going out of yourself, pulling out the triggers in your life, and so on. It has to do with intentional consciousness or intentional good will, willingly doing things out of choice, not just singing, screaming, shouting, and hoping that God will come and do something. Through this intentional good will, you carry an intent into the content of your worship and, using that as an instrument or a handle for stirring the cipher, you do it until there is a chemical transformation of the atmosphere and your own body. Then

137

MOED

when you walk out of it, your reaction to the world is different.

God created this whole concept of *moed* as a set time, but a man or woman can also set a time, and that time can become sacred before the Lord. You can use sacred time to change whatever walks into it. So when you say in your gatherings, we are going to meet at 5 o'clock, the person who sets the time must then do some spiritual work to set that particular time. If it is a particular space, they must set that time in that space so that it becomes a space for transformation and transmutation. You are not just gathering for gathering's sake. In the Jewish tradition, ten men create an atmosphere that controls time called the *minyan* (מנין). Right now, you cannot start a prayer in the Jewish community without ten people. They will sit and wait until the ten are complete. You can call them religious if you want. The problem is everyone wants to be among the first ten to get to the synagogue, complete the *minyan,* and start the prayer. Yet Jesus says,

For where two or three are gathered in my name,
there am I among them. (*Matthew 18:20*)

If there are two, there are three. If there are three, there are four. If there are two, plus one more (Jesus), there are three. If three, then there are four, which means there are seven. This is how it works. You may think this is "crazy Jewish mysticism!" It is this capacity to take particular time and imbue it with boundaries and to bring angels into that context to get things done within the context.

When you create a space, and you take a time and create a space within that time, you can literally bring an angel into that place. The angel will be bound by the parameters that you have created and work with you within that context to do what you want to be done. You can create a specific atmosphere for the angel to function in the particular purpose for which that space and time have been set apart. In the same way, God set apart a certain time at which He visited Sarah.

The LORD said, "I will surely return to you about this
time next year, and Sarah your wife shall have a son."
And Sarah was listening at the tent door behind him.
(*Genesis 18:10*)

**The LORD visited Sarah as he had said, and the
LORD did to Sarah as he had promised. And Sarah
conceived and bore Abraham a son in his old age at
the time of which God had spoken to him.**
(Genesis 21:1-2)

In other words, God set the time and, within the context of that time, He accomplished what He said He would. You can do many things in a time that you have set apart. Here is the catch-22,

Everything is intentional.

however. If you set apart a time and then you decide you are not going to use it, the next time you set it, the angels will not show up. It requires a lot of discipline (which we do not have) to function this way. Do you wonder why? You may have experienced the presence of the angel last week or last month, but the angel did not show up the next time. You have to ask yourself, "Did I set the time. Did I really keep my word? Did I do what I said I was going to do?"

Do you know why people do benedictions at the end of a service? Have you ever thought about that? We do invocations because they open the atmosphere for angels to be present and set a boundary for angels to work with us in the service. We are not just thanking the Father for being together. We are setting boundaries and creating time and space for angelic work to take place and for things to happen in that atmosphere. When we finish, we collapse the boundary and release the angels that are present. That is why we give benedictions in church. Everything is intentional. You finish a work, end it in gratitude, and dismiss whatever help you had in that context. But this takes consciousness, does it not? It takes you being aware that, when you are praying, angels are truly helping you. At the end of every one of my conferences, I close the session by releasing all the workers who have come spiritually and who have come to be with us in that season. Most people think that the church is not mystical because it hides everything in plain sight. They put the candle in plain sight, the symbols, the

139

MOED

baptismal font, etc. People may think it is nothing but religion because most people think physically rather than spiritually. For many years the church got away with talking about spiritual mysteries and people did not know what they were talking about.

The church initiates someone in front of you every few months, but you may not realize. Do you realize most baptized believers, despite their wickedness, will not behave in certain ways? If you catch them, they will say, "I shouldn't have done that." As unconscious as they are, they have been initiated and when they are activated, they act differently. What do you think you are doing when you pray over somebody, really? What are you trying to do? You are giving a piece of yourself to that person. If you do not understand how to build up your own energetic system, how to build up your essence, you are going to be continually depleted if you are praying for everyone else. Many people who are prayer warriors are having frequent attacks because their defense systems are always down. Their essences are always depleted, and they do not know how to build it back up.

> When anointing becomes essence, it is different from when it just operates from personality.

If you go after an issue for someone, you are going to have to use your built up essences to do it. You have to figure out the technology for constantly drawing more essence and pulling essence into yourself and developing anointing. Personality can only take you so far. When anointing becomes essence, it is different from when it just operates from personality. You probably know people who are in intercession and warfare who are sick all the time. In that case, they do not know the secret of building up their essence to keep them from actually getting sick. All of us get like that. You need to have the knowledge so that you can renew your essence because your essence protects you. Those of us in ministry tend to overextend ourselves and deplete our essence without actually knowing how to replenish it while we are working. Then when we get sick, the same people who stole the essence think we have committed a sin!

Moed creates the space for not only for transforming or transmuting other people, but also for creating an inflow of essence back into your life. You must create an inflow of essence to renew yourself because your essence is your power. The old Pentecostals had it right; they just did not have the language. After the preaching concludes, they all stretch out their hands and say, "Lord, bless your woman servant. Virtue has gone out of her." It is true that virtue has gone out of her, but raising their hands provides them only quick relief. They will have to do something else to rebuild their essence. You must have a technology. You do not even have to rest. You just need to know the technology to do it. A guy came up to me and said, "Bishop, I have watched you. You can stand and speak for 10 hours and get up the next day and speak again. You just do not seem to tire. Can you tell me what you are using?" Building my essence means I have developed the technology of accessing Christ while I am talking. I split myself into several bodies and I keep drawing with the rest and changing my bodies. You renew yourself and stay in a place of renewal. You keep going in and out. You can do the same thing. Your strength can be unabated.

If you are going somewhere that will deplete your essence, you need to know beforehand what it is going to cost you. Counting the cost does not mean how much money it is going to cost you. You need to know with whom you are going to war and figure out if you have enough essence to last you. It is not when you finish because after you finish certain spiritual activities, the strength of your immune system, your soul, and your emotional systems can decline, and then you become open to an attack. One of the reasons I do not talk about things like that is because I learnt how to build the system. If you give me a day to myself, I can build enough essence for the next five months. I can take 15 minutes and do it as well. You must learn how to go in and go in deep enough to stay and draw from your source. You can really do this.

God told Israel to come before Him three times. He could have told them to come seven times, but He said three times. In other words, every time they came before the Lord, it lasted them for four months. They were filled and replenished by one meeting at the time and space appointed by God. You can do the same thing in your spiritual life. Find those places in the spiritual realm where you can go in and, using that

141

MOED

technology, renew both your body and soul. Each time, it will last you longer and longer. That is why the Bible says, "He renews my youth as an eagle. (Psalm 103:5)" The scripture also says:

...but they who wait for the LORD shall renew their strength; they shall mount up with wings like eagles; they shall run and not be weary; they shall walk and not faint. (*Isaiah 40:31*)

It does not say God shall renew their strength. They themselves shall renew their strength. God renews our youth while an individual who waits on the Lord renews their strength. God has put the capacity inside you for the renewal of your strength.

The believer can create the frequency of *moed*, just like God creates it. You can create it and use that time for as long as you want. For example, you could decide that you will get up at 7 AM every day and you will use the time from 7 to 10 to transmute and change whatever you want to change. I bring something into that context and, when I do it consistently, things begin to change because I have set that time for transmutation. Everyone who comes into my life and connects with me at that precise moment gets something. I could set time with specific people. When I spend time with people, whether I or they set the time, I imbue it with certain boundaries and structures so that when I am talking to them, something is happening in their life. I do not want to waste people's time. It is your life and it is my life. I am just suggesting some things you can do. The old Pentecostals used to say, "Set a time with the Lord," but they never told you what could happen in the time. They just think it is a time for you to talk to God and God listens but it is actually a time of revelation. It comes by process and progress. Our church fathers had revelation. A lot of them had experiences, but they were never able to tell you how they actually got the experience.

These words and their frequencies can give us an idea of what they experienced:

Hebrew Word	Hebrew Spelling	Gematria
Yom	יוֹם (Yod Vav Final Mem)	10 + 6 + 600 = 616 = 13
Thirteen represents priesthood embedded in the kingdom and manifested in a particular realm or dimension. The number of Israel is 12 and the number of Israel with a priest is 13.		
Moed	מוֹעֵד (Mem Vav Ayin Dalet)	40 + 6 + 70 + 4 = 120 = 3
Eth	עַת (Ayin Tav)	70 + 400 = 470 = 11 = 2
Two is an arc. Two is also 1 and 1, which is 2 pillars. The frequencies in the 400s have a lot to do with healing and opening. *Eth* is a form of the word *et* (עֵת) which is 1 + 400 = 401. When you subtract *et* from *eth* you have 470 – 401 = 69 = 15 = 6.		

I am doing that deliberately because I want you to see how much the number 6 occurs in time. In fact, both six and four occur frequently as it relates to time which means that time responds to the frequency of the name of God and the substance of God as well as the nature of man. You will notice as we go through these things that there are numerous fours and sixes relating to words that are used for time when you do a complete gematria. I am showing you a "simple gematria." It is the simplest gematria there is. (We are not using the Albam or the Atbash systems. These systems follow a logical sequence of dividing the Hebrew letters according to certain structures and exchanging letters to learn different and deeper meanings of the word. If you really want to push yourself, you can learn a lot by using these other systems of gematria. I recommend that you start with memorizing the Hebrew alphabet so that you will have an easier time understanding the gematria of a word).

Eth is a deformative of the word *eth (Ayin Tav; עַת)*. Ayin (ע) is the sixteenth letter, which is 1 + 6 =7. The value of Ayin is 70. These things are not accidental. You can exchange Ayin with Zayin (ז) because they come from the same thing. You can also exchange Ayin with the Final Nun (ן). Once you make these exchanges, you now realize that, while

Ayin means "nothingness," it can also mean a sword (Zayin). Likewise, a Final Nun looks like a straight tack that also looks like a Vav. This means that the Final Nun becomes a longer nail than the Vav.

Eth is time that is timeless because it has nothing in front of it. However, *eth* is a time based on a certain sign. What is a Tav? The pictograph in Hebrew is a cross. It is actually the sign. When you put *eth* and Tav together, it means that you are trying to create and elongate time. You are trying to open up time so that it lasts longer or it is a longer daytime. It used to be called "timeless time." Yet it is more than that—*eth* refers to a season that is open to productivity and progression. *Eth* is the word that is used repeatedly in the Ecclesiastes 3.

For everything there is a season, and a time for every matter under heaven:

> **a time to be born, and a time to die;**
> **a time to plant, and a time to pluck up what is**
> **planted; a time to kill, and a time to heal;**
> **a time to break down, and a time to build up;**
> **a time to weep, and a time to laugh;**
> **a time to mourn, and a time to dance;**
> **a time to cast away stones, and a time to gather**
> **stones together; a time to embrace, and a time to**
> **refrain from embracing; a time to seek, and a time to**
> **lose; a time to keep, and a time to cast away;**
> **a time to tear, and a time to sew; a time to keep**
> **silence, and a time to speak; a time to love, and a**
> **time to hate; a time for war, and a time for peace.**
> **(*Ecclesiastes 3:1-8*)**

You have three types of time already. *Eth* is the word you use to open and to close. There is also a time that means "season" which is *zeman* (זמן). The *eth* can be used to open and close seasons. Isn't it amazing that Solomon does not talk about seasons, but rather about time throughout? He does not introduce the idea of season because it is an *eth*. Everything he talks about is open in nature. Even death is considered open. So, *eth* means that in every moment, there is a possibility and a capacity to elongate time. Now then, you have this

ADONIJAH O. OGBONNAYA PH.D.

time that is connected to nothingness where you draw by the power of the cross, by the power of the sign to elongate time and open it up.

Everything in nature, everything in the world can serve as a doorway to greater experiences for someone who is a mystic. A true mystic does not need a good thing to happen to them to be able to use it to enter the other realm. For this person, everything is a doorway. Let me say that again. **Everything is a doorway.** *Sacramentum mundum* — the whole universe is a sacrament. Everything is a doorway. A mystic can use a rock to open a gateway to God. He can open a gateway by walking in the forest and open gateways through nature itself. Every experience is a doorway to a greater experience of God. The idea of time consists of particular daily experiences that allow you to elongate time or to open up to other times. This is your key to experiencing other times in other dimensions. That is why *eth* is a deformative of eternity, which is Aleph Tav. Ayin Tav, Aleph Tav, Ayin Tav. Ayin refers to nothing, but it also refers to a spring of water that is rising continuously. Aleph Tav is also the name of God. Ayin Tav is a deformative of that name which is mimicry of eternity. It means that if you are operating in *eth*, you can actually imitate eternity in a particular moment. When you come across this in scripture, you will always notice that something is happening when the person is using time to mimic eternity. It looks like time is imitating eternity and they can hold that time and elongate it until they accomplish what they want to accomplish. This is the principle. Joshua elongated the day (Joshua 10:13). He is not the only one who did that. These are the ones about whom we read, but the fathers of Israel who went into Egypt could do things like this as well.

> It looks like time is imitating eternity and they can hold that time and elongate it until they accomplish what they want to accomplish.

145

MOED

אָז

Az

The next word for time is *az* (אָז). *Az* is a temporal principle for opening the gateway for increase and multiplication. This is the symbol for infinity: ∞. *Az* is a time that taps into infinity for multiplication and increase. It is the word for power. Some call it *oz*.

AZ:
THE POWER OF TIME
AS A WEAPON

Oz is the "power" or "might," or what the Greeks call Kratos. This is what the Bible means when it says God gives you the power to get wealth. It has to do with the ability to find the right timing. The power to get wealth is not to just to go and work. The power to get wealth has to do with timing. The people who know the timing of this process are the ones who make money.

This is the time of Issachar that reveals the capacity to look at the movement of the earth and find a specific time when multiplication is getting ready to burst open upon the scene. It is to ready yourself to receive because there is a specific time, if you look at the natural principle, when certain movements of prosperity are much more ascendant.

What if you can create this time within yourself? What if you can create it yourself and carry it wherever you go? If that is true, it means that you are not affected by seasons, time, or government processes. It means you can actually walk into a place, any structure, and then insert yourself, draw prosperity from it, and walk away.

Look again at the word *az* (אָז). Aleph is the name of Yahweh and Zayin is a sword, a weapon of war. *Az* allows us to use time as a weapon. I keep asking believers, why is the world so scared of you? You do not have guns and you do not rule governments, so why are they afraid of you? Why is the world scared of a woman who does not have a gun, who has three children and is sitting in the house trying to feed her children? Because she is a believer. Why is the world afraid of a retired woman who is not controlling governments What is scaring them? The fear from the world is that, if you get to know yourself, then they cannot be in control of you. If you actually get to know yourself and know how you are supposed to function, they will be afraid. Have you ever thought why the Roman government put pregnant women and women holding babies in front of lions to maul them? What are a few women from Carthage going to do to the Roman government?

Why does the world hate you? Jesus says it is because you are not of them. The part of you that is a part of them gives you the capacity to impact the system they have created. Do you know what danger it is when you can walk into a system, direct the system to yourself, draw what you want to draw from it, and leave people wondering what happened? Right now, it is only those practicing the occult who can do that. They can set the market up, get money out of it, and walk away. They actually set it up, withdraw money, let it fall down, let it build back up, and make each other rich by working this system. The dangerous thing for them is that a believer can do the same thing spiritually. They will be looking for you. They will start trying to stop Christians before they ever get to the level where they can do these things. They realize if you ever come to a full understanding of your spiritual power, it would be disastrous for them.

Psalm 149 speaks of the saints of God executing judgement upon all the nations. In verse 9, it says:

...to execute on them the judgment written!
This is honor for all his godly ones.
Praise the LORD!

Part of the execution of judgement is the capacity to get into a system, use the system against itself, get what you want from it, and keep walking.

Someone once asked me about the Babylonian system. Which system is *not* a Babylonian system? Did you go to school? Are you working for someone? Even if you start your own business, it is a Babylonian system. It is an excuse for Christians to be lazy and not to participate in fighting, in actually standing up to the system. Instead they say, "I don't need to work for the government. I don't need to work for the bank." The truth is that you want to reap where you have not sown. I do not believe in that. Any Christian who has built a business without the participation of unbelievers should let me know. If unbelievers do not buy your product, will Christians make you a multimillionaire? Can someone please define the Babylonian system? It is one of those Christian catchphrases, but most people do not understand it. The Babylonian system works because nonbelievers took God's principles and applied it in a wrong way for themselves. They are benefitting from the same principles God created. They created a new system, but they did not create a new foundation because the system would not work if it did not come from God.

The names of God are the highest principles of substantiation

The name of God carries effulgence with it. It carries numerical, alphabetical, and metaphorical principles. It carries symbolic power within itself. The name of God is the epitome of how structures are imbued with this power. In spite of everything about which we disagree, all mystics, whether Christian, Kabbalistic, or occultic, do agree that if we use the name of God, something will happen. We may not agree on anything else, but we agree that, if we can find a way of using the name of God, something can happen because we bring these numerical, alphabetical, metaphoric, and symbolic principles to transmute anything. That is what we believe.

149

AZ

The names of God are the highest principles of substantiation—something you can use to change anything. Do you know the name you use for God is the same name the occult uses? Do you know they use the name Yahweh? Do you know they use the name Jesus? They also use the names Adonai and El Shaddai. They know how to use these names and imbue them with such substance that when they speak, things happen because the names of God are independent of any system.

You can get upset that they are using the names of God this way, but if you are upset, then learn to use them in the right way. We are the children of God, and yet we do not even know more than ten names of God. Do you? Of the 72 names of God, how many people have memorized them? Do you have them memorized? People who are not believers or Christians have them memorized and imbue then with power. It is true we have the name of Jesus. It is the 888 that I mentioned earlier. The Bible says the name of Jesus is above all names.

> **Therefore God has highly exalted him and bestowed on him the name that is above every name, so that at the name of Jesus every knee should bow, in heaven and on earth and under the earth, and every tongue confess that Jesus Christ is Lord, to the glory of God the Father. (*Philippians 2:9-11*)**

I like to read it this way: "the name *inclusive* of all names." You know the name of Yeshua and you need to know all the names included in it. Every time you pray and you start your prayer with "Father," you are already using two of God's names, Jesus and another name. Most of the time, you put other names in your prayer.

> ...just because you say the name of Jesus does not mean you know how it functions.

You end your prayer with Jesus because all those names are inclusive. However, just because you say the name of Jesus does not mean you know how it functions.

As a Christian, you have the capacity to become one who carries the *az* (אֵת), the first and seventh letter of the Hebrew alphabet. So, you carry both the name of God and the sword. It is a weapon. It is time that you can use to impact anything to bring forth this productivity. Therefore, you must know that time.

The children of Issachar understood the time and they knew what Israel should do. I love the way the children of Issachar worked. Did you know that it was not labor intensive for them? Hebrews called the children of Issachar lazy because they figured out when to sow and when to harvest without having to labor like everybody else. The Sons of Issachar had access to specific times that they used to create increase among them.

ADONIJAH O. OGBONNAYA PH.D.

Az: Cleaving Time

From the time that he made him overseer in his house and over all that he had, the LORD blessed the Egyptian's house for Joseph's sake; the blessing of the LORD was on all that he had, in house and field. (*Genesis 39:5*)

So far, we have discussed the familiar concept of *appointed* or *set* time. The word that is used for time in this passage about Joseph in Potiphar's house is *'az* (אָז). It means *then* or *at that time*. This word is extremely important for Joseph.

Joseph, as you know, had problems with his siblings because of his own immaturity. However, Joseph knew something that his brothers did not. Remember that God told Abraham to go out and count the stars:

And He took him outside and said, "Now look toward the heavens and count the stars, if you are able to count them." And He said to him, "So shall your descendants be." (*Genesis 15:5* [NASB])

God is telling Abraham to go decipher or check the coding of the stars, and if you can decode the stars, then you will understand how many your seed will be. Abraham did not just step out of his house. God actually took Abraham outside and into the realm of the spirit. From that realm, he sat above creation, looked into the stars, and then decoded them. Because of his friendship with God, in the process of decoding them, Abraham also directed the stars on how to relate to Israel. This is very important because when God told Abraham to *count* the stars, He did not mean to actually number them one by one. The word for *count* in the Hebrew is *saphar* (סָפַר), which is where we get our word for cipher. God was actually telling Abraham to decipher or decode the stars for so shall his descendants' seed be. We know the story. Isaac had two children, Esau who worshipped the sun and Israel (Jacob) uses the moon. Jacob had thirteen children which represents the star system. In fact, even though people may not like to hear this, Jacob's children look exactly like the constellations of the zodiac. Most people on earth do not really know God and yet use the zodiac to determine the direction of their lives. The Bible tells us in Deuteronomy 32:8 that in the day that the Lord God divided the nations, he did so according to the number of the children of Israel. That means every nation on earth answers to a divine destiny written in the genetic code of Israel. If you read Torah the way the rabbis say you should, you will see the first word of Torah is in Genesis 1:1 is *bereshit* (בְּרֵאשִׁית) and the last word is in Deuteronomy 34 is *Israel* (יִשְׂרָאֵל). In other word, it says, "In the beginning, Israel." That statement is not a reference to Israel as a nation. Rather, it is the whole idea of the nations living in this context of rising up to the heights of divinity and that the world was created for the righteous.

Some would say the world was created for Israel, but the scripture is speaking of Israel from the position of the righteousness that God imputes upon her. It is from this perspective that God uses Abraham to tune the stars, ensuring that for generations and for almost all eternity, Israel shall always supersede fate. The wheels of fortune have no effect on Israel. Even Balaam said,

For there is no enchantment against Jacob,
no divination against Israel. (*Numbers 23:23*)

People use the elements and the star system, the sun, and the moon for divination and sorcery. However, if you move above the heavens and you are seated, like you are, in heavenly places, that means neither the sun, the moon, or the stars can actually affect you. Those who bend the wheel of the sun, the moon, and the stars cannot affect your life.

Keeping all that in mind, Joseph dreams that the sun, the moon, and the stars were bowing to him. I think Joseph knew Abraham better than Jacob because Joseph is the one who understood the stars. He looked and he saw the stars descend to bow at his feet, which means that he was above the stars. It is true that Jacob asked Joseph if he and his mother and brothers would come to bow before him, but I think it is beyond that. We know there is a physical meaning to an esoteric concept, something natural for the spiritual. That is why Paul said,

**But it is not the spiritual that is first but the natural,
and then the spiritual. (*1 Corinthians 15:46*)**

So here is Joseph with this experience and his father keeps it in his mind, but that gets him in trouble. I have come to believe as I studied Joseph that everything Joseph did was deliberate. Everything that happened to Joseph was brought about by the Lord, but Joseph knew how to tune both the stars and time. The sun, the moon, and the stars are the bodies of space that we use to determine time. God tells us that they shall be for signs and seasons. This means that Joseph carried this sense of being able to split time and to make something happen that could never happen any other time.

> There is one way to tune time and another way to cleave it and open it.

One of the ways that Joseph was able to cleave time was through visions and dreams. There is one way to tune time and another way to cleave it and open it. Hence, a thing which is said will never happen in creation can come in and happen. Every forerunner who opens up a movement upon the face of the earth must be able to use both dreams and visions to cleave time and cause what is afar to come near.

Watch what Joseph was able to do at every house he entered. the scripture always refers to "at that time." Why not just say when Joseph was there, the household prospered? The reason is that you cannot prosper on earth if you do not understand what time is and how it works. Even Jesus's cry over Jerusalem was that their destruction would come because they did not recognize the time of their visitation (Luke 19:44). However, it is one thing to know the time of your visitation and it is another to have the tool for creating a time of visitation. "At that time," when Joseph entered the house, it began to prosper.

Why was it that when Joseph entered the house, both the *season* and *time* of the man's life changed? Remember that the Bible verse says "at that time" which is *az* (אָז) in Hebrew. The numerical value of Aleph is 1 and Zayin is 7 for a gematria of 8. In Hebrew, the number 8 describes

153

AZ

the capacity to combine two dimensions or to cause two dimensions to interpenetrate each other. Time is given to you as a tool to open up or to cleave and enter into eternity. As a human being on this side, you cannot disregard time and have access to eternity. Remember that Paul said it is first the natural and then the spiritual. A problem is we want the spiritual first before the natural. We treat what is given to us in the natural as if it is meaningless. This is an issue. We put our heads in the spiritual when in fact the spiritual has been summarized and given to us in the immediate experience of our own reality. For example, you may want to be a millionaire, but every time you are given $200, you go somewhere and waste it. You still wait for God to drop a million on you from heaven! Do not misunderstand me—there is nothing impossible with God, but if you cannot handle $200 or $2000, you do not understand how to access eternity. It does not matter how much you pray.

> Time is given to you as a tool to open up or to cleave and enter into eternity.

Why does God take natural things and little things and put them in your presence? It is as a way for you to harvest or to access the abundance that you carry and the abundance that the world carries for you. This is how Jesus said it:

One who is faithful in a very little is also faithful in much... (*Luke 16:10*)

Time is the one commodity that we have and it is also of which there is plenty, but we believe there is not enough! We actually do have plenty of time, yet it is the one commodity is wasted because we think that time is not that expensive.

What we learn now from Joseph is that he understood how to use time. Time was not outside of him. There is something called soul. Your soul has a clock and your time is not actually outside of you. The time and timing of your life is determined by the structure of your inner being. In other words, you carry with you your time and your timing. If that is not the case, how did Joseph who was just sold by his brethren, who was away from his own country, who was in a foreign land, who was a slave in a man's house become the aperture by which abundance flowed into the house of an idol worshipper? The real principle is inside of us. God even says that He has placed eternity in your heart (*Ecclesiastes 3:11*). In other words, the gateway of time is inside of you.

The way that Joseph worked was to discern the movement of his own soul in order to open gates that people said could not be opened. When we listen to the clock inside, we will hear things that are so unique, sometimes frightening, and sometimes that sound impossible. The difference between us and Joseph is we hear those things and then think it is only going to happen in the spirit realm. We ignore the physical reality of where our timing is supposed to intersect. Then we go looking for something spiritual to fall from heaven when all along it is inside of us and around us. What we need to do is learn the timing of our soul and connect it with the timing of our environment to make things happen.

How do you do this? Let us look at Joseph again, a slave in the house of Potiphar. He could have sat around and complained about his brethren selling him and doing all kinds of things to him. His father did not even know he was alive! The Midianites bought him, sold him to the Arabian Ishmaelites, then the Ishmaelites sold him to the Egyptians, and the Egyptians sold him to Potiphar. Joseph really is a mess. However, Joseph has the interior sense of the movement of divine timing, which is the harbinger or the carrier of his dream. He was not prospering. However, he knew what he carried even before his own prosperity was manifested. He created an atmosphere for prosperity everywhere he went. I have come to understand that it is not your environment or what anybody else is doing to you; it is how you understand what is happening within you and how you choose to structure your inner consciousness in relation to your external reality. There is no reason for Joseph not to mess up the man's house out of bitterness and anger. Many of us have one or two experiences and we become bitter. We think everybody in the world should run to help us and if they do not, then we get angry, bitter, and complain. Yet, we still expect the timing to match up with heaven's movement.

AZ

Nonetheless, in spite of all his circumstances, Joseph understood. I wish I could see Joseph praying and worshipping the God of the Hebrews, allowing his heart to connect while he was in the house of the person watching his every movement. How does Joseph know that you prosper by the movement of God in the world? God moves the earth in order to have things flow from the eternal realm into your life. The aperture of hours and movements of minutes and seconds, the movements of seasons, months, and time is God's way of telling you that every time the world moves, there is something new available for you. However, it can only come through if you yourself understand the timing of your own inner being.

To know the timing of your soul is to have power. You can create time if you want to. That is what Leah did. It is not a contradiction. Not everybody is able to do it, yet everybody knows and can feel the movement of their own soul to some degree. However, we overemphasize the external movement of time and we do not understand that there is a clock in the soul. The hand of time in that clock is the spirit of God working in the background with our souls to tune our beings to a timing that will open doors for us. Your job then is to discern times. If you do not have the technology for changing time, then develop the technology for discerning the time. If you can discern the time, then you can go one step further and redeem the time. This is what Paul means when he speaks of making the best use of your time or making the most of every opportunity in Ephesians. You cannot redeem time unless you discern it and understand the Lord's will (Ephesians 5:16-17).

You must develop a dream that nobody can take away because then your soul will be looking for the right time to manifest it. I do not believe daydreaming is necessarily a bad thing. When you daydream, you are bringing a dream that is from the night into the reality of the day. I believe when you ground your life in reality, your dreams will be drawn to that reality. For example, if you say you want to be the designer of the greatest building on earth, but then you do not draw buildings because you are waiting for God to make it appear on your paper, what happens? You wait and wait and wait for something to be downloaded and nothing happens. However, listen to me carefully—when you begin to do the little that you know in your heart, you will begin to shift the clock in your soul to align with the principle of eternity for your manifestation.

Never stop doing what you know as a way of having access to your dream. If you are doing what you know, do not get discouraged because those things attract the reality that you desire. It may take a while, but do not give up. It may not always make sense and others may not understand what you are doing, but sometimes it takes using an uncouth, unnatural, and sometimes unsophisticated reality to tap into the vastness of God's resources.

I used to get upset with my son. When he was a child, he would open up my tape recorders and take them apart. When I would ask him what he was doing, he would tell me he was fixing it. Usually, I would end up throwing the recorder away because he removed all the wires and left them sitting there. I would think he destroyed my nice tape recorder, but when children do this, are they really destroying something? Today, he can take apart anything and put it back together. He can also apply these same techniques and skills to composing music.

> To know the timing of your soul is to have power.

My point is doing these types of things is the secret of timing. Do not give up! Do it as if only God is watching. Our problem is that we give up and say we are dreaming without any physical or normal construct that can serve as a vessel of attraction. It is hard to have anything done on earth if you do not have a seed. If you say you want an avocado and I give you the seed, you will say it is useless and you throw it in the neighbor's yard. Later, you will buy avocado from your neighbor! This is how life works.

So then Joseph understood that he had been given a vision, but he did not let the vision stop him from creating a context for its manifestation. In fact, he first opened up the timing for someone else to prosper before his own dream was fulfilled. He did that for his first master and then for Potiphar. Everyone Joseph is around he makes wealthy while he is still struggling. The idea is that the capacity for finding the right time is not just about you trying to get blessings for yourself. When you help other people come into consonance with their timing, you will gain a greater sense of what your own timing is and you do not even have to do much. One day it will happen.

Remember how Joseph, the dreamer, got out of prison? It was somebody else's dream. It was not his dream. Before his dream could become reality, he had to help somebody else understand their dream. As long as some of us continue to think that our life experience excuses us or justifies our unwillingness to help somebody manifest their dream, we will not manifest our own. There is no way for it to be manifested until we wholeheartedly help someone find his or her own time.

When you ascend and travel to heaven, you will understand what I am saying. I ascend a lot. I have learned that something on Earth always serves as a magnetic principle for what is seen in the realm of the spirit. Part of you learning how to redeem, discern, structure, and access your own time includes you not having a problem helping others align themselves to their own timing. Look at Joseph. Everything he did seemed to fall into place even though it began with something terrible. At the same time, all of his experiences still structured his timing. Sometimes timings cause you pain, but nonetheless, you must understand that aligning with the pain, with the suffering, whatever is happening, propels you to another kind of time. You cannot have a time of resurrection without a time of suffering.

> Your own suffering is another way to help someone find his or her own timing.

Recall that Ecclesiastes 3 describes that there is nothing new *under* the sun. However, there are two sides to that coin. In heaven, there is no time of death, no time of mourning, no time of crying, no time of seeing, no time of ceasing to embrace, etc. The 28 principles are not there in heaven. Nonetheless, when you bring your vision from heaven and your timing is supposed to align with heaven, it first goes through the process of pain.

We look at a time of pain and suffering as if it is useless, so we do not embrace it and push through. We are afraid that the experience is going to kill us but there is always a reason for the time. Solomon said a time to kill and a time to heal (*Ecclesiastes 3:3*). The positive aspects are always at the end. So how I handle the timing of my suffering will structure my experience and the timing of my joy.

Be a dreamer because it is by the dream that time dilations happens. Have a vision—it is the instrument for cutting through the veil of time and bringing what is over there to here. Most of all, discern the timing of your soul. Know the time of your own visitation. The way to make sure you do not miss your time of visitation is to take the natural things that God has given you and treat them as if they are completely divine.

Your own suffering is another way to help someone find his or her own timing. Your suffering is not an excuse for you not to help other people. Your struggle actually is an opportunity for you to open up your own structure to the possibility of your being. When you use your struggle to help someone, your soul is free to move the clock for you because you are not self-absorbed. If you do not take care of that which belongs to another person, who shall give you yours? This is a lesson that many people are not learning. You do not get your timing or dream by just pursuing your own. Remember, pursue it without bitterness, and pursue it with joy! Then we begin to realize how to use what is in our hands as a tuning fork for time. The key is learning how to love people in a way that allows love not only to transmute their lives but also to transmute your own inner being.

Whenever you begin to walk in love, your inner being tunes itself to the aperture of divine time. Your soul begins to move its own clock to the right time. How can Joseph, a boy in slavery, be the key to everyone else's prosperity while he is still in slavery? It is the same key to Jospeh's personal timing as yours. Because he used it for someone else, that same key released him from his own prison house. You see that thing you are holding in your hand that you think is useless, a waste of your time, or looks like it is not working? God will use that very thing to open up somebody else's life and it will become a great blessing for you.

His brothers called him a dreamer and Pharaoh, because of a dream, called him the wisest of men. Something that was already in him became an instrument to fine tune Pharaoh's life. In the same way, if I accept that the things already in me—even simple things like cooking, drawing, mechanics, music, speech, driving—have been given to me for tuning my soul, then I must also use these things to tune other people's lives. In doing so, someone beyond my environment with greater power and greater possibility will reach out to me based on that which I carry and that which I do. With the little things I do, one day a president will call, one day a fortune 500 company will call, one day a production company will call, or one day somebody wants to go into business with me. These things can happen as long as I understand that the thing I hold turns my life towards my time. I am not just focused on using it for myself, but also for serving others.

Do you realize that every time Potiphar prospered, it was Joseph's timing? It was Joseph's time; it was not Potiphar's time. Joseph was the one who carried the system of the stars in himself. He was the one before whom the stars bowed and before whom the sun and the moon bowed. He was the one and yet you do not hear him complaining. When the time of his heart had been tuned, Pharaoh took him out of the prison house. It was that same principle of time and timing that Joseph used to interpret Pharaoh's dream. It contains so much mystery!

The thing that is in your hand is the key to your timing.

Az: Redirecting Time to Fulfill Destiny

> *From the time* that he made him overseer in his
> house and over all that he had, the LORD blessed the
> Egyptian's house for Joseph's sake; the blessing of
> the LORD was on all that he had, in house and field.
> (*Genesis 39:5*)

In the previous section, we talked about the timing of the inner being of Joseph. We realized that Joseph's capacity to operate within his own time from the inside of his being is what opened the atmosphere for Potiphar's house to become prosperous. Everywhere Joseph went, suddenly there was a shift. The word *az* (אָז), which is used in the scripture here, actually has two definitions. First, it means *"at that time"* or *"then,"* referring to a specific time. However, the second meaning indicates timing for something to be changed: *if this, then that*. In other words, *az* (אָז) refers to the transmutation and the transformation of an event into a different model.

I am not just focused on using it for myself, but also for serving others.

Az is a particular kind of timing that, when it is used correctly, can change direction and destiny. It is that inner consciousness of divine timing and awareness of what is happening around you. Being able to direct what is happening inside you as a way of transforming the moment is a powerful thing. Abraham uses the phrase in Genesis 13 when he talks to Lot about separating. Recall that Abram and Lot were traveling together, and their herds were becoming so large that their herdsmen began to fight each other because the land could not support all of them:

161

AZ

> **Now Abram was very rich in livestock, in silver, and in gold. And he journeyed on from the Negeb as far as Bethel to the place where his tent had been at the beginning, between Bethel and Ai, to the place where he had made an altar at the first. And there Abram called upon the name of the Lord. And Lot, who went with Abram, also had flocks and herds and tents, so that the land could not support both of them dwelling together; for their possessions were so great that they could not dwell together, and there was strife between the herdsmen of Abram's livestock and the herdsmen of Lot's livestock. At that time the Canaanites and the Perizzites were dwelling in the land.**

> **Then Abram said to Lot, "Let there be no strife between you and me, and between your herdsmen and my herdsmen, for we are kinsmen. Is not the whole land before you? Separate yourself from me. *If you take the left hand, then I will go to the right, or if you take the right hand, then I will go to the left.*" And Lot lifted up his eyes and saw that the Jordan Valley was well watered everywhere like the garden of the Lord, like the land of Egypt, in the direction of Zoar. (This was before the Lord destroyed Sodom and Gomorrah.) So Lot chose for himself all the Jordan Valley, and Lot journeyed east. Thus they separated from each other. Abram settled in the land of Canaan, while Lot settled among the cities of the valley and moved his tent as far as Sodom. (*Genesis 13:2-12*)**

Lot, if you remember, was the son of Abraham's older brother. Lot chose first because, in this culture and tradition, the son of the older brother still represents the older brother. If the youngest person in the group comes from the oldest tribe, they get to choose first. It is the law or right of the firstborn. So Abraham says to Lot that there should be no warfare between them because they are brothers. Then he says, "*If you take the left hand, then (az) I will go to the right, or if you take the right hand, then (az) I will go to the left.*" Lot probably did not understand that Abraham was using the structure of his inner timing to direct the situation. The same guy ascended to heaven, sat over heaven, looked on the stars, and structured them for the future manifestation of his children. Lot chose to go to the valley that the Bible describes as "like the garden of the Lord." Abraham goes up to the dry mountains. But in that moment of aligning with the divine timing of his soul, Abraham set and structured destiny. Today the families of Lot are no longer in existence, but Abraham's families—all the way from Asia into Africa (and even according to some researchers, the Navajos!)—still exist all over the earth.

> If you tell me you are saved, then I know you carry this divine clock.

Things, of course, did not change immediately. Sometimes when you set the *az* from your inside, it takes a while to work out the soul time and it does not always work out immediately. In the case of salvation, soul time works out immediately, but in the case of prosperity or destiny, soul time takes several years.

In order to work with this time that is embedded in our souls, you and I need to be cautious. Jesus even said this to the disciples after He prayed in the garden:

> **Watch and pray that you may not enter into**
> **temptation. The spirit indeed is willing, but the flesh**
> **is weak. (*Matthew 26:41*)**

When you do not know external time, you watch and pray. Our problem as believers is we are always watching for external signs, but we are not watching for what is happening inside of us. If you learn how to read the clock of your soul, it is much more precise than chronological time. In fact, each of us has a biological time that actually tells you when things within you are going to change. Women know this better than men do.

So Lot chose what appeared at the moment to be the best land and Abraham chose the mountains, dry as they were. However, a few years later, time caught up with Lot. By then, Abraham had opened up a different dimension. The salvation of your soul is a way in which God recalibrates the clock of your being so that it is able to direct cosmic affairs. If you tell me you are saved, then I know you carry this divine clock. Remember, God has placed eternity in the *az*. The soul also carries a clock that helps you access eternity and tune the cosmos to destiny. From our perspective, it may look like Abraham does not have anything and that he made the wrong choice. After all, he was the stronger one. He could have told his nephew to go to the mountains, but he knew what he could do with the structure of time in his being.

Let us discuss a different aspect of the power of Aleph Zayin (אָז)—freeing ourselves from curses. One of the ways you and I can release ourselves from a curse or from an oath that we made which haunts us is by having access to the time-altering principle of Aleph Zayin.

Look at the account of Abraham sending his servant to find a wife for his son Isaac from among his own people:

> Now Abraham was old, well advanced in years. And the LORD had blessed Abraham in all things. And Abraham said to his servant, the oldest of his household, who had charge of all that he had, "Put your hand under my thigh, that I may make you swear by the LORD, the God of heaven and God of the earth, that you will not take a wife for my son from the daughters of the Canaanites, among whom I dwell, but will go to my country and to my kindred, and take a wife for my son Isaac."
>
> The servant said to him, "Perhaps the woman may not be willing to follow me to this land. Must I then take your son back to the land from which you came?" Abraham said to him, "See to it that you do not take my son back there. The LORD, the God of heaven, who took me from my father's house and from the land of my kindred, and who spoke to me and swore to me, 'To your offspring I will give this land,' he will send his angel before you, and you shall take a wife for my son from there. *But if the woman is not willing to follow you, then you will be free from this oath of mine*; only you must not take my son back there." So the servant put his hand under the thigh of Abraham his master and swore to him concerning this matter. (*Genesis 24:1-9*)

Abraham uses the word *az* when he tells his servant that if the girl refuses to come with him, then he would be free from this oath (or curse) that Abraham put on him. The way I read the text is that by using this principle of az, Abraham understood the timing from within his soul and recalibrated the time so that the servant could never be free from the curse unless his oath was fulfilled.

Likewise, the only way you are free from people people's curses and words over you is by an internal recalibration of the clock of your soul.

ADONIJAH O. OGBONNAYA PH.D.

People will say cursing things to you and you even say cursing things to yourself. You tell yourself how terrible you are because you think that by doing that you are actually being holy. You continuously tell yourself what a mighty sinner you are because you made a mistake in your life, but by doing so you are actually creating a time for condemnation. You are reliving the same moment repeatedly.

When we look more deeply at the structure of Aleph Zayin (אז), we can understand another layer of meaning. Aleph (א), which is made up of two Yods and a Vav, is the name of God (the self-existent One). Zayin, which is made up of a Vav and a Yod, is an implement for cutting and for digging. When you use the name of God and the word of God (a two-edged sword) together correctly, you create a particular restructuring of time. That is why the name of God is given to you. That is why the word is given to you. Again, *az* is the Aleph Zayin, the name of God and a sword that is also a hoe for digging the ground. Zayin is also a tiller of the ground for planting a seed. *Az* uses both principles to open up a portal that allows you to access a different time other than the one you are in. The way to overcome what people have said about you is to access a different time either in the moment that they have spoken to you or after you remember it. In this way, you create a different time, and you find a different word.

I use the name of the Lord and I use the word of the Lord, but you can do it with your own name. I am not talking about your personal name now. You can do this with your identity

> You can find your own word and identity, and you can create a portal for the manifestation of something else other than what somebody has said about you.

and with your words. For instance, you can say, "I am..." and declare something positive over yourself. Or you can say, "No" to something and it will not happen. You can find your own word and identity, and you can create a portal for the manifestation of something else other than what somebody has said about you. I prefer to use the name of God (Yod Yod Vav), the self-existent One, and the word of God (Vav Yod) to transform the time:

165

AZ

The sun shall not smite thee by day, nor the moon by night. (*Psalm 121:6*)

No evil shall befall you, Nor shall any plague come near your dwelling. (*Psalm 91:10*)

The angel of the Lord encamps around those who fear Him and rescues them. (*Psalm 34:7*)

I do not know about you, but when the word tells me I am the apple of His eye (psalm 17:8), or that I am exalted and seated in heavenly places in Christ (Ephesians 2:6), I am changed and encouraged. So I use the name of Yahweh and then I use the word of Yahweh because, by His name and His word, I create a portal that brings a new dimension of time into my presence.

> If you bring a bad identity and a terrible word, you open a portal for diseases, sickness, fear, and anxiety.

Do not let just anyone tell you what you can never become. Whether you are married to them or whether you came out of them, you all have to learn what God has given to you. How can someone born of a woman tell you what you can never do? As a child of God, you have a name and a word, so you have an identity from God. You have a promise from God. You have these two things working for you. Every time a curse arises or someone rises up to say something about you that bothers your being, take the identity that comes from God, take the word of promise from God, and match them together. You will create a portal, a gateway, and open up a dimension that will direct you into the context of your own word and promise.

It works both ways. If you bring a bad identity and a terrible word, you open a portal for diseases, sickness, fear, and anxiety. You must stop telling yourself those things because you are affirming a false identity that God did not give you and you are creating a false word that is not a promise from God. This is how Reuben got himself in trouble— by aligning himself with a false identity, false word, and false action.

He misused his timing and it created a problem for him. That is what his father Jacob said in Genesis 49:4: "...you went up to your father's bed; then you defiled it...!" He used his time as a way of accessing something that did not belong to him.

Somebody else who was an incredible user of this kind of time is Zipporah, the wife of Moses, the daughter of the priest of Median (and maybe a black African woman). Her father Jethro was a priest of Yahweh and taught Moses how to operate as a priest. Zipporah is the daughter of a Melchizedek-type priest. Remember, Zipporah's father taught Moses how to administrate. Her brother divined and navigated the path that Israel took in the wilderness. When the father-in-law came to see Moses, Moses bowed down and worshiped him about seven times (Genesis 18) which is what the in-law is supposed to do.

The next day Moses sat to judge the people, and the people stood around Moses from morning until evening. When Moses' father-in-law saw all that he was doing for the people, he said, "What is this that you are doing for the people? Why do you sit alone, and all the people stand around you from morning till evening?" And Moses said to his father-in-law, "Because the people come to me to inquire of God; when they have a dispute, they come to me and I decide between one person and another, and I make them know the statutes of God and his laws." Moses' father-in-law said to him, "What you are doing is not good. You and the people with you will certainly wear yourselves out, for the thing is too heavy for you. You are not able to do it alone. Now obey my voice; I will give you advice, and God be with you! You shall represent the people before God and bring their cases to God, and you shall warn them about the statutes and the laws and make them know the way in which they must walk and what they must do. Moreover, look for able men from all the people, men who fear God, who are trustworthy and hate a bribe, and place such men over the people as chiefs of thousands, of hundreds, of fifties, and of tens. And let them judge the people at all times. Every great matter they shall bring to you, but any small matter they shall decide themselves. So it will be easier for you, and they will bear the burden with you. If you do this, God will direct you, you will be able to endure, and all these people also will go to their place in peace.

So Jethro pulls Moses up, kisses him, and asks him why he is sitting in the tent with a thousand people lined up for prayer. The father-in-law said, "What are you doing?" Moses says "I'm trying to tell the people what God wants." Jethro says, "Are you crazy? You are going to wear yourself and these people out! This is not the way to do it!" Some academics believe Jethro was actually an Ethiopian priest of the Midianites, but not necessarily a Midianite. In those days, people groups would hire priests and other people to come and do things for their tribes. Jethro knew God, but the Midianites, as we know, were idol worshippers. Also, Aaron and Miriam were upset with Moses because he married an Ethiopian woman (Numbers 12:1). So Jethro was not a Midianite; he was a priest of the Midianites.

Now we know that the priests in those areas were not circumcised. Only the Egyptians were circumcised. In fact, Abraham learned circumcision from Egypt. All the priests of Egypt were circumcised which is why you never hear the Bible calling the Egyptians uncircumcised. When Moses returned to Egypt to free the Israelites as God instructed, Zipporah went with him (Exodus 4:18-31). He is going to meet Aaron who has been chosen by God and whose DNA vibrates the things that Abraham did in the star system. You see, his physical body did not carry the mark. I know his children's physical bodies did not carry the mark. In other words, Moses had not done circumcision as was supposed to be done for his children. The Bible says God himself met him on the way in order to kill him. Moses did not even probably know what was happening to him, but Zipporah grabbed a flint knife, removed her son's foreskin, and threw it at his feet. The blood hit his body and he was released from death. Zipporah then told him that he was a "bridegroom of blood" to her, indicating that he is someone who lives by bloodshed.

Zipporah is actually speaking prophetically here because, first, Egyptians do not sacrifice animals, and second, Moses had killed a man. All of Israel's religion is going to be changed. The word *az* is used in the passage because of the capacity to reset time. In fact, without that act of circumcision, the future of Moses would have been completely closed. Even though her father was not circumcised, she performed a circumcision on her own son, which is something she had never done. How does a woman who has never seen circumcision perform a perfect circumcision? This is a combination of the movement of time and the soul. If you and I know how to use the technology of the Aleph Zayin correctly, we can have access to knowledge of things we have never learnt.

That one act of Zipporah changed the destiny of Israel. Sometimes we look at a certain act and just walk past it. What if Moses had died? God would have had to look for somebody else. The funny thing is that it was God who was trying to kill Moses — not Satan. That fact might challenge those in the deliverance ministry. How do you know it is not God dealing with the person? Just because something may not fit your religious constructs or your cultural worldview does not necessarily mean it is from the devil. If we learn how to use that inner structure, we will know when it is God and when it is the devil, not because somebody told us so. If I looked at this situation outside of this context and saw Moses, the man of God who had just seen God, I would not automatically think that God was going to kill him. I would think that the devil did not like the fact that Moses would become a great man of God and therefore wanted to kill him. There goes our theology out of the window!

> You just need to learn the purpose.

Oftentimes, God is probably disciplining someone when you think it might be the devil. Remember if the doctor cuts you, it is painful, and if your enemy cuts you, it is painful. You just need to learn the purpose.

The technology of *az* is illustrated often in the Bible. For instance, in Exodus 12, *az* is used when servants, slaves, or strangers in Israel are permitted to participate in the Passover as long as they are circumcised. These outsiders, by virtue of circumcision, gained access to the time of Israel's deliverance. However, that timing was opened not by the slave and the stranger, but by the master of the house who knew how to do it.

Jesus came as the word and as the promise. Through His body He opened up the dimensions of time. If you and I use correctly the promise, the name, the word, the identity, we can open up those portals. Remember, Aleph is also the same as the name of God as well as the principle for transmutation. This is *why* the scriptures in the Hebrew do not begin with Aleph, which means it is outside the system. When *Aleph* is used, it informs, transforms, and redirects creation. *Zayin* is used as a sword for cutting things open and opening the ground for the sowing of seed. *Az* represents your capacity to find a particular time from inside of you that tunes the cosmic clock.

Study the people in scripture who do things and tune their futures around a vision. Do you have a 10-year plan? A 20-year plan? How about a 25-year plan? Planning is one of the ways you open up dimensions and use your soul to set the cosmic clock. If you do not have a plan, you are not using your cosmic time correctly. We may think that if we do not have a plan, then God will do it. Why would God tell Abraham about a thousand generations to come? Because He needed Abraham's soul to tune time. Take your life by the horns. If you do not have it on paper, have it in your head because it helps you to tune the cosmic time.

Take the word, take the promise, and develop a plan. It is not a waste of time. Let the Holy Spirit work a few minutes and let it sink in. Close your eyes for a second, breath, and relax. The capacity to redirect time is inside of you. Has someone told you it is not your time? Then you can tune it to your time and can speed up time. Has someone spoken evil of you, cursed you, said things that bother you, or cursed your body? By the movement of your soul, you can recalibrate

> If you do not have a plan, you are not using your cosmic time correctly.

your time and enable your body to receive new energy and new virtues. You can remove the curse by living in a different plane through the power of the blood of Jesus Christ and through the power of the name and the promises of God.

If you are you hitting a wall in what you are trying to do, tune your soul to open up a door. Do not be afraid! I do not care how old you are; your season is not over. I do not care how young you are; your season can be now. You carry the timing. Be like Joseph—everywhere you enter, change the structure of time, and allow that which God has embedded in you to come through by the power of God in you, by the grace of God in you, by the blood of His Son. By His name and His word, create your own time. Nothing is impossible and you are loved! Your body is healed! Your bones are healed! They said you are not going to be healed, but I say you are healed, your neck, your back, your shoulders, your organs. Receive healing now; receive health now in the Name of Jesus! Amen.

Communion will activate these things in our lives to open up doors. Taking communion transmutes our lives. As you take communion, have in your mind what you are trying to manifest and what you want God to do.

As you participate in the Lord's Supper, time stands still and dimensions are opened so that you can draw from the future into the present. As you hold the communion, focus on what you want to see happen. Have no fear about where you are trying to go in your life. Nothing is impossible with God.

Az: Accessing Time, Eternity, and Rest

Sometimes the scholarly reading of scripture, which is mainly linguistic, rubs of esoteric and arcane meanings. What I mean is that I do not think the scripture was written to be given to us as a script. There is great value in the simple meaning of scripture because if you do not have the simple meaning, you cannot have the deep meaning. There are people who do not know the Bible who are trying to be deep, yet many people want to be deep without being scriptural. You cannot do that.

I disagree with scholars who look only at the linguistic and literal meaning of a word and forget that the Hebrew script is a glyph. A glyph is a painting or a structure you use for accessing something beyond the ordinary. I am not talking about Modern Hebrew, but rather, ancient Hebrew. The Hebrew scripture itself was written as glyphs or pictographs. The glyphs convey more meaning than just the word they create. For example, we have looked at the word az (זָא) which is translated in the scripture as "then." However, we miss the fact that *az* (זָא) is a word that speaks of timing. In fact, we saw how it is used when Joseph transforms the house of Potiphar because he creates a time portal that allows Potiphar's house to become an attraction for abundance.

We also saw how Zipporah, the wife of Moses and the daughter of the Midianite priest, Jethro understood how to function in time. By her understanding of time, she was able to create an atmosphere or a circumstance through which God released Moses from death. Let us talk about Leah, who was Jacob's first wife and the older sister of Rachel. Leah was one of those women who knew how to use time. She used time to access the realm of descending souls in order to have three of the most important people in the history of Israel and the world as her descendants. Jesus is a descendant of Leah because of her understanding of time and how she created that moment of access into the future. She had Rueben, who was the firstborn, and Levi and Judah. She accessed that time by the way she structured her life. This is not time management because you cannot manage time really. Time will just pass you by if you try to manage it. I am talking about using your inner structure to access or calibrate outside time to give you access to something that you actually want.

The word *az* means much more than "then." Let us look at the song of Moses in Exodus 15:1-18 where he sings a song of redemption and, in that very moment, creates access to Israel's future:

Then Moses and the people of Israel sang this song to the Lord, saying,

"I will sing to the Lord, for he has triumphed gloriously; the horse and his rider he has thrown into the sea.

The Lord is my strength and my song, and he has become my salvation;

this is my God, and I will praise him, my father's God, and I will exalt him.

The Lord is a man of war; the Lord is his name.

"Pharaoh's chariots and his host he cast into the sea,

and his chosen officers were sunk in the Red Sea.

The floods covered them; they went down into the depths
like a stone.

Your right hand, O Lord, glorious in power,

your right hand, O Lord, shatters the enemy.

In the greatness of your majesty you overthrow your adversaries;

you send out your fury; it consumes them like stubble.

At the blast of your nostrils the waters piled up;

the floods stood up in a heap; the deeps congealed in the heart
of the sea.

The enemy said, 'I will pursue, I will overtake, I will divide the
spoil, my desire shall have its fill of them. I will draw my sword;
my hand shall destroy them.'

You blew with your wind; the sea covered them;

they sank like lead in the mighty waters.

"Who is like you, O Lord, among the gods? Who is like you,
majestic in holiness,

awesome in glorious deeds, doing wonders?

You stretched out your right hand; the earth swallowed them.

"You have led in your steadfast love the people whom
you have redeemed;

you have guided them by your strength to your holy abode.

The peoples have heard; they tremble;

pangs have seized the inhabitants of Philistia.

Now are the chiefs of Edom dismayed; trembling seizes the
leaders of Moab;

all the inhabitants of Canaan have melted away.

Terror and dread fall upon them; because of the greatness of your
arm, they are still as a stone, till your people, O Lord, pass by,

till the people pass by whom you have purchased.

You will bring them in and plant them on your own mountain,

the place, O Lord, which you have made for your abode,

> **the sanctuary, O Lord, which your hands have established.**
> **The Lord will reign forever and ever."**

Read it again. Moses sings the song as an access to the future that Israel is not in yet. In the Jewish exegetical process, "song" refers to a Sabbath so the word itself is an access to the Sabbath rest of God that allows for the flow of abundance and grace. As Moses sings, he talks about God and gives a prophecy that unlocks a certain future for Israel.

Now let us look at Numbers 21:17-20:

> **Then [az] Israel sang this song:**
> **"Spring up, O well!—Sing to it!—**
> **the well that the princes made,**
> **that the nobles of the people dug,**
> **with the scepter and with their staffs."**

> **And from the wilderness they went on to Mattanah, and from Mattanah to Nahaliel, and from Nahaliel to Bamoth, and from Bamoth to the valley lying in the region of Moab by the top of Pisgah that looks down on the desert.**

There are many mysteries in this place of the well. The passage begins with *then* or *az*, which tells us that Israel is accessing something in their future. From the wilderness they went to Mattanah, which means *gift*. Then they went to Nahaliel. Nahaliel comes from the root word "to lead someone to springs of water" or "to lead someone to a place of abundance." When the word "-el" is added to the end of the word, it becomes the word referring to an angel. That is why you have Gabriel, Michael Uriel, Sachiel, Haniel, Ariel, and so forth.

> It means a particular time that coincides with the inner time of somebody's life that opens up another dimension to get what he or she needs for the present moment.

The passage says it took them from the gifts to the angel that led them to the place of overflowing abundance and then through the gate of death. If you keep reading, you will notice that

Israel goes to war just down the road. The verse is set up so it takes them to Bamoth, which is the valley of death in the country of Moab. Then God leads them to the top of Pisgah, which is a mountain that looks towards Yeshimon, a place of listening, to prepare them to face the Amorites. In Hebrew, the word Amorite means and spells the word "flesh." So the passage that says, "you shall deal with the Amorites all your life" actually translates to the word *basar*, meaning flesh. When God said, "you shall do war with the Amorites all the days of your life," He told Israel, "you shall always do war with your flesh." The thing that concerns me here is that for Israel to be able to move through this process and on to victory over the Amorites, they had to open a gate. It is a gate of time. As I have said, *az* means more than "then." It means a particular time that coincides with the inner time of somebody's life that opens up another dimension to get what he or she needs for the present moment.

Our biggest issue is timing. Everybody has opportunity. The issue is that the *az* is not in the present. The dials that we should use to align with the moment of our visitation are off kilter. We may cry all the time for not having opportunity, but the problem is that our inner clocks are off. The number one thing that throws our inner clocks off kilter is emotionality or sentimentality. It could be sentimentality drawn from personal hurt, race, or even family, and these can impact your internal clock. Your clock is determined by an event that has already passed and so your clock is constantly five minutes late because your whole life is about what somebody has done to you.

It is funny that Israel is singing this song after having come out of slavery. Do you know that the alignment to their timing is what allows the waters to flow in the wilderness? The water did not come from God. The scripture never says that the water came from God. It says the elders took their staffs, which is a deeper meaning than this, and began to pound the ground. This is what the elephant does, in the bush to find water. It stamps its feet on the ground. My father used to say that when an elephant walks, his body will vibrate to the frequency of the water. Then he will make a purring or mooing type of sound to communicate to the other elephants and they will start stamping until the water bursts forth. In the case of Israel, they were in the wilderness where there was no water, yet the water was created by how they structured it. You can actually structure your inner life to attract something that is not there.

To look for water in the village, not only do we use the staff, we dance. It is like the Native Americans doing a rain dance. However, the evangelical church calls it witchcraft because God must come and provide water, because God is your water-fetcher. But the scripture does not say God brought the water. It says the water springs up with digging and singing. The verse says *then* or *az*, referring to timing, and it is also a Sabbath that is opening a dimension of rest. Here is the text in Hebrew:

הַזֹּאת הַשִּׁירָה	יָשִׁיר	יִשְׂרָאֵל	אָז
this song	sang	Israel	Then

What the scripture is saying here is the *az* through Yod sang over Israel.

It actually says that the dimension of rest, a certain dimension of time which is not now and not yet, which is the place where God rested, the day when you are not supposed to do anything, began to sing over Israel through the Yod. Notice that the word for singing begins with a Yod. Remember that Jesus said in Matthew 5:18 that heaven and earth shall pass away, but not one Yod or tittle? We teach in Hebrew that the Yod is the letter by which God created the heavens. Yod is also the first letter of the name of God.

So the dimension of rest sang over Israel along with Israel. *Az* opened up the dimension of singing through the Yod over Israel. They are digging the well in the earth. In Hebrew, the word is ath (אֶת) which is the phrase Jesus uses to describe himself: "I am the Alpha and Omega." In Hebrew, it is the Aleph Tav. (Incidentally, nobody should translate ath as "that" because Jesus uses it to describe Himself). When we synthesize all of this together, the verse actually describes the name of God being sung by the Yod which is the seed of God's creation of heaven and earth. The first letter of God's name is sung into eternity because the Alpha and the Omega signify the beginning and the end for which there is no beginning and no end.

ADONIJAH O. OGBONNAYA PH.D.

Watch what is happening here. Here is the Sabbath of God singing over Israel through the Aleph Tav, which is the principle of eternity. In doing so, the scripture also uses the Aleph, the other letter of the name of God that God gave to Abraham and Sarah. When God changed the name of Abram to Abraham and Sarai to Sarah, He added the Hey to both of their names, speaking the two letters Yod Hey together. Now we know what God is doing here— He is connecting Israel with the promise that He made to their parents.

> Sabbath rest is not just the seventh day of creation, it is that which is inside of you.

In this one moment of their singing, God crosses the heavens to speak to Israel in their presence and in the song to sound out their need in the heavens. By doing this, He moves Israel through the principle of eternity so that the same letter that was given to their father and mother will come upon them for the presence of increase and abundance. God does this before He leads Israel through all of these other processes because, unless Israel operates in rest and the inner clock operates by the clock of the Sabbath, they will not walk in the promise. *Az* is not just a sign. Through the name and the word of God, a song came from heaven upon Israel. It sang through the Yod into the realms of eternity. Then out of eternity came the voice that went through the Hey as God changed the names of Abraham and Sarah. Now He begins to speak to Israel so that Israel can bring forth life. When Hey is given to you, there is no death that can hold you. No famine can kick you down. When Hey is given to you, the wilderness will provide for you.

Looking at ourselves, we can understand why we have our problems because either our timing is off or we are in so much of a hurry that we miss the opportunity. The actual principle for operating in *az* is finding rest in the midst of your trouble. This Sabbath rest is not just the seventh day of creation, it is that which is inside of you. You must find this rest inside of yourself because when the rest of heaven calls, it calls to the rest in you. Then when it comes to rest in you, then the name of God begins to sing over you. And when the seed of God sings over you, it sinks through the first Hey to the second Hey and

177

AZ

becomes the opening for creation. You will become a foundation for manifestation.

We sometimes forget why Jesus ascended into heaven. There is a reason He did not stay. He had to go to the place of rest in order to sing through the Yod, which is the seed of Himself back into your life. When He sings in you, He sings through the principle of eternity. When He speaks from above, He speaks from the seat of rest. He is looking for someone who also has the timing of rest in them. So the earth sang to the (upper) Hey and the (upper) Hey sang to the (lower) Heh. The Yod sang to Israel and Israel sang through the eighth son and through the Heh—from the (upper) Hey to the (lower) Heh.

What is the word Jesus gave to us in Matthew 11:28-30?

> **Come to me, all who labor and are heavy laden, and I will give you rest. Take my yoke upon you, and learn from me, for I am gentle and lowly in heart, and you will find rest for your souls. For my yoke is easy, and my burden is light.**

We like to say, "Be strong and courageous," as quoted from the book of Joshua. Remember when God commissions Joshua to lead the Israelites after the death of Moses?

> **Be strong and courageous, for you shall cause this people to inherit the land that I swore to their fathers to give them. Only be strong and very courageous, being careful to do according to all the law that Moses my servant commanded you. Do not turn from it to the right hand or to the left, that you may have good success wherever you go. This Book of the Law shall not depart from your mouth, but you shall meditate on it day and night, so that you may be careful to do according to all that is written in it. For *then you will make your way prosperous*, and then you will have good success. Have I not**

commanded you? Be strong and courageous. Do not be frightened, and do not be dismayed, for the Lord your God is with you wherever you go. (*Joshua 1:6-9*) [emphasis added]

God did not say, "*Then* I will make your way prosperous." He said to Joshua that if he understands timing and it is structured the way it should be, he will prosper everywhere he goes. He will become the clock of his own season. The same word is used when Joshua stopped the sun and the moon. When I was growing up, I learned things about Hebrew by some seemingly crazy guys who I did not understand, and they would teach things like this. Sometimes I would argue and say, "But it just says this or that here." Then they would tell me that English linguistic studies do not work well when trying to understand the arcana (deep mysteries). You see, these words are not just for communication.

...when you access the rest above you and the rest inside of you, a sound will come from the realm of the depth of the heavens and will sing a song over you.

There is more to it. We cannot ever say, "If this, then that," and call it a causal statement because even that means that something changes in the temporal realm that allows for something else to emerge. In fact, even native peoples do not use words merely as linguistic handles. Words and letters are pictures that, taken both individually and together, have broader and deeper meaning. He who has not seen will not understand and he who has not experienced will not know.

In the world we have so many people trying to teach us who have not seen and have not experienced. However, when you access the rest above you and the rest inside of you, a sound will come from the realm of the depth of the heavens and will sing a song over you. The song creates a different rhythm that allows you to access what the world says you cannot access. My brothers and my sisters, we have access! This is what has kept me throughout all my struggles and sufferings in life, from a war as a child all the way until now. This is what has kept

179

AZ

me, knowing that there is a place of interconnection in the human soul. I did not understand it when I heard this as a child, but I know it now. I know that if you tune your soul, the heavens will bend to you. When the sound of heaven hits the frequency of your heart rightly, the song will cause the heavens to bend to you and the voice of God will open up eternity for you and in eternity you can do whatever you want.

If the sound comes through eternity, you can cause it to create any harmony you want. There is no chaos, just what you make of it. Through eternity the Hey speaks to Hey, the male and the female come together, and impregnation and breathing happens. Jesus looked at Jerusalem and said,

> **And when he drew near and saw the city, he wept over it, saying, "Would that you, even you, *had known on this day* the things that make for peace! But now they are hidden from your eyes." (Luke 19:41-42) [emphasis added]**

Again, it is all about timing. Your timing is right inside of you. You can ride on your own time that rolls in your soul. Through it, you can frame the external clock around you. Seasons are not a factor for the one who understands the timing of his soul. As the princes and elders sang their song, they used their own staffs, not the staff of Moses, and they pounded the ground. The Bible does not say that God sent water. They commanded the water to come forth and they prepared themselves for every eventuality. That one timing allowed them to reach the place of Mattanah, the place of gifts. It allowed them to encounter the angel that leads into abundance and overflowing water. This angel leads them to the place of gifts, through the valley of the shadow of death, and up to the mountain of Pisgah. Pisgah is where they could listen and hear the voice of the Lord, and get the energy for facing the Amorites (flesh) with whom they will do battle all their lives and gain victory.

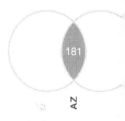

שני

Shney

We have been looking at words that imply time and the usage of time in the Hebrew. We want to continue to deal with the sacramentality of time because our whole life is structured around time.

We have dealt with Jesus Christ as a sacrament, life itself as a sacrament, and you as a sacrament. We are going to come to deal with your body as a sacrament. You see the body of Christ as a sacrament, but you may not yet see your body as a sacrament. First, let us look at time.

One thing I have learned is that time is actually a boundary-creating mechanism. It makes distinction between moments. I think that God gave time to protect man and to give him a moment and a period by which a human being can choose how to deal with the past and how to anticipate the future. Time is actually given to us as a key to life. Let us deal with a new Hebrew word: *shney* (שׁנׁי). For those of you who know Hebrew, *shney* is spelled *Shin Nun Yod*. Shin represents the three flames of fire, Nun represents water, and Yod represents the seed or principle that carries the creation of heaven and earth. The Yod is a very serious principle.

The word occurs on its own very few times in scripture and it always has a prefix or a suffix. The prefix is Hey. The suffix is usually a Mem or a Tav. When the suffix is a Mem, it means water. Tav refers to a cut in space and time or a cross. So the cross itself is something that stands in space and time to open up another dimension. Remember that in the word *az* (אָז), Aleph represents the name of God, and Zayin is a sword that is the word of God and also a tool that digs up the ground for sowing seed. Therefore, the way to create a time of transformation is to use the name of God with the word of God, taking the word and the promise together, as we saw with people like Joseph and Abraham who used it in scripture.

Now we want to use the word *shney* which means *"second."* Hebrew may use the word *second* but, as I am sure you have realized, it is more than just saying the number two. To understand what a Hebrew word really means you need to begin with scripture and find out when the word *second* is used. In English, you and I think about words like *first* and *second* as chronological. However, I will give you examples from scripture that reveal deeper levels of meaning for the word *shney* and as I teach more, you will see what I am doing.

The first time the word *shney* is used is on the second day when God divided the waters. God created space by dividing the waters above and the waters below. In so doing, He allows for the earth to have creatures it can bring forth and for the heavens to have a firmament. The firmament becomes a filter of what God is thinking and keeps things from the other realms from destroying humanity. So the firmament is created as a protection for human beings.

Shney is used is used a second time concerning the Gijon, which is the river that flowed through Egypt. I believe the Gijon is the Nile. In any case, it is a river of abundance and it determines the timing of planting in Egypt. The Nile was a river that overflowed and flooded everything every year, making it necessary for the Egyptians to re-divide their land. Every year in Egypt was a new year—even a poor person got a piece of land. The waters came and cleaned up the boundaries annually so they had to start afresh. Someone once said that time is the greatest physician there is for man because time really does heal. Time is meant to be a physician. It is meant to remove certain pains and ameliorate the impact of pain.

The third time *shney* is used is when Lamech marries a second wife. The fourth time it is used is when God speaks to Noah about building the ark and where to place the windows on each of the three levels. *Shney* talks about the window in the lower level that is below the water line. Do you ever wonder why you have to have a window on the lower level? The fifth occurrence refers to when the windows of heaven opened and waters from heaven came down. The sixth one has to do with when God shut the windows and dried up the water. We are going to see more of this.

What I notice as I look at all these occurrences is that the idea of *second* has a lot to do with how water operates. Understand that when the word *second* is used in the context of time in the Hebrew, it is not about counting something.

It is actually about creating an opportunity by restructuring the time through what is happening inside of you. I think the way to accurately translate it is *"second chance"* or *"second opportunity."* When you read the various texts including the word *shney*, this movement is not just that God gives a person a second chance. In fact, it alludes to something in the person that is structured to actually allow the person to reverse time by the way he or she relates to God.

> Time is actually given to us as a key to life.

Let me illustrate further. The gematria of *shney* is 360, which is a reference to a circle. The circle starts and ends at the same point. In other words, the circle comes back to its beginning point. So if God gives you a second chance, He is taking you back to a starting point where you can redo. There is a redo in God. There is a restart button and this word seems to be a restart button. People like Lamech, for instance, used it to start something new for themselves. If you understand this, then you realize that a person whose soul is structured to restart does not have to run around in circles like the proverbial lab rat. Most of the time when the word *shney* or "second" is used, God is doing something to turn somebody's life around.

Jesus is called the "second Adam" because He is God's reset of man. He was not second because He was inferior. He was second because He is the one through whom God brought man back to the beginning and redirected humanity. *Second* in God's mind does not mean you come after. It means that He has placed you where you can actually begin again. This concept of second is hard in America because the one who takes second place is never mentioned.

The idea of the time of the second is so incredible! Let me give you an example. If you read the Hebrew mainly from a linguistic perspective

185

SHNEY

and consult your concordance, you are not going to get it. I am sorry, but your concordance will not tell you what I am about to tell you. Do you remember when Israel made the golden calf and God wanted to destroy Israel?

> **But Moses implored the LORD his God and said, "O LORD, why does your wrath burn hot against your people, whom you have brought out of the land of Egypt with great power and with a mighty hand? Why should the Egyptians say, 'With evil intent did he bring them out, to kill them in the mountains and to consume them from the face of the earth'? Turn [Repent] from your burning anger and relent from this disaster against your people. Remember Abraham, Isaac, and Israel, your servants, to whom you swore by your own self, and said to them, 'I will multiply your offspring as the stars of heaven, and all this land that I have promised I will give to your offspring, and they shall inherit it forever.'" And the LORD relented from the disaster that he had spoken of bringing on his people. (Genesis 32:11-14) [Commentary added]**

When you enter through repentance, God hits the reset button.

The Bible says Moses stood up to God. Moses looked at God and said, "What's wrong with you?" He told God to repent. He asked God, "Why does your wrath burn hot against your people, whom you have brought out of the land of Egypt with great power and with a mighty hand?" Moses is giving God a long lecture about realizing what He is about to do; "What will the nations say?" It is like your mama talking to you, "What will the neighbors say?"

Moses tells God that the neighbors will say He is a terrible God and no one will want to believe in Him again. They will say, "Isn't this the God who brought them out of that land and into the wilderness just to kill them?" At first, God says He will destroy them and make Moses the king. God even says He will make Moses a great nation, but Moses refused and said that if God will not forgive them, he wanted his name removed from the book where God had written it. Essentially, Moses is saying that he will go to hell with them.

Do you realize how difficult that is, especially in the world in which we find ourselves unable to stand with other people under the judgment of God? When Moses retells the story and reminds Israel in Deuteronomy 9:7-21, he tells them that he went to God the second time using the word *shney*. When he went to God the second time, he reset the button. He says the same thing when Aaron sinned against God and God said He was going to kill him. Again, Moses went up the second time, did a 360 degree turnaround, and Aaron was allowed to live. You have heard people say, "God's going to give me a second chance," but there are also people who are able to do this.

Remember we have been talking about the soul time. There are people who are able to link into this time because they have a clock in them by which they are able to create second chance moments. One of the things that God has given his children is the spirit of repentance. I am not talking about you sitting around and mourning for 500 years. I am talking about you having a spirit of repentance that allows you to rethink moments, rethink matter, and enter into the presence of God with humility, acknowledging who you are and what you have done. When you enter through repentance, God hits the reset button. That is why you are a believer today. You were heading to hell, whatever that is. You were heading to destruction, whatever that is. You were heading to your own nowhere when you said to God, "I'm sorry." Something in your soul caused God to reset the button of your life and now you are a child of God. Now you are redeemed. Now you are saved. Now you have a future!

For you and me to do this after we have repented and become believers, we must still live a life that says we understand there is more to do. We are supposed to reset moments so that people around us have a second chance. We are supposed to reset time so that our children have a second chance. We are supposed to reset time so the nation has a second chance. However, we cannot do this unless something in us or the clock of our soul operates rightly. For our soul clock to reset time, there are certain things that must happen in the maturity of our soul. Believers are called to be time setters, but why are they unable to do it? Because believers are stuck in the past and they are stuck in bitterness. They are stuck in disappointment and regret. They are stuck in unforgiveness which means that they are not actually resetting the button. Rather they keep repeating the same experiences because, when you live in that context, you repeat the same pattern over and over again. You are not going anywhere.

Remember, everyone who lives in repentance knows how to reset their life. When you say to God, "I'm sorry," He removes everything. I hear believers say many things that are not biblical. For example, they ask someone "Have you truly repented?" However, I wonder what they mean by that. There is not one person who knows what that really means. When you say that to someone, what you mean is that they should be groveling at your feet because you said they have not repented! What does someone need to say or do so that you actually know they have truly repented? It is false righteousness for you to say you really know how the penitent person is supposed to behave. Then if a person makes the same mistake, you will think that they never repented. That is false logic because somebody can truly repent and still make the same mistake. It is a false doctrine in the church to say that if you really repented, you are not going to make mistakes again because you are saying that repentance changes the person's behavior immediately. Did it change yours? The answer is no. You repented and the Spirit started working with you. You are willing to give yourself an opportunity to change, but you are not willing to give somebody else an opportunity to change. In so doing you are refusing the second chance (*shney*).

We refuse to let people have a reset. When this happens in marriage (and all marriages go through this), the couple repeats the same process and you end up with the same headache, the same quarrel every day. Neither the husband nor the wife is willing to reset. It happens to friendships, families, business partners, and co-workers. This refusal to allow a person to press the reset button and continually bringing them back to the idea that they never truly repented is called unforgiveness.

A believer whose soul is growing and working in maturity has this capacity to reset other people's lives. The way you look at and behave towards them, and the way your presence resets their lives, encourages them to start over and gives them an opportunity to emerge again. This is what God did for you and me. I know everyone I read in scripture who was able to reset nations, reset families, reset friends, reset communities, and reset their own lives has a mature soul. Let me list the seven things that you must walk in so it will be easy for you to stand as one who commands second chances and creates it for yourself and other people.

> A believer whose soul is growing and is working in maturity has this capacity to reset other people's lives.

1. I AM

The number one thing is you must have a conviction of a sense of "I AM." You must be convinced of your intrinsic value as a being. You are dealing from the place of I AM, which carries with it a sense of immortality. In other words, to be able to reset someone's life, you have to know and develop a sense of your own immortality. Intrinsically, you have life in you, and if you know you have life in you, you will always bring forth life. Life begets life. Jesus said;

I came that they may have life and have it abundantly.
(John 10:10)

He means we have a second chance at life more abundantly. "I AM the way, the truth, and the life," is connected to the identity of I AM. If you do not know who you are, you do not have life in you. Your knowledge of your own I AM means you have life in you. As a believer, being conscious of the sense of immortality is what makes you want to reset other people's lives towards life. You do not live a life of this epistemic condemnation, which is the mindset that everyone must be punished (although this is the mindset of a number of the churches).

Now we have this confusion within the church where we have those who believe everyone must be punished, and then we have those who believe nothing is wrong. Both conservatives and liberals do the same thing. For them it is about preserving an ideological situation that supports someone else's view of life rather than transforming human beings. If you want to be able to reset life in the context of *shney*, you and I must access this sense of immortality that is an intrinsic understanding of ourselves as life-givers.

> Raise your consciousness to the level where you realize that you are actually inside God and God is in you. You are not separated from God.

2. Obliterate Fear

A person who can reset time must obliterate fear completely, and must overcome and transmute fear and hate into love. What I mean by fear is trepidation—the things that cause your stomach to churn. I am not talking about the reverence of God. I am talking about the fear of man. Even the Bible says the fear of man is a trap (Proverbs 29:25). You can become entrapped by fear of what someone is going to do or say. However, if you overcome that fear and you transmute it into love, then you are able to reset any timeline. When you overcome fear and love becomes your reality, it produces an unassailable confidence that is not based on the flesh, your occupation, or your accomplishments. Rather, this confidence is based on a sense of being that is unassailable because YOU ARE and I AM.

3. Make Love the Eternal Point of Reference

As weak as your love may be, nobody has a perfect love yet. Our love is not strong enough yet. It is always weak, always gets tempted. You always want to say, "Not this time." If you make love your eternal point of reference, you hear even in the midst of darkness and evil, even in the midst of disappointment by others. If you make love your point of reference, time becomes meaningless. When love is present, time is subject to the lover. You can change time.

4. Remove Self-righteousness and Self-condemnation

A person who will change other people's lives must remove from the depth of their being any sense of self-righteousness and self-condemnation. Self-condemnation and self-righteousness go hand-in-hand. People who condemn others tend to be self-righteousness. Ironically, they also tend to be self-condemning because they cannot meet their own standards. It is psychological bondage. They tend to set very high standards for themselves and for others. Yet deep inside they know they cannot meet their own standards and so there is a deep self-condemnation. They use the veneer of self-righteousness to condemn everybody else that comes around them and so refuse to reset other people's lives. They want others to stay at a place where they can continue to condemn them. However, if I remove self-righteousness and self-condemnation, it allows me then to look at other people from the perspective of their possibility and the inherent desire of Divinity for them. Therefore, I meet them at the point where I restart. I reset at the point of their mistake. I remove it and give them an opportunity to start again. Still, some of us are like Peter, asking Jesus how many times we should forgive this guy. Seven times? Or as Jesus said, seventy times seven (Matthew 18:21-22).

Listen to me! You know that thing you have been carrying all your life? Press the reset button! That thing she did to me? Reset! That thing he did to me? Reset! This is what time masters do. They hit the reset button. That is why God is the master time master. For those of you who like to complain to God about other people, while you are complaining, the person has gone to God and God has already hit their reset button while you are complaining. Part of it has to do with the fact that you really do not love yourself. I think there is some sort of spiritual masochism going on. We feel that the more we self-flagellate, the more God will be honored.

We feel the same thing about everybody. We think the more people suffer, the more righteous they can become. So let the poor be hungry because it will teach them a lesson. They committed the crime so they must pay the time. Yet the Bible says forgiveness transforms an individual. In our self-righteousness, we say, "No, forgiveness just makes them do it again." We have created a system where there is no reset button. I do know how civil society is supposed to work, but civil society is different from the divine setting and it does not serve us to confuse our social system with the divine system. It is amazing that people who benefit from the system think the system is divine.

Do you remember the old symbol of the *Ouroboros*—the snake that bites his tail? The whole idea is that there is always a possibility of starting again. Always! I can even push that and say that even after someone dies, the gospel is still preached. I do not believe that the passage says it is appointed unto men once to die and after that comes the judgment.

> **Thus it was necessary for the copies of the heavenly things to be purified with these rites, but the heavenly things themselves with better sacrifices than these. For Christ has entered, not into holy places made with hands, which are copies of the true things, but into heaven itself, now to appear in the presence of God on our behalf. Nor was it to offer himself repeatedly, as the high priest enters the holy places every year with blood not his own, for then he would have had to suffer repeatedly since the foundation of the world. But as it is, he has appeared once for all at the end of the ages to put away sin by the sacrifice of himself. And just as it is appointed for man to die once, and after that comes judgment, so Christ, having been offered once to bear the sins of many, will appear a second time, not to deal with sin but to save those who are eagerly waiting for him.**
> **(Hebrews 9:23-28)**

Paul said the only appointed death in the world is the death of Christ. Your death is not an appointment. Your death is a punishment. That is why you do not know when to die because you do not know how to lay your life down and take it up again. There is only one person who had an appointed death and He is the only one whose appointed death decides judgment. Read the whole passage. It deals with Jesus, not with you. It talks about his one eternal sacrifice. There is a time when the reset button is going to go away—it is going to happen, but it does not happen after you die. As a believer, you have the capacity to reset peoples' lives! We have been preaching this to unbelievers that it is appointed unto men to die and after that comes a judgment, as if that is what the Bible teaches!

> He gave you a second, second, second, second, second, second, second, second chance.

Jesus himself said He that does not believe the son of God is already condemned. He said He that does not believe is already judged, so time is not waiting for you to die before you are judged. It is the death of Christ, His *appointed* death, which removes judgment.

5. Remove Guilt

Strip away the guilt from your inner consciousness. I do not mean you strip away the idea that you have done something wrong because guilt is deeper than that. The thing about guilt is that when it takes hold of your conscience and consciousness, it debilitates you. It actually keeps you from doing anything else. Everything you are trying to do is informed and inflated by that guilt so that everything you do becomes ineffective.

How do you remove guilt? We started with it in the beginning—repentance. If you have repented and you are still carrying your guilt, you are either living in the wrong structure or somebody has done something to you and has created a system that does not allow you to accept forgiveness and cleansing from God. It is a human system, not a divine system. As a believer, be conscious of God's presence in your life and be conscious of your presence in God. Raise your consciousness to the level where you realize that you are actually inside God and God is in you. You are not separated from God. When you realize your interconnection with Divinity and that you are not separated from God, then it is easy for you to help other people reset their lives. If, however,

193

SHNEY

you are living with separation consciousness, you are still living as one whose sin is not forgiven.

Listen to me! You know that things you have been carrying all your life? Press the reset button!

Paul says your sins have separated you from God. If your sin is removed, are you separated? We have to come back to actually dealing with what Jesus Christ has done for us. He removed sin so that our conscience and our consciousness can become that of interconnection with Divinity at the very depth of our being. He removed sin so that which is in the mind of God can enter into our minds. The Bible even says we have become the righteousness of God.

For our sake he made him to be sin who knew no sin, so that in him we might become the righteousness of God. (2 Corinthians 5:21)

I did not write it! It says that we are the righteousness of God in Christ Jesus. This means that our consciousness is one of righteousness, not of our own doing, but that God has transferred His inner consciousness into our being. It is that consciousness that resets life at every moment. Every time the enemy or my own thoughts come to me and tells me what I have done before, I press the reset button.

6. *Allow Joy to Invade Your Being*

If you want to be a resetter of time, you must develop a blissful, joyful, enthusiastic, ecstatic mode of living. To do this, you must allow your being to be invaded by joy, bliss, crazy enthusiasm, and ecstatic movement.

The cellular memory in your body needs to become a memory of joy, enthusiasm, and ecstatic exuberance so that you make no room for regret, self-pity, and overshadowing sorrow and depression. If you allow yourself to operate in kindness, love, and joy, you orient yourself to constantly shift time. That level of being makes you a master of time. If, on the other hand, you live in regret, you are marking time and staying in the same place. If you develop joyful exuberance, and your whole being is filled with joy, it resets the moment. You are a master of time.

7. Develop Complete Union with God

Finally, get yourself to the place where your whole idea is union with God. Release your being through Jesus Christ into this intimacy with God. Intimacy with God raises you above time, allows you to restructure time, and allows you to redirect time. When your soul is matured at the level where the I AM of God becomes the I AM that you are, His I AM becomes your I AM. "I am that I am" becomes the "I am that you are." When your being is completely saturated with a sense of divine presence, divine nature, and divine identity, you can press any button at any time. You can press your restart button at any time in your life and begin it anew. So you lost your job! Press reset. So the doctor says you are going to die. Press reset. Though they say your family has this genetic problem, it started in time. Therefore, you can reset the time. Maybe they say it is a problem with the men in this family or that depression is in your blood. Yet when your soul's identity is based in the nature of God, and you understand that your soul is not just a visitor on earth but that it was released from the depths of God to express His rulership on the face of the earth, then time is not your master. Your Father made time. It does not matter how many years have gone by. That is why for the believer, every day is a new day and His mercies are new every morning (*Lamentations 3:23*).

There is no end for believers. Every day is a new day. He renews my strength and my youth. If they say the world is suffering from famine because of sin, I hit the reset button. I was on my way to hell. I was on my way to be destroyed. I was on my way to suffering, but somebody hit the reset button. The enemy does not like this. He gets me in a corner and says, "I got you now, I got you now! You did this and you did that! You are not going anywhere." That is what the enemy hates most about me: I have a finger on the reset button. God has actually made it so easy for us! Is it sin? You go to God, your daddy. Is there somebody in your job that has decided they are never going to allow you to move forward? You know what to do.

We are the ones who allow things to be the way they are. It usually comes from our human kindness. We know my Father would not behave that way. Sometimes it is good to just reset the button. Aren't you glad that God resets? He gave you a second, second, second, second, second, second, second, second chance. It is funny—the Bible always calls it the second chance even though it is the hundredth chance. It is based on the fact that God gave a second Adam.

תחילה

Techila

We are delving deeply into what we are now calling times and seasons, but really we are discussing the value of time as a sacrament in and of itself.

TECHILA:
RETURNING TO
THE BEGINNING

In this chapter I want to shift us and deal with a term for time that is not so common. I want to look at what happened when Joseph finally meets his brothers again. We are using the text in Genesis 42-46.

Some philologists might take issue with me, but from what I know about those who were ascended in the early time of the Hebrew tradition, they received the revelation of the Torah by ascending, harvesting from that, and then seeing the reflection of what they had seen in the heavens or in the Torah. In those days they engaged with the angel called the Prince of the Torah. We are going to talk about the word "techila" (תחילה) which means *first*. The word is pronounced like the alcohol 'tequila'. Take it from me—it is not the one you drink!

I want to look at what happened when Joseph finally met his brothers again and this idea of beginnings. You could use the word *reshith* (רֵאשִׁית), which means "beginning" in Hebrew, but the word *techila* is used a lot when referring to beginnings. It is found in Genesis 13:3, several times in Genesis 40, and in the book of Judges when they talk about who will go to war for the Israelites and who will go first. They chose Judah and then, when they talk about going to war against Benjamin, they say Judah should go first. So I am going to pull revelation from the text itself and from ascension in the early Hebrew tradition. I studied the word and I want to look at what it actually does in the scripture. It is one thing to see a word used in a text and it is another thing to engage the way that the word is used spiritually. Let us do both.

Techila means first. It means the word *first*, but it also means the word *"beginning"* (It is not the word *reshith*). It is used initially when Abraham returned to where he first made an altar to God. Understand that an altar is something that opens up dimensions. In this context, we will look at this word as what Mircea Eliade, the famed Romanian religious historian, referred to as "il tempore," which is the "time before time" or the "time that starts every other time."

Now in the context of a human being's life, it refers to the moment when an act commenced. It is used several times when Joseph's brothers come back to him with the bags of goods that he gave to them and with the cup when the cup is taken. This word *techila* is important because Abraham went back to where he first started, where he entered in the beginning.

> **And he journeyed on from the Negeb as far as Bethel**
> **to the place where his tent had been at the beginning,**
> **between Bethel and Ai, to the place where he had**
> **made an altar at the first. And there Abram called**
> **upon the name of the LORD. (*Genesis 13:3-4*)**

I was wondering why Abraham would go back there. Was he missing something? Abraham had been everywhere. Abraham had criss-crossed the land and he had also gone to Egypt, yet he came back to the place where he started. Why? Interestingly, *techila* can also mean *"before,"* depending on which commentary you are reading. So Abraham returned to the first time in order to access the moment prior to everything he had ever done. In other words, it is a word meaning *beginning*, but refers to foundations that are not yet manifest.

Remember, Bethel has not been named by Jacob yet. Later you read the story about Jacob naming Bethel (Genesis 28:10-22). So how did Abraham go back to Bethel when Bethel was non-existent? Still, Abraham went back to where he first started, to the foundation. When you have access to first principles, you have access to their fruits. He went back to Luz. However, in the Abrahamic narrative, it is called that which is the house of God, although it was not yet a house of God. What made it the house of God is the fact that Abraham accessed something outside of the reality that was in front of him. He went back there because there was something there where he built the first altar.

The thing about being first is there is nothing behind you. When there is nothing behind you, you have access. Access to nothing is access to everything. When someone is first, they become the foundation for whatever is built later on. In using this phrase "at the beginning," a foundation to nothingness is established, which is essentially a foundation to everything. It means that everything in the universe is possible because nothing is present.

We can apply this concept to all the firsts. Being the first is not easy but, in one sense, I think it is the easiest thing because there is nobody with whom to compare yourself. Abraham went back to where he first started in order to have access to nothingness. When I say nothingness, I mean "NO thing." Nothing you can grasp, nothing you can touch, nothing you can taste. You have to stand on nothing in order to formulate something. This is how God operates. Even in the beginning, before all creation, it does not mean there was nothing when God speaks. His word is something. Even though we say God created the world out of nothing, God did not really create the world out of nothing. He created the world out of His word, which is a substance.

> He created the world out of His word, which is a substance.

When this term *techila* is used, then you know this person has access to possibilities. This person has access to divine potential and to things that are not yet manifest. Abraham returns here because he wants to restructure how he enters the land. Remember he is already in the land so he does not need to do anything. He has built this altar and he goes back to the first place because he wants to have access now. I want to suggest that he missed something when he first entered the land (but I am not telling you he went to get something he missed). He also went there to borrow from the future. Again, remember the place is called Bethel but it is not yet named Bethel. So who is writing the text and why are they writing in this way? It is because they know Abraham is accessing through time, into the future. He is going to the first place in order to access that which was not, but that which shall be.

201

TECHILA

Let us refer now to the story of Joseph in Genesis 42-46. His brothers come, they are hungry, and they want to get food. He recognizes them, but they do not recognize him. I want you to see this. When his brothers leave, he puts all their money back into their bags. When they get home and see the money, they get scared. They decide to take this money back. Now God is doing something significant here. This group of people has gone crazy. They sold their brother, Judah is shacking up with his daughter-in-law, and Levi and Simeon have killed off a whole village. These men have forgotten what God has done for them. Who knows what the other brothers were doing? We only know about these because God picked on Judah, Levi, and Simeon because of their position in Israel.

> Love had become transactional. It was not until that moment when Judah began to give his life for his brother that love became real again.

Now when they come back, they return the money and they are afraid, and this time they brought Benjamin with them. They tell Joseph the whole story and they use the word *first* several times. His brothers were so far gone that they did not understand what Joseph was doing to them. Joseph was not just trying to get them to recognize him. You see, their language was betraying what Joseph was doing spiritually. They were the ones using the word *first,* but it was Joseph who was trying to take them back to the time before they created all this mess. Joseph was the alchemist. In other words, they were saying it, but Joseph was the one operating the system.

These are the same men who sold Joseph and who sat to eat while their brother was in the well. Something had happened that removed them from where they were in the first place. So how does Joseph bring them back to using the language that they did not even understand? They thought it was about the money, but it was not. The money came afterward. This is all about the journey of Joseph. Joseph was the first one in the family to leave home. He was the one, with no example before him, to be taken to a foreign land. He was the one sitting in prison, having been accused with no defense.

His brothers, on the other hand, had their father and everything they needed; however, they had forgotten how they left the land of Laban's house, the story of their childhood, and their father's fear. How easy it is for us to forget the first moment of our connection? One of the things I discovered is that *techila* is a relational term. When Joseph gives his brothers the money and puts the cup in Benjamin's bag, he begins to prick their conscience, but they do not get it because they have built such a deep life of fear by their actions—killing, sleeping with a daughter-in-law, having babies by her, and threatening to kill her even though they were more unrighteous than she was.

How do you get people who are judging other people more harshly than they judge themselves to move from there to a different position? Joseph was an alchemist. He could change things. He knew how to take nothing and produce something. He knew how to be in an empty place and call forth abundance. He knew how to stand in the place of slavery and yet be the master of the house.

When his brothers returned the money and started using this language, Joseph told them that he received the money and that God put it back in their bags, but they still did not get it. He invited them to eat with him, but they still did not get it. Everything he had done was what they learned in the first place. They used the word *first,* but they did not want to go back to the beginning. They regarded the beginning as the point of coming into Egypt, but Joseph was pointing them to look at the beginning, unto Abraham the rock and Sarah the rock "from whom you were hewn." However, they were still standing on the immediacy of the environment. They thought this had to do with the current situation, but Joseph was a man who had access to primordial principles. So he let them eat and he gave Benjamin, his brother, five times the portion (five is the number of multiplication), yet they still did not get it. I want you to notice everything Joseph did was to help them remember and to bring them back to first things. He fed them and they did not get it. He gave them drink and they got drunk and they still did not get it. He asked, "How is your father about whom you spoke?" and they still did not get it. "Is this your youngest brother?" and they still did not get it. Joseph brought Simeon out from the prison house. Remember Simeon and Judah were the ones around whom the rest of the brothers rallied.

203

TECHILA

Judah in particular was instrumental in selling Joseph.

Joseph put his cup in Benjamin's sack. This cup is actually a divination cup. It is the cup used by chiefs and leaders to drink and to look into to see the future. Joseph sent his messenger to accuse them of the theft of the cup. They thought they were innocent, but when Joseph's messenger discovered the cup, they tore their clothes and cried out in despair. They were sure they were doomed! Now watch what happens here because this is the amazing alchemy of Joseph. Through all of these orchestrated events, he worked to bring his brothers back to *tehillah* (תְּהִלָּה) which means praise.

When the brothers returned, they were still screaming and crying. They pleaded with Joseph to release Benjamin and said their father would surely die if he lost his other son, too. Joseph actually got them to tell on themselves, although they still did not admit what they had done to him. Joseph could see that they were getting close to the first principles. In spite of their pleading, Joseph said he would imprison the thief and make him his servant. Yet who stepped up to offer himself in place of Benjamin? Judah! Judah is the same guy who was instrumental in selling Joseph and sat by the fire eating while ignoring Joseph's cries from the pit. Yet now he said he would rather be Joseph's slave than to let his father die and go to his grave. He returned to first principles.

Let us circle back to Abraham now. Abraham went back to what would be called Bethel to recover something. In his original journey, he had had to interact in ways that did not demonstrate first principles. In fact, he acted as if God was not his shield, an exceeding reward. So he went back to the place he began to draw from the future—not just from the altar he built in Bethel, but from a future point in which he is applying first principles.

Joseph did the same thing in our text. Judah stood up for Benjamin and said he would be willing to take his place! This is where I am going to play with words a bit. Remember Judah's name means praise. Judah had forgotten the meaning of his name. The name Judah itself conveys the idea of kingship, a strong one and a defender. These are first principles. His name carries the very nature of himself as one who stands in a place that praises God.

ADONIJAH O. OGBONNAYA PH.D.

His father said to him that he was first among his brethren. As a result, every time there is a war, Judah goes first, even when they are casting lots. I wondered why and what it was that Judah first had access to that he had lost. What is it that the children of Jacob had access to that which Joseph knew they had lost?

One of the first principles that they lost was that feeling of fraternity. There was a loss of the depth of relationship and that feeling of brotherhood. For some reason, when it came to Joseph, they had lost the capacity to love. Love had become transactional. It was not until that moment when Judah began to give his life for his brother that love became real again. What they had lost was the first thing that kept them together. They lost their love of family. This was not about the money. It was about the first principles that they had lost. This situation probably illustrates the first time in a long time that they had actually kept their word.

> The person with this particular capacity can go back to where things started and pick up what was left out or restore what others have lost.

Do you remember how they first conspired to kill Joseph in Genesis 37:18-33?

> They saw him from afar, and before he came near to them they conspired against him to kill him. They said to one another, "Here comes this dreamer. Come now, let us kill him and throw him into one of the pits. Then we will say that a fierce animal has devoured him, and we will see what will become of his dreams." But when Reuben heard it, he rescued him out of their hands, saying, "Let us not take his life." And Reuben said to them, "Shed no blood; throw him into this pit here in the wilderness, but do not lay a hand on him"—that he might rescue him out of their hand to restore him to his father. So when Joseph came to his brothers, they stripped him of his robe, the robe of many colors that he wore. Then

TECHILA

Midianite traders passed by. And they drew Joseph up and lifted him out of the pit, and sold him to the Ishmaelites for twenty shekels of silver. They took Joseph to Egypt.

When Reuben returned to the pit and saw that Joseph was not in the pit, he tore his clothes and returned to his brothers and said, "The boy is gone, and I, where shall I go?" Then they took Joseph's robe and slaughtered a goat and dipped the robe in the blood. And they sent the robe of many colors and brought it to their father and said, "This we have found; please identify whether it is your son's robe or not." And he identified it and said, "It is my son's robe. A fierce animal has devoured him. Joseph is without doubt torn to pieces."

> As a believer you have this capacity to take people back to the first point and open up for them the worlds to come.

The second thing they did was agree not to kill him and instead threw him into the pit to leave him there to die. The third thing they did was decide not to let him die, but to sell him instead, so they sold him to the Ishmaelites. The fourth thing they did was took his clothes, dipped them in blood, and gave them to their old father with the lie that Joseph had been killed by an animal. They are so removed from brotherly feeling, filial piety, and filial faithfulness that they even told their father that his son was dead. How many years did they keep that lie secret? All those years they kept lying to Jacob and Jacob felt like he was going to die. Now he was threatened with losing Benjamin, too, and Jacob was certain this would kill him.

At this point in the story, they still had not come to terms with the fact that they had lost something. Judah acted out of guilt, not out of first principles. Judah is more worried about the guilt he will carry the rest of his life if his father hears about losing Benjamin and dies. He is more worried about the consequences to himself. This is not even about love. The first principles are still not there. Joseph's job, therefore, was to keep moving them alchemically until they came to the point where they could actually handle a return to foundational principles. Sometimes we are too quick to try to return people to first principles. Most people we encounter who are not doing what they should are not ready.

Finally, Joseph tells everybody to leave and he introduces himself to his brothers. Watch the process—they do not embrace him because they are still afraid and they feel guilty. How are they going to cross the threshold back to the first foundation? They can only come by invitation because they had forgotten the first principle. They did not know who they were. All they knew now was how to save their own skin. Even Judah's plea about his brother was not about Benjamin, but it was a start, right? For the first time, Judah was putting his own skin on the line. They looked at Joseph, wondering what to do, and then Joseph revealed himself as their brother:

> **And Joseph said to his brothers, "I am Joseph! Is my father still alive?" But his brothers could not answer him, for they were dismayed at his presence.**
>
> **So Joseph said to his brothers, "Come near to me, please." And they came near. And he said, "I am your brother, Joseph, whom you sold into Egypt. And now do not be distressed or angry with yourselves because you sold me here, for God sent me before you to preserve life. (*Genesis 45:3-5*)**

Joseph was the only one who had never left the first principle. He was the only one who knew how to survive by accessing that pool that stands between nothing and something.

You can access so much with this word *techila*. As I said before, Hebrew word usage is not just philological or linguistic in terms of sentences and structures. It is also used for communicating emotion, divine purpose, and things that are outside of the realm of creation. It is a revelatory process. The person with this particular capacity can go back to where things started and pick up what was left out or restore what others have lost. By standing at the point where he built his first altar, Abraham reclaimed the first principles he had left when he lied

TECHILA

about Sarai being his sister. Abraham was able to access Jacob's repairing and renaming of the gateway. Jacob actually reopened the gates of himself, even though he did not know what he was doing. So Abraham was able to access the first principle. When you stand on this issue in particular, you are able to step back to where you started and access what was not and what will be.

Jesus said to the church in Ephesus:

> **But I have this against you, that you have abandoned the love you had at first. Remember therefore from where you have fallen; repent, and do the works you did at first. If not, I will come to you and remove your lampstand from its place, unless you repent. Yet this you have: you hate the works of the Nicolaitans, which I also hate. He who has an ear, let him hear what the Spirit says to the churches. To the one who conquers I will grant to eat of the tree of life, which is in the paradise of God.' (Revelation 2:4-7)**

He said that when you return to the things you did at first, you will have access to the fruit of the tree of paradise. I believe that people who have conscious access to divinity are able to bring other people back to the first principle to recover whatever it is that they have lost. This included issues such as relationships or friendships. You and I are standing in this place of remembrance and being drawn to the first principle. Let me be Aristotelian and say it this way: God is the first cause. He is the "uncaused cause." This means that when you meet God, you are standing in the place of all possibilities and, therefore, everyone who comes to you who has lost who they are, or who has lost their connection to the foundation, can be drawn to that place through your interaction. In that place, all things become possible for them also.

I think this is the principle Paul drew from when he spoke of first fruits in 1 Corinthians and several of his letters. You will often see the phrase, "You who are the first," or "You who are the first fruit." I know he could have been using the word *reshith* (רֵאשִׁית), but I think he is not just referring to the beginning of creation. He is referring to us being the first act of God that allows for access to the point of creation. He is talking about us as those who stand on the edge of nothingness and make an open door possible for everyone who steps into our presence. In the same way, the sons of Jacob could come into the presence of Joseph and in one moment have their whole life recalibrated and brought back to the place of the foundation. The place where they know their purpose as a family, where they become brothers again, rather than antagonists. They become a loving and caring family rather than jockeying for the top position.

I have learned some things about Joseph in this process and how he moved in the spirit to restore the foundation of Egypt, the house of Potiphar, and the house of

Where you are standing now, nothing is impossible.

everywhere he went. There was something unique about Joseph. He knew how to step to the first place, get to that place and stand there allowing himself to become the access point for those who could not do it themselves. As a believer you have this capacity to take people back to the first point and open up for them the worlds to come. You open up for them a dimension behind them that has no baggage. When Abraham came back to that place, he dropped every piece of baggage he had gathered. Joseph gave his brethren an opportunity to drop the baggage, remove all the clutter around it, and tell the story until it becomes an authentic and genuine story of their future again.

I think Paul would say we are the first because, through us, the world will come to know God. Jesus was not the first one to rise from the dead, but He was the first one to come out of the grave. What makes Jesus coming out of the grave so unique is that, in doing so, He stood between this world and that world, allowing you and me to go here and there. He raised you and me to do the same thing. Did you know that you could be the gate through which somebody can go back to first principles? Just by being in relationship with you, someone can have access to primordial realities and, not only that, but also have access to future things.

209

TECHILA

The reason God used Judah to activate this technology is because where there is *techila* there is *tehillah*—pun intended! This is a way to restore the joyful exuberance through and into which Judah was born. It is amazing that in the dance of Israel, Judah always leads. It is the idea that the one who stands in this time also reactivates or activates kingship. If you look at Jacob's blessing, he blesses two kings: Joseph and Judah. This blessing provides the capacity to take people back to the point where they can start anew, pick up what they left behind, and drop the things they were not supposed to pick up. In the presence of a king like Joseph, his brothers had to drop everything they had and then pick up what they had left. They were able to drop hatred, pick up the brotherhood they discarded and the honesty and love they threw away.

I call these places the "places of elemental manifestations." Do you realize that because of your position here, nothing is impossible? Nothing. Where you are standing now, nothing is impossible. You can access things that are a thousand years out of this generation. You can access the things that are in the mind of God which are not yet here because He has allowed you to stand in that place. That is what you did when you gave your life to the Lord! Where there is a *techila* there is a *tehillah*! Everyone who is brought to the first place revives joy, grace, mercy, and power. Everyone who is brought to this place begins the process of repairing the world.

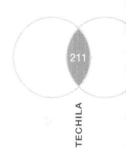

רָצוֹן

Ratson

We are delving deeply into what we are now calling times and seasons, but really we are discussing the value of time as a sacrament in and of itself.

RATSON:
FREE WILL AND THE CONNECTION BETWEEN TIME AND SPACE

We already know the basics when we talk about the heavens and the earth. You know all the theory that space is infinite. It is not, but it has an infinite possibility. There is a boundary to space and that boundary is God. God is the one who is not finite. God is the one who encapsulates, surrounds, and saturates the universe. All things in the universe are in God. I recently read a book in which the author said hell is not in God because no horror can be inside of God. My point is if hell is not in God, then hell is independent of God. The reason it is hell is because you are in God and you cannot access God. This means space and time includes all the good, the bad, and the ugly. Everything is there. God does not look at something that is bad and say, "Ooh, get away from me. I can't get too close to you!" because it is in God.

He does not react the same way you react, which is why He is a redemptive God. In redeeming what is within God, God is redeeming part of Himself. So, if you do not want to be redeemed, it is not God's fault; it is because you choose not to be redeemed. The only thing that can become irredeemable is a being with a free will. Everything else is redeemable. Nothing else in the world is irredeemable. Of all the races and beings of the universe, only man and angels (that is, angels before the fall) have the capacity to be lost and irredeemable. When somebody tells me that everyone is going to be saved, I always ask them a few very simple questions. Is God a free being? The answer is yes. Can God make any being in His image that is not free? The answer is no. Otherwise, His creation would not be in the image of God. If the creation is in the image of God and it is created free, it means this being has the capacity to withstand God, say no to Him, and to refuse to do what God wants to be done. This free being can actually choose not to be connected to God. God will have to honor that choice because He is the one who made that being in His image. Otherwise, God is a liar.

The free will of a human being is what makes the human being divine. It is what gives him sovereignty because God is sovereign by His will. Yes, you are dependent. Yes, you cannot do anything on your own without Him. And, yes, you can actually exert your will without Him. He gave you the will, but that is the one place that God allows you to be sovereign. Otherwise, you are not like Him. In order to be like God you need a sovereign will and to make decisions out of your own free will without compulsion by God or by Satan. This is why Satan is Satan because he forces you to do things. God does not. Your will is the foundation of your sovereignty. Thus your will is wider, stronger, and more expansive than where you are. *Your* will touches the will of God, and *your* will is as expansive as space. Your will is as expansive as the universe because it can impinge upon the will of God.

> Your will is as expansive as the universe because it can impinge upon the will of God.

God will want to do certain things in the world, man will stand in the way and God will say, "I could have done this, but you did not let me." That is a hard theology for some people, yet it is the basis of the argument about whether or not God is a good God. People do not actually think about evil. They are, in fact, actually thinking about their own wellbeing. So, if I am in pain, God must be a bad God. It is childish thinking. Even the higher scientists do that. "If God is such a good God, why did my grandmother die?" We are being emotional when we say this (even if you happen to be a scientist). We are not looking at the facts. We are thinking about what affects us and then decide that the whole universe is bad based on our experience. That is how children think! We are determining whether God exists based on our bad experiences. Those conclusions all boil down to the emotional residue of childhood and the emotional pain of empathy with other human beings. It is not based on fact.

So then, what is the human will? Why is it so important to God? It is because it is the handle for space and time. Your capacity to make a choice really is a key to how the universe is structured. The problem is you are not making choices deliberately. What humans have called free will merely refers to mechanical structures through which we make decisions without actually thinking. It is not a choice. People are hit by things and react. It is not that they do not have free will. They simply do not operate with it. Therefore, when I say your will is actually the handle for space and time, they say, "Well, it can't be because things just happen to me." Or they begin to think they can control the world, which leads people into the same situations over and over again. What they run into is not the transformation of the world. What they run into is themselves over and over again.

If you learn how to become observant, then you should become self-observant because that is how you learn to actually operate dynamically and know how to make choices based on intention. Then you begin to learn how to be free. When your will begins to operate from the place of your personal observation, then you will know freedom. When you know freedom, the universe will bend towards you. If we act in such a way that our free will is subsumed under our mechanical activity, then the universe becomes a boulder that runs over us. So things just happen to us. God did not create you for things to "just happen to you." He gave you a will. In spite of all the arguments that human beings cannot do anything to change the world when they say, "What will be, will be." That is not the case!

God gave humanity a will because He does not want things to "just happen to us." He does not even want God to just happen to us. He does not want salvation to just happen to us. Even when we think salvation just happened, God somehow has found an aperture, an opening into our will. At that moment when the will opens, something happens to the person. However, because we do not think based on free will, when we become a believer, we think we did not do anything. We think thoughts like, "I didn't really want to be saved." We think thoughts like this because we are not very observant. If you are observant, you will notice you actually did want to be saved. It may have been in a single moment, but that aperture of the will affects the whole universe and brings salvation towards you.

Remember, your will is one thing that makes you like God. If that is so, what happens when you actually use your will intentionally towards something that is connected to the rectification of the universe? I am not saying you have to know what you are doing. It just means you have to will it. It is hard to explain, but if God created you in His image, then there is more to you than meets the eye. There is also more to you than you know about yourself. There are things you are doing that you are not aware of because you have never been trained to observe your will. When you become a believer and give up your life to the Lord Jesus Christ, the task of your whole life is training your will. You may not realize it, but everything you do is directed towards training your will. Training the will is much more important than you going to heaven. Training the will is what releases your divinity. Training the will is not just self-control—it is having a *good* will. I think that is where Immanuel Kant, the famous German philosopher, hit it right when he said, "The only thing that is good without qualification is a good will."

Good will is a development of the will. What is going to save the world? What is going to rectify the universe? It is God's good will and man's good will. This understanding affects the way free will is translated in scripture. The King James Bible translates Luke 2:14 as:

Glory to God in the highest, and on earth peace, good will toward men.

Yet other translations say, "peace to men of good will" or "peace among those with whom He is pleased." Those who like to point out contradiction in scripture always say, "You see. It says, 'good will to men,' in one place and 'to men of good will' in another!" They do this because they do not want to read the text of scripture as dealing with two sides at all times. The gospels are written according to the Quadratic Principle; that is, one deals with the south, one with the west, one with the north, and one with the east. They are actually written in a cherubic nature. They are written according to Yod Hey Vav Heh. The people who selected the gospels did not just select them because they were the only gospels. They selected them to communicate something to you. Actually some of writings they selected, apart from the book of

John, do not exhibit the best writing. They selected them for a purpose. Even the ancient ones understood that there are four gospels for a purpose. Our church fathers called one the lion, one the ox, one the eagle, and one the man. Sound familiar? It has always been taught in the church. A Jew would look at the four gospels and say, "Oh yes, four gospels makes sense. It aligns to Yod Hey Vav

So then, what is the human will? Why is it so important to God? It is because it is the handle for space and time.

Heh." Likewise, there are four angels around the throne and four realms in every age. Four is associated with every larger principle. The whole thing is structured that way. Therefore, when I read scripture and it says, "good will to men" and then it says, "to men of good will," it is not a contradiction because both come from God. We must have these two wills come together to rectify the world. If man does not bring good will, God will have to destroy the world.

The reason I do not believe in the destruction of the world is that you are here. There are people of good will. The only way God can destroy the world is if he cannot find good will to align with His good will. God did not destroy the world of Noah. The world of Noah is still here. You are living in it. He just renovated it, cleaned out all the critters, and helped humanity so that there can be good will on the face of the earth. He did not destroy the world. He says, "…never again shall there be a flood to destroy the earth," (Genesis 9:11). He is talking about the same world that came through the water. Did God say there was another earth that He had to recreate? He never said that. On the contrary, He found a man with a good will in order to rectify what had been.

The world is only destroyable when there are no men and women of goodwill. That is the reason why I do not believe God would just destroy the world today. You do know that even though Babylon was destroyed, the Babylonians were not completely destroyed because the Iraqis are still here. The Jews are still here because they became part of Babylon. The Babylonians destroyed Jerusalem, but destroying the city is not destroying everything. God destroyed the Tower of Babel,

RATSON

but He did not destroy the people. Even in Sodom and Gomorrah, He saved the seed and the people of Sodom in the daughters of Lot. He made the Moabites and the Amorites survive because there was one man with a good will.

We underestimate who we are and how God looks at us. When some modern prophets talk, I always ask them, "Are you not a child of God? Why God must destroy everything. Why would God look upon the earth and destroy you and the whole world when you already have a good will and you are actually in relationship with God?" Not even a father, a mortal father, would do that. Does that mean that God does not discipline? Far from it! He disciplines those He loves. So I am not into the gospel that says that God does not discipline people. I get my own chastening. He will be the whip. The Bible says,

> **For whom the Lord loveth he chasteneth, and scourgeth every son whom he receiveth. If ye endure chastening, God dealeth with you as with sons; for what son is he whom the father chasteneth not? But if ye be without chastisement, whereof all are partakers, then are ye bastards, and not sons.**
> **(Hebrews 12:6-8 [KJV])**

The Bible actually says that if God does not chastise you, then you are a bastard. Many modern translations say "illegitimate children" instead. I suppose it sounds better, but it is the same thing. The reason God disciplines you is because you are His.

When you become a believer and give up your life to the Lord Jesus Christ, the task of your whole life is training your will.

This thing about the will is what I have been working on. I have been asking the Lord. "What is it that actually connects time and space?" One day He just said to me, "Your will." I said, "Really? That's just too simple." Then He said, "It is not as simple as you think." He then began to show me how my will can affect His will and how my will and the structure of my will can actually affect how things operate in space. There is more to us than merely what we think every day.

ADONIJAH O. OGBONNAYA PH.D.

The chaos in space, right now, has to do with the chaos in man. God is working from chaos to order, while some 'prophets' are working from order to chaos. What is really amazing is that they believe they are doing the work of God! They see the order created by humanity as being completely evil instead of understanding that it is human beings trying to be like God and doing what God created them to do—calling order out of chaos. It is not calling chaos out of order. That is what people in the occult do.

The problem for most of us is that our ideology is stronger than scripture and better than Jesus. Actually our ideology supersedes whatever Jesus commanded us to do. If that is the case, we can insist on our unforgiveness because Jesus did not know what He was talking about. We can insist upon treating strangers badly because Jesus did not know what He was talking about. Our ideology supersedes. Again, that is where our bad will shows its effect. When you have a bad will, then you notice that everybody in the world begins to tune to that frequency and begins to act the same way. Because Christians do not operate by clear observation and intention, they operate by being affected mechanically and by what is going on around them no matter how much God says, "Treat the stranger right!" The Christians close their ears and do not want to listen. Their ideology and their feelings are greater than the command of God.

We are talking about the frequencies of time and space. The people who have the actual frequency are not pushing the frequency. They are pushing the frequency of somebody else. Who is the one with the good will? You. Who is the one with the love? You. Who is the one with the sound of the blood? You. So why is it that someone coming out of nowhere, who has never been to church in his life, becomes president? When that person makes a statement about anything, it influences your frequency if have been acting mechanically all your life. You have never really acted intentionally. It is easy to push other frequencies on people. This is not political. This is how the people, who carry the frequencies of God, have allowed one statement to go around the world. Christians come to church and want to rebel, yet they cannot stand up to something that is blatantly against the gospel that they preach. Why? It is because somebody has learned

RATSON

how to tune the atmosphere. If you do not think frequencies affect the atmosphere, ask yourself why every nation that was Christian has been going towards hating strangers. Where are the people with the frequencies of God? We really do not know who we are. Someone should have asked, "Chaos? Didn't Jesus say in Luke 9:56, 'For the Son of man is not come to destroy men's lives, but to save them'?" James and John were two of the apostles who wanted to create chaos. Jesus even called them sons of thunder or destruction. He said, "No! No! No! You have got it all wrong." Go and learn about the good will of your master! Stop learning from politicians! I have been watching the Royal House of England. I have been so impressed with how they carry themselves. Every throne is established by righteousness and mercy, and they know it. Each time you and I make a decision about something and our wills are truly involved, we put out a frequency into the universe.

I read most of the things written by our church fathers. I highly recommend that you read Clement of Alexandria and Lactantius. All of the church fathers, from the beginning through medieval times and even the late church are very clear. If they can hone their will and be intentional, they can imbue the atmosphere with their intentions, whether they intend evil or good. People will just fall head over heels to follow, thinking it is the right thing to do. Most of us operate mechanically. Think of it this way. Why will a parent who is raising children and teaching them to live a righteous life then sit them in front of television to watch everything that goes against what they are teaching their children? Have you ever wondered why parents do that? These people are good parents! After training your children and talking to them about all the wonderful things you want them to accomplish, you put them in front of people who make fun of God and talk to them about things you do not believe in. The issue is when you debilitate and weaken the will of a people, you become the determiner of their destiny. So you keep striking, striking, striking, but you do not strike with force. You strike with softness. You give suggestions.

Do you know that Christians on Facebook are doing more damage to Christianity than atheists and unbelievers? Why? What is the problem? They are affecting the will of people. You will not see unbelievers attacking Christians when they write on Facebook. They are letting us attack each other, because they understand they do not have to do the job anymore. You have seen how Christians talk to each other. Let there be a controversial political statement and they all forget they are brothers and sisters in Christ and one blood bought them all. It affects the frequency. Then when Christians want to witness, it is ineffective.

> Each time you and I make a decision about something and our wills are truly involved, we put out a frequency into the universe.

The greatest attack that anybody in the spiritual world can bring against you is an attack on your will. It is not an attack on your body. If your will is focused and strong, there is nothing anyone can do to you. An unbeliever whose will is focused is stronger than a Christian who is busy wondering where the devil is coming from. The will is the crown of humanity. The will is what connects you to divine space. It is the distiller from the upper realm. The will, then, is a lock that needs to be opened. The will is *not* the soul. The will *informs* the soul, not the other way round. If the will is in the soul, how does it get the soul saved? If you believe the will is the soul, you have conflated two things that do not belong together. As a result, you do not know how to use your will because now you think your soul is in charge of your will. If that is the case, you have never really used your will. What you have used is your emotions. Oftentimes the emotion you are using is not in your soul, but rather, in your body. You have two types of emotion: that which operates at the ethereal level which is your soul, and that which operates in your body. You may think you are using your real emotion when, in actuality, you are using residual pain and pleasure that is in your physical body. The will is what will stop the emotion of both the physical body and the soul. You can actually exert your will to cause that emotion to go away.

So the will is king in your life and when your will is weak, you are a slave. Everyone who practices the dark arts or practices any spirituality knows that when you can influence people's will, you can change

RATSON

everything about their lives. How did you get saved? You willed to be saved. Forget about stray thoughts that tell you that you did not want to be saved. You were willing to be saved. You just did not want the kind of salvation that was being offered to you. Your will is what attracted the person who ministered to you. Although it may not be immediately obvious, your will is what Jesus was referring to whenever He said, "Whosoever will." There are, however, people whose goal is to direct the evil of nations and the masses. They operate on the basis that a few deaths can provide blood to fuel their occult rituals. However, they quickly lose control during such rituals because a covenant with any devil is never kept as it is written.

> The will is the crown of humanity. The will is what connects you to divine space. It is the distiller from the upper realm. The will, then, is a lock that needs to be opened.

The Hebrew word for the (good) will is *ratson* (רָצֹן) or Resh Tsade Nun. The word for that powerful and intentional will to get something done is ratsah (רָצָה) Resh Tsade Heh.

This is what you are activating when you make your declarations. Jesus taught the Lord's Prayer and declared, "Thy will be done on earth as it is in heaven." You cannot declare or will something on Earth if there is no will that conjoins with that which is from above. People say that God's will cannot be thwarted. No, that is not true. People do it all the time. God never intended to remove Israel out of the Promised Land. The Israelites, most likely by willful choice, made the decision for God. When we look at the entire narrative structure around the tribes of Israel, we see that God warns them about doing certain things, yet they go and do them anyway. What was that about? Forgive me for saying it, but I think they forced God's hand.

Believe me, the will is an incredible thing that God has given you. If human beings really have a good will, I do not see a meteor hitting the earth. If human beings continue acting in chaos, it is not God. The Bible says that the righteous are the foundation of the world (Proverbs 10:25).If you are the righteous person at the foundation of the world, doesn't that mean that God has given you greater control than you are actually willing to exercise? It is always easy to control people when they are in chaos and then to give them what they do not want. They are desperate to receive from you. God is not a creator of chaos. Death is not chaos. It is an orderly process of the disintegration of an entity to bring it forth into another realm. Chaos is just chaos. It does not produce anything. Chaos needs a will placed upon it for it to become order. That is what creation is. Creation is the will of God checking chaos and bringing it into order. God created man to have His will to sustain the order.

We know from science that time and space are interconnected. They are not separate things. If time and space are interconnected, it means that their source or their place of manifestation is somewhere. I suggest to you that the place where time and space are actually interconnected is in the heart of man. One Jewish philosopher wrote that there is "clock time," "event time," and "soul time" (similar to the views of Thomas Aquinas). He argues that time as we know it is only made known through the apertural process of the soul. In other words, the soul opens up for us to experience temporality. It sounds crazy, but the Bible says that eternity is in your heart (Ecclesiastes 3:11) and time cannot exist unless eternity releases a bit of itself. The only vehicle through which eternity releases a bit of itself is the human soul. It comes through the heart which means that time itself is a telescopic lens into eternity.

So what is the human soul really? We know that the will rules the soul which means that the soul cannot operate effectively unless the will rules it. When the will is weak, then the soul acts without restraint. You have experienced this in ordinary life. When your will is not strong, then you give in to things you do not want to do. However, if your will is trained, it is different. Your soul immediately comes under control. It obeys your will because your will is sovereign. It is amazing what you can actually do when your will is trained and it becomes king. You can say to the soul, "Shut up!" and the soul shuts up. It can say to your emotion, "Enough!" and your emotion is cut off. The Holy Spirit wants to sit in your emotions, but many of the emotions you have are not soul level emotions. They are the work of the flesh, which means they are based on your body in its unrefined, unredeemed, fallen state.

Did you know that all of the fruits of the spirit have no limitation? The Apostle Paul said, "Against such things there is no law," which means there are no boundaries for them. The problem with all the works of the flesh is that they are limited. In dealing with someone who has the fruit of the spirit, we say the person is free. In dealing with someone who has the works of the flesh, we say the person is under bondage. So why is one free and the other under bondage? Because in the one with the fruits of the Spirit, the will is operating according to infinity while the other one who operates according to the flesh is subject to temporality. There is no end to joy. There is no end to patience. There is no end to longsuffering. It does not mean you suffer long now. Does it mean I am going to be suffering throughout eternity? Maybe, because God suffers throughout based on the creation. He has been suffering you from the moment He created a free being. He has had to operate in the depth of His being from patience. He knew what He was doing when He created those who saw His glory and still rejected Him.

The idea that if you actually see Jesus, you will not reject Him is not true. Keep dreaming! There are people who actually see Jesus face-to-face and say they do not want Him. Emanuel Swedenborg was a Swedish Christian theologian, scientist, philosopher, and mystic from the 1700s. He tells a story of a vision he had about going to heaven. He saw these beautiful angels and a man who had been a terrible sinner on earth coming towards them. They had opened up a way for him to come in, but the closer he got, the angrier he became. All of a suddenly, he saw the glory. He saw everything, but he still had to make a choice whether to determine his own way or to follow God's way. Anyone who tells you that everybody is going to be saved, ask them what happens then to the human free will?

How your will affects eternity, space and time puts you in a position where you realize you can be here and control what is happening in another dimension. However, you just do not do that by pretending in your head. One of the best ways to have that kind of impact without actually going to another galaxy is by being intentional with your will. Going is better. If you go and you do not have a trained good will, you will come back empty-handed and nothing will be done. At the same time, someone who has an incredible will can sit in their house on earth and speak to something billions of light years away and it will do what they want. Again, if you do not have a trained good will, you will travel there and return without having any impact. That is why people are going to heaven, coming back, and not fixing anything. People are ascending over their nation and nothing is changing. Their wills are not strong enough or properly trained. The will is wishy-washy. It lacks focus.

All over the world there are ascension groups, yet in the nations where they are ascending, there is chaos. People are praying and creating chaos in the atmosphere, their will is creating it. People say to me, "Why don't you just change something?" I say I have done it. We have established governments and atmospheres over nations but the church was too busy casting out demons to protect what we had won. For example, my home country of Nigeria went from being the 19th largest economy in the world to being the fifty-something because believers were busy having prayer meetings instead of actually controlling the atmosphere. They had weak wills. When a politician suggested to them that their Christian brother was evil, they all bought into it. That is the impact of an untrained will.

> I suggest to you that the place where time and space are actually interconnected is in the heart of man.

It is the same thing in America. We throw away the Christian to elect a man who has never been to church because we think that, since he is a billionaire, he is going to make a better president. Then we abrogate our Christian perspective. Somebody made a suggestion spiritually and we bit on it. It is a spiritual process. We did not do it because we wanted to. We did it because somebody made the suggestion and we bit on it so hard that we could not pull ourselves back. As a result, the Christian brother or sister is being kicked out. In America, Christians are crying because their fellow parishioners, who have been in the nation legally for thirty-something years, are being kicked out and not given opportunities. (I am an American citizen and I believe you should come into the country legally. I am very clear about that. However I will protect a believer who is running from their home with my own life).

What happens when your own persecution comes? Where will you go? We forget the British nation hung Christians many years ago. Anyone who thinks that they are safe because they are part of a nation as a believer is lying to themself. In London, some of our brethren who tried to translate scriptures were hung. So what makes you think that you are safe when you do not protect other Christians? Every time something happens in our nations, we need to ask ourselves, "Why was my will so easily moved?" Say, for instance, that someone approaches you with the intention of creating chaos in your family. It is very easy. They just make a negative suggestion to you about your spouse and walk away. Then you go home and fight with your spouse or you start suspecting them. You start thinking, "I know my spouse loves me, but there are certain things they do that bother me." I talk to many people who have problems in their marriage that result from a suggestion from another person.

Believers do not realize how people are working against them. These enemies know what to do. They know your moral make-up and they use it as a meme to control you. They do not have to do much. Self-righteousness is the hook that they use to make you act for them because your will is not free. If it was actually free, you would see that manipulation coming from miles away. You are the one that God has called to stand in that gate. Nobody else. So if it is easy for me to control you, you are going to have a problem. I am telling you to develop your will because it will let you be in charge and look at things more deeply so that you do not blindly accept everything you are being told! It is not good for a king to take words at face value.

Now that we know what the strategies are to derail our will, how do we train our free will so that we are the ones in charge? How do you train your will now to ensure people do not come into your family and make suggestions to

> It is not good for a king to take words at face value.

cause you to be at odds with each other? You know it happens, right? Remember, everything we struggle with in this world is directed toward our will. Weakening our will, as believers, is what gives the enemy power. We are the only ones with the capacity to have a good will and when our good will is weakened, things happen that we do not intend. One of the reasons why gossip is not good is because it is one of the patterns of witchcraft. Things are said so everybody's free will bends against you. They know the power of the will of a human being, even an unsaved human being, when it is directed against someone.

Christianity is a system of mysteries for the transformation of the lives of people and the world in which we live. In every system there is a process of initiation. You were initiated by baptism. What do you think they were doing to you when they baptized you? Just pouring water on your head? No! They were actually initiating you into the mystery of Christ, making you qualified to know the mysteries. Baptism is burying your old soul and bringing you up with a new soul to give you this incredible access to the mysteries of Christ. Although that word *initiation* may trigger you, we are the true initiates of the mysteries of God and Christ. Many try to imitate us. Every time you participate in that system, the goal of anyone training you is to strengthen and solidify your will. The goal is not to make you strong willed so that you become rebellious—it is to help you become powerful enough to move universes. Baptism is putting you back into the chaos before creation and bringing you through the waters of creation to this realm. What you thought was just religion was actually an act of *initiating* you into the mystery of your Lord. It was not just religious activity. When you are baptized, you become a different being. You are no longer part of your former world.

There are people who say baptism is useless because they have learnt more than Jesus. They know better than the apostles because they have had, so they say, a mystical experience that supersedes the person of Jesus Christ. As you know, I am a Jesus freak. I am a Christological fanatic. I believe that the fundamental valuation of man is in the person of Christ and that God's value of humanity is in Christ. We are valued based upon God demonstrating how much He values us by giving His Son to die for us. Ask God, "How much do You value

227

RATSON

me?" and He says, "Here's Jesus." This is serious! What is the price for my life? God puts His hand up and proclaims, "I am the price for your life. What other price do you want? I am the price for your life." He says there is no greater price. Furthermore, that price is for your life and inside of it is a price for your divinity, which is the price for your capacity to rule the world. That price is an amazing price which is why your salvation began with your will. It does not begin with anything emotional. Your salvation did have emotion tied to it, but in reality, you willed it. The person who led you to Christ said, "Say this prayer with me." They ask, "Do you believe that Jesus Christ is the Son of God?" Through that question, they implicate your will in your own salvation. They make you put your will into it. At that point, you are a baby so you do not realize it, yet your will is already entangled with God. Once that happens, the goal of your life is to start disentangling your free will from other entanglements and to ensure that the beams of light and the refractions of your will are clear and straight and connected to the world in the way God intended.

What is the frequency of the will if you were to put a number on it? Let us discuss the Periodic Table for a moment. Within the first 83 elements on the Periodic Table, two elements, Technetium or Tc (43) and Promethium or Pm (61), are not sustainable and can only be created in labs. These two elements can dramatically change a lot in the things they contact, yet they both come from the human will and not from nature. Quite a number of elements higher on the Periodic Table also come from the human will. They do not last long because they are chemically unstable, but they can change things. By creating a fusion with them, you can actually change, kill, destroy, and sometimes heal. When you combine Tc and Pm with natural elements, you can even create something new, but their function and effectiveness is based entirely on the function of the human will.

So then, if your medicine is poison, it is because a human will infused it with that. How powerful are you? How glorious are you? When I started teaching people how to make decrees and declarations, I wanted three things to happen. I wanted you to inscribe your will, structure your will, and lift up your will so that your will operates at a level where everything else in your life is subject to your capacity to "will it,"

Ratson: Man—The Ultimate Trading Floor

The word for the will in Hebrew is *ratson* (רָצוֹן) which is Resh (200) Tsade (90) Nun (700). The numerical value of *ratson* is 990. If you add a Vav, which has a numerical value of six, it becomes 996. The gematria of ratson is as follows:

9+9 = 18 (without the Vav)
18+6 = 24 (with the Vav)

So then the numerical value of the will is 18, which also equals 6+6+6. What if I told you that 666 was not the number of the beast? What if I told you that 666 is a good trading floor that God set up in heaven and that Satan used it for trading? It was not, in fact, Satan's own trading floor. What if I told you that 666 is actually a key to some of the trading you are doing in the world and, because you are so scared of the number, you do not want to use it?

> The human DNA is one of the greatest bargaining chips in the universe. The truth is you cannot buy or sell without it.

666 is an important mystery. Do you realize that one of the reasons Christians do not work effectively in the world is because they do not really know that the codes used by the world were stolen from them? Why does the beast need the number 666 to be on a human being? Why not just use it in the air? It is because a human being is God's highest trading floor. Nothing else can be that. The only place that 666 works is the body of a human being. Think about it. 666 is the number of a man. There is nothing God does in creation for which He does not need a man. You are God's ultimate trading floor. Why would the beast *not* want to use you as a trading floor? Where else is he going to go?

The human DNA is one of the greatest bargaining chips in the universe. The truth is you cannot buy or sell without it. However, if you sell your DNA as a bargaining chip, then you have a problem. You are indeed the trading floor because when you put the mark on your head and your hand, it means that you have sold both your will and your action.

The number 666 occurs several times in scripture. For instance, the son of the King of Tyre gives Solomon 666 talents to have advantage in the temple and to insert his bloodline into the lineage of Israel:

Now the weight of gold that came to Solomon in one year was *666 talents of gold*... (*1Kings 10:14*) [Emphasis added]

Jezebel's blood and the blood of Tyre are still in the blood of the Jews today. They bought into the Messiah's seed by setting the trade into the temple at 666, the number of a man. And it was the Messiah's ancestor who did it!

Again, your will is the highest place where God trades. When your will is in alignment with Divinity, God can trade Himself with you.

You would not have the computer or the internet today without 666. Try figuring something out without *www*. The "www" in an internet address is actually Vav+Vav+Vav (vvv) which is 666. The Church criticized the use of *www* when it came out because they knew what it was. It is the frequency of man. That is precisely why you can get hooked in it. You try to unleash yourself from it and you cannot. Come on! You never used to have the internet! Then why is it that, now that you have it, you cannot do anything without it? They have keyed into the frequency of trading with your mind and trading with your soul. You just need to know that they are trading with *your* soul. Take it back and use it for yourself.

Numbers and what they mean are very important. For instance, 0-1 (zero one) signifies primordial possibility while 1-0 (one zero) signifies primordial potency. I want to show you something interesting with the gematria of triple numbers like 222, 333, and so forth.

$111 = 1+1+1 = $ **3**
$222 = 2+2+2 = $ **6**

333 = 3+3+3 = **9**
444 = 4+4+4 = **3**
555 = 5+5+5 = **6**
666 = 6+6+6 = **9**
777 = 7+7+7 = **3**
888 = 8+8+8 = **6**
999 = 9+9+9 = **9**

Isn't that amazing? I am no mathematician (although I am the son of one), but the fact that all these numbers are often emphasized in scripture lets us know that God wants us to know they are significant! I tell people that there are at least seven different ways of seeing scripture. Some scholars would even argue that there are up to 70 different ways to see scripture, but in my opinion, they are overstating its complexity. No man could ever understand all of those layers of meaning.

Again, the numerical value of *ratson* or the will is 990, which is 9. If you divide 990 by 2, you get 495, which is also 9. Are you getting the picture? The number 9 was considered the perfect number by the ancient world. That is why most nations have 9 gods. Nine is the highest form of trading across creation and keying into the potential of creation. For trading in heaven in the throne room itself, you need the number 12, which is what God put on the ephod of Aaron to allow him to trade at that level. If you look at Ezekiel 28, Ithobaal, the king of Tyre, traded on 9 because he had the nine stones (v. 13).

Going back to 666, did you know that all the people who defeated Israel and were able to insert their seed into Israel, all traded on 666? We are talking about Jezebel and Solomon's temple. Then there was Adonikam who had 666 children (Ezra 2:13) and was a noble of Israel. 666 is associated with Nebuchadnezzar as well as the prince who will conquer Israel in the book of Daniel.

Solomon knew the power of 666. How did Hiram of Tyre learn about 666? David was Hiram's best friend. Just look at the letter Hiram wrote to Solomon when Solomon comes to power. He offered one of his most skilled craftsmen to Solomon for building the temple because he realized that Solomon was the bearer of something greater: the

231

RATSON

Messiah. If you were Hiram or Ithobaal, what would you do? Would you trade into that? I would trade into that, especially if I knew from divination that my priesthood was going to be destroyed in the future. I would preserve my seed by sowing into a lineage.

Let us go back and talk about the world's market system. Because of the way believers have looked at how world economies operate, and because they have thought it was completely evil, they have not even considered that this principle. What believers do not understand is that this system is not evil or good. How are you going to be effective if you go into this system thinking that these very foundational principles are evil in and of themselves? The devil has had you! As a result, your mindset will always work from the position of doubt and fear, which means you cannot really succeed in that system the way you desire. If you want to talk about prophecy and insight, these guys listened to their intuition. You cannot really have the Holy Spirit working if it has had not quickened and awakened your intuition. You may say it is not intuition, but if your intuition is not functioning, the Holy Spirit cannot really use you effectively.

Do not forget the number 990 — it will help you one day. It is the number of the will. Again, your will is the highest place where God trades. When your will is in alignment with Divinity, God can trade Himself with you. You become "god" trading with God, not just someone sitting on the ground. You say, "Well, what can I trade?" Actually, you are trading all the time with the blood of Jesus Christ. You may not think of this as trading. Remember, if something is given to you, it belongs to you. If Christ is given to you, His blood belongs to you and you can use it, therefore, as a trading commodity. The blood of Christ is literally the instrument of trade that you use. You use it everywhere as an instrument of exchange. If you sin now and you know punishment is coming, what are you going to use as a commodity? Your confession is not enough. The only trade you have is the blood of Jesus. Do you remember the line from the song?

**"For my cleansing this my plea,
Nothing but the blood of Jesus!"**

The coin (or instrument) of trade that God used to purchase you was the blood of Jesus. When you give your will to God, you are trading at the same level as God. It is amazing what God does; He makes everything so simple. Yet, because we think we know better than He does, we fight and come up with all kinds of arguments as to why that is not the case.

If my will becomes the will of God, does not it mean that I am actually acting as God in my circumstance? If you align your will with the will of God and they become one, are you still operating as an ordinary human being? A man said it on national TV in Nigeria and they almost shot him. He said, "When I become one with my Father, I command and I get interaction with God, so much so that He is my true Father. In that situation, I do not just pray for the will of God to be done, I pray for *my* will to be done." Everybody got offended. He said, "I can do this because my will is *good* will. My will is my Father's will. I am so tied with my Father's will that my will ought to be done on Earth." That, my friend, was me! People get offended and say, "You are not thinking when you say that" or "Oh, you are being very arrogant." But God said,

Remember, you cannot do the will of God on Earth if there is no goodwill on the face of the Earth. It is not possible.

If you abide in me, and my words abide in you, ask whatever you wish, and it will be done for you.
(*John 15:7*)

If that is true, then whose will is being done? Believers always talk about how they are looking for the will of God, and I always remind them: find your own will. Align your will to the Father when you find it and then your will shall be done too, because your will shall be goodwill. You should not do that when you know your own will is only mean and wicked. Then you ask for somebody else's will, because your will is not worth the penny for which it is exchanged. But if your will is aligned with your Father's will, then your will also can be done. How are you a son if your will cannot be done? I can hear some of you thinking about

233

RATSON

what Jesus said:

Father, if you are willing, remove this cup from me.
Nevertheless, not my will, but yours, be done.
(Luke 22:42)

Jesus said this in the context of surrendering His will and aligning it with the Father. When you talk about the will of God that way, you are talking about how Jesus gave His will over so that He could die on the cross. However, once you are a child of God and your will is aligned with your Father's, saying "Not my will but your will" is actually an aberration. You do not say this in the context of suffering like Christ did. There is no pain involved. In the Lord 's Prayer, He did not say, "Thy will be done." He said "Thy will be done on earth as it is in heaven." Remember, you cannot do the will of God on Earth if there is no goodwill on the face of the Earth. It is not possible.

Who is it that does the will of God and whose will is aligned with the Father's? You are the one! I say it again: You are the one! If you do not want to have a good will, an aligned will, then go get a life! Good luck to you. For you who have aligned your will and say you know God, then you must come to the point that your will is so aligned with the Father that when you speak, it is done because your will gets done in your context. That is why you can be a dangerous person. Otherwise, you are nothing but just another fallen human being, walking around the face of the earth, pleading and begging God to help you. You and I do not work this way. You and I work with a different kind of will. We have the will of our Father. If you say you do not know the will of God, you lie because you do! Don't you? What is the will of God apart from being one with you? And when that happens, doesn't your will become the will of your Father? If you are functioning in the context of fear, then you say, "I don't know what the will of God is." The problem is, every time you are told what the will of God is, you

> The servanthood of a son is stronger than anything else in this world. When a son serves, he changes the world.

go again and pray to see if it is the will of God. It gives you an excuse not to do what God has asked you to do. Referring to ourselves as bearers of the will of God means we believe ourselves to be those who influence the universe.

We know from our studies so far that certain sound frequencies are good. 440, for instance, is good because it is a healing frequency. However, shift it just a little to 441, for example, and it can hurt someone. You do not really need to shift it that much. 443 can really mess things up. Likewise, we know that 333 is good because it is 9. Remember the triple numbers in the previous chart.

We know that these frequencies have to do with different aspects of creation because they are in Scripture. The first 3 in 333 carries a witness in heaven and bears witness on earth. The frequency 333 carries the record of heaven, which is revealed on Earth. The first place that this record is revealed is in the body of the human being. When man was created, the Spirit of God would come upon him, but did not live in him. Therefore, one 3 by itself is missing the complete testimony. Adam did not have the complete testimony of God. God did. God brought the record and had to affirm it on Adam every time He was with him. Then He would lift it up when He parted from Adam. When Adam fell, the testimony was incomplete on earth. The second 3 is the frequency of the record in heaven and carries a witness in heaven. The first two 3s, which add up to 6, is the frequency of the completed man.

444, which is 12, is the frequency of creation and of our kingdom as a proxy. This is not the kingdom of sons. This is the kingdom of proxies because the scripture says Moses was a servant in the house (Hebrews 3:5). It is true God calls Israel a son, but Israel never came out of his servanthood to actually act like a son. It is one thing to be a son who becomes a servant, but what makes the servanthood of a son redemptive is that he does not have to serve. In other words, sons can be the laziest people on earth because the house belongs to them. Do you understand why Jesus' servanthood was so powerful in heaven? As a son, He did not have to do any of the things that He did, because everything already belonged to Him. While the servanthood of sonship is redemptive, the servanthood of a slave is destructive and more binding. What makes the difference? A son serves by will, not by compulsion! This is why many Christians are lazy. Did I just say that? Many believers do not want to do the work that God has told them to do and God still blesses them. When you talk to them, you wonder how someone like them is blessed, but they cannot come into rulership and kingship because their wills are not trained. Such sons develop a sense of entitlement. Of course, they are entitled, but a sense of entitlement always removes your ability to function effectively as a ruler.

Entitlement was the problem with the Israelites who stayed home. Those who were scattered learned how to survive among the people. Those who stayed became entitled, which is what is happening in Israel right now. They do not want to work because they think that just by believing in Yahweh and praying, everybody else should take care of them. Israel is one of the most atrocious welfare states in the world. When people become so entitled, they regard every stranger who comes into their land as their enemy who has come to take something away from them. As a result, they cannot open the ark of the covenant because there are 10 names that open the ark of the covenant and one of them is "Lover of the stranger." It is in the Bible! Moses gave a key on how to open the Ark of the Covenant and touch it without dying. Do you realize that Moses could touch the Ark of the Covenant without blood? He could go in and out of the Holy of Holies without doing what the High Priest did. Have you ever wondered why that was so? Check Moses' life.

The number 12 is the number of kingdom. Let us look more deeply into the frequencies of 400. We may know that a piano is out of tune, yet it still makes good music. You can tune it back, but if you do not practice, it will not matter because your frequency will still be off. This is the problem with believers. They think that just by grabbing hold of a concept, they have produced something. That is why believers sit around and play songs with three cords throughout. Are you getting my point? Why should I buy your music just because you are a believer and called by the name of Jesus? Everyone sings the same tune. Nobody comes up with anything new. I want to go to a jazz club and listen to a blues singer who changes his music. Sometimes he sings out of key, but he is creative. Are you getting the point now? I am not trying to push; I am just saying we know it is wrong. What makes Beethoven's, Mozart's, Bach's, Bernstein's, or even Yanni's music so good? What makes some of these neoclassical musicians so good when they are playing with an instrument that is off key by 0.0001%? What makes the Christian music so terrible? Go listen to it and listen to the structure of the music. You will notice that there is no creativity in it. I am sure that all believers have heard some music composed by unbelievers that has moved them deeply.

I have told the young people in my church to find their own sound, create music, and stop trying to sing everyone else's music. I am very serious about that. How do people like Mozart, Beethoven, or Tchaikovsky compose such good music? Do you think it is the instrument? No, it is the will that is placed upon the music! It is an intentional fusing of the will with the music. When you listen to it, it touches you. Secular musicians, even rock 'n rollers do the same thing. Listen to music infused with the will of Michael Jackson. You cannot listen to it and not move; I do not care how strong a believer you are! Sometimes when you have Christians making music and saying the Holy Ghost is the one playing, you can hear that their will is not involved.

I do not let my church musician go into the Spirit when they are playing music. I want them to hear what they are playing. It used to get them frustrated. Sometimes in the middle of a sound coming from heaven, they would kind of space out and I would tell them to wake up now! There is a time for them to go into the Spirit, but not when they are leading us because their lack of alertness is messing up the frequency that is coming in. A priest is not allowed to be caught up in the Spirit when he is ministering to people. If he is going to move in the Spirit, he must be aware because he is the watchman. As a leader, you must be aware about what is going on in the Spirit and be intentional about what you are trying to manifest. People may say this is controlling, but if you allow their will to flutter all over the place, it will cause everybody else to have a problem. I will not let people get hurt under my watch.

Seriously, people get scared. Some people, on the other hand, will come into our meetings and act in certain ways just to see what they can stir up in the people of God. I will not tolerate that behavior and

237

RATSON

I will address it in people who know what they are doing and doing it deliberately because they know the children of God are open. So I make my musicians be the watchman. I say, "You have to watch. I know you want to be in the Holy Ghost. When the time is right, I will release you, but you must wait until I tell you to go because it is not good for me to do this alone. We all need to be involved in taking care of this atmosphere." You may be leading worship when, suddenly you go into the Spirit because it is so sweet. However, because your will is not alert, you do not notice what is happening around you. Now when I go into the Spirit I know when to pull myself back, especially when I am with my brethren. You must have one person guarding. Everybody cannot ascend because that means there is no active will standing at the gate.

When I was learning meditation as a child, they always told us never to do it alone. In fact, the Jews did not teach Kabbalah to single men and single women, or people who were not disciples together in a group. Your wife does not need to go up with you because she needs to be able to pull you back. So if both of you ascend and something happens, they will carry both of you into the hospital. You should take turns. The job of the one who is keeping vigil is the same as the job of the one who goes up.

I have people in my church who are watching. There are about seven or eight people who are watching. Nobody knows who they are, but they are watching. I tell them, "Today I am going up. I am not going to be in charge, so you had better watch! If I start going off the deep end, pull me back down." Really! You have no idea what happens to me when I am alone. My wife has had to wake me up. Once she poured water on me so that I could come back. I did not know where I was. I have learnt to ascend at will. Once you have learnt to ascend at will, an angel can wake you up. Most of us don't know how to get an angel to wake us up. We do not even know when an angel is touching us. We do not know whether it is a touch to wake up or a touch to keep going. I know now in my church what an angel is saying when they are touching me. If I need to stop in worship, the touch of an angel in the congregation will make me stop. Sometimes, if you are watching our videos on YouTube, you will see I will just abruptly stop; and then the Holy Spirit just takes over. So, as you are doing this, watch each other's back.

Can I tell you that we have not yet truly gotten into the Spirit? A lot of the things we are doing, we are really doing in our heads, which is okay. The other day, I was with one of my spiritual daughters online. I went up in the Spirit and I literally took her up with me. When I came down, she was still there crying with tears in her eyes, shaking and I had to go in there and wake her up. I clapped my hands and said, "Get up!" She said "Oh, Papa!" And I said, "It's alright, get up." If you are leading people into this realm, do you know how to get them out if they become stuck?

Let me tell you about a young lady in my church who has never been in this mystical stream. She went into a vision and was caught in a forest. She actually left her body. She was walking around and the people with her wanted to take her to the hospital. For two days she was in this state. She finally said, "Call Dr. Ogbonnaya; I need help!" When they called, I had them put her on the phone and asked for permission to come into her vision. After she said yes, I went into her vision and saw where she was. It was her first time to leave her body and to leave this realm. She was stuck. I said, "Okay, you need to look at me." Her eyes were closed. She started crying and saying, "Dr Ogbonnaya, it's you! It's you! He is in my dreams!" Then I called on the Lord because sometimes that is necessary. She did not know I did that, but when she said "Jesus," she became calm. Then I asked her if she could follow my voice. So, she followed my voice, and in the Spirit, I picked her up, carried her with Christ, brought her to the front of the house, and watched as she walked back into her body.

I do not mean to scare you, but you have certain powers and certain things you have not yet practiced. Some things remain "revelation" to many of us and have not yet become actual practice. This may scare some of you. People need to know that this works!

In all of these things, why is the frequency of the will so important? It is because those people who cause things in the world, imbue it with their will, and make the sacrifice to trade with their will. You do not make a sacrifice with your soul as an individual. All your sacrifices are directed at your will. They are meant to align your will and to strengthen your will to do what you are supposed to do. Remember, a son's servanthood is based on will, and a slave's servanthood is based on compulsion. The servanthood of a son is stronger than anything else in this world. When a son serves, he changes the world. A servant can serve and the world will remain the same, but a son cannot serve intentionally without the world changing.

The number 666 and the number 999 are the same because they both come to 9. 666 is the frequency we use to open up, operate, and trade in the material realm because it has to do with our body. 999 is nine, but it is on a higher octave, which means we are trading beyond just our physical realm and in other realms.

If we take 444 (12) and add another 12, we have 24, which is also the number 6. However, this 24 is higher even than 444, even though it is a 6, because it is a combination of two 12s; it is not just a 6. The number 24 is actually the kingdom of sons, or what we call the kingdom of the crowned ones, who themselves become gateways. This means you carry these positions of an altar that can be traded upon. You become multiple altars that serve as a junction and gateway to other realms. So then, if I sow into your life, you have an altar that receives my blessings. When I bless you, the altar receives my blessing, which opens a gate that I travel through to share in your destiny.

> If God can get your will, He can do anything He wants on the face of the earth.

Consequently, when I serve you or bring into your life any blessing, a certain altar opens and allows me to share some aspect of your destiny. There is an actual exchange that happens, which is what the Bible means when it says we are members of one another. It is not just that we are members of the body of Christ, but that we are members one of another. There are, then, certain things I must do to share in the destiny you carry because it is not yours alone. In addition, I must do it by my will. It cannot be something I am forced to do.

There are different ways of writing 777 in scripture. If I say the number

49, 7×7 probably comes to mind. If you look at it that way, you will say that 49 is not 77; however, it is for the Jew. Let me explain. What is 49 in the Bible? It is jubilee. And what is jubilee? Jubilee represents rest. Remember this: 777 is the frequency for trading into rest. So then, 7 is the number of rest. 49 is 7x7. It is more than a reference to rest. Its meaning applies to periods of 7 years and 7x7 years (or 49). 777 is the principle of rest. Now, this is rest in the present, but it is also rest in the past. It is a rest that reaches into the future and draws back.

Now let us talk about 666 again. Six is a number through which you trade for yourself, you trade for someone in your life, and you trade for the future. In other words, you are trading in three different dimensions of your being. All of these are the frequencies of trading in different aspects of your life: for rest, for man, for yourself, for your seed, and for your future.

555 is multiplication and the sowing of light. You can see there are all kinds of frequencies in scripture.

Are you seeing how these numbers occur in scripture now? They are all over scripture. How many elders are there? There are 72, which equals 9. What is 144? It is 9. The number 144 is not about people going to heaven; it is actually 72 x 2. In reality, it should be 72 above and 72 below.

Let us have a little fun with the number 144,000. When you read about that number in Revelation, you think there must be 144,000 people who will be saved from Israel. Really? That is not what 144,000 means. It is a key towards binding heaven and earth. There are 72 elders and 72 disciples sent out. I am just trying to get you to understand how the number 9 works in scripture. It is so serious, but it is a number we have not studied. Churches do not study the number 9; we do not talk about it. Yet 9 is in every high culture that has ever accomplished anything. What is 9 anyway from a pictorial perspective? Six is a man sitting with his butt on the ground or with his head on the ground and his feet up. Nine is the man standing on his feet with his head in the heavens. It is the same number just turned upside down. All these things we are dealing with were developed by people who were engaged in alchemy. Writing came from divination and soothsaying. Before that, language was written in pictures or pictographs. All the Egyptian alphabets are based on animals and the like, just like most ancient alphabets. And almost all traditional writings have gematric forms.

Again, remember that your will is bound to that the number 9 because your will is the highest trading principle in creation. That is what God is looking for. If God can get your will, He can do anything He wants on the face of the earth. If your will can be aligned to His, you become like Him on earth. It happens by way of submission. Somebody once argued that when Jesus submitted His will to the Father in the garden, His Divinity was restored. If His Divinity had not been restored, He would not have been raised from the dead. Jesus was God, but His Divinity was not allowed to function in its fullness. He was just allowed to function as a human being. He could raise many people from the dead. To raise other people from the dead is one thing, but to raise yourself is quite another. Never say you cannot raise the dead. The real question is whether you can raise yourself from the dead because only God can raise Himself. Do you get the point? So, rising from the dead was Christ's act as God.

Some scholars have said that the resurrection was not important for the Divinity of God. Do you disagree? You cannot raise yourself from the dead. Even in ancient Egypt you needed other people to do magic for your body to be raised. In all the other cultures, you needed the other gods to speak over your body. You needed Zeus to gather your body together, but Jesus says,

> **For this reason the Father loves me, because I lay down my life that I may take it up again. No one takes it from me, but I lay it down of my own accord. I have authority to lay it down, and I have authority to take it up again. This charge I have received from my Father.**
> *(John 10:17-18)*

In case you do not understand that statement, He is telling you that He is God. Anyone who understood the system of the ancients would have known exactly what Jesus was saying immediately. Jesus was adept in the mysteries. Anyone who heard Him would have realized what He was claiming. He actually claimed to be the Most High God! In all the cultures, from Egypt all the way to India to Tibet, the Most High God always says of Himself, "I am the One who raised Myself upon My mount when I was all alone, by Myself." It is the self-raising principle that makes Him God. Imagine Jesus saying that. Everyone who heard Him surely thought that Jesus was crazy!

> **There was again a division among the Jews because of these words. Many of them said, "He has a demon, and is insane; why listen to him?"** (*John 10:19-20*)

Everyone needs God or somebody to raise him. Yet Jesus never said the Father would raise Him. Rather, He said He would raise Himself. It is in the Bible. The structure in the commitment of the will allowed Him to do that. Then He sent out 72 in order to change the land of Israel to a place of supernatural trading with the souls of men. There is much more to it than that, but that is essentially what He did. Likewise, Moses did not take the 72 up the mountain just so they could eat and drink. It was a way of opening a trading floor for Israel because they had access to the sapphire pavement.

The decision to willingly (and not by compulsion) to lay your life down and take it up again is the expression of the will of the Son of God. We are called to be like Him. We are one with Him. By this good will we can change creation.

243

RATSON

פַּעַם

Pa'am

Pa'am (פַּעַם) is Pey (80) Ayin (70) Mem (40). *Pa'am* means hoof beats or the striking of the horse's hoof on the ground, which is a term used for the clock.

PA'AM:
THE BEAT OF TIME

You did not know there were so many words for time in Hebrew, did you? God has a lot to say about time. Hoof beats are connected to actual clock time. Time made by a device has nothing to do with human intervention. If you put a dial under the sun, it merely points you to where the time of day is. You do not have to do anything about it. It is mechanical time.

The funny thing about mechanical time is that you can adjust it. The dimension of mechanical time is one of the places where man gets himself in bondage. When you deal in mechanical time you begin to forgo "event time" and "soul time" so that your time is no longer relational. How people perceive time is the difference between Europeans and Africans. We say Africans are late and they say they are not late. They will tell you that if an event is still going on, there is time. You are late only when the event is finished.

We do not consider how other people live in time. When I go somewhere like a doctor's office where people have appointments, I always watch how people get completely irked if their time is missed. You should know, however, that in the doctor's office, your time means absolutely nothing because it is the time of life. I am learning this more and more because I have a couple of physicians in my family now. They will confirm your appointment time and then tell you it is not your turn if a patient who has a greater need than you comes into the office. You cannot do anything about it because that is life.

The problem with mechanical time is that, although we use it to set time and control the hour, it does not work very well in relationships. Europeans may think mechanical time works, but it causes problems when you come to something one minute late because you were feeding your baby in the car or there was traffic, etc. When you cannot give enough excuses for people to accept that you are late, life becomes a nuisance. I love the Europeans for their time keeping because I am a time person as well. I do not like being late. I do not do late because there is laziness with it. Also, I think part of what happens to us when we build mechanical time and we set things up by it, we become mechanical ourselves. True, we are successful in some things, but it is hard to relate to people whose major emphasis is time. I start on time, but I do not finish on time. I do it deliberately in my church just to the people who are crazy about time shaking. I just keep teaching. I know the time is over. People will say, "But you're not keeping time?" But I say, "Whose time? That clock on the wall?"

I should tell the Holy Ghost to stop moving because I need to stop the service. You know people do that right? We do that. I have been guilty of that; the Holy Ghost is moving and I say I need to go home. I could be like John Wesley. He would be preaching to 20,000 people without a microphone, the Holy Ghost would come down, people would scream and roll around on the ground, and he would just leave because he was off to another town. He did not close the service. God dealt with the people and Wesley just moved on. You see, it is a great thing to control mechanical processes, but it is not very good for human relationships.

However, clock time does something that is very important. Clock time allows you to understand the times of the openings of gates in the day. It also allows you to pinpoint which angel is functioning at each time. This is the reason the clock was invented, not to merely tell time. The clock was developed to understand the gates that are open at specific times within the day and which angel to call specifically at that time. It was developed as a mystical device to open gates in other realms because the first clocks were all 24 hours. The 12-hour clock was standardized not all that long ago when we divided the day into two time periods, AM and PM. The 12 is a division of the two.

There are certain angels that govern the day and the hour based on 24 hours. In fact, the throne room of heaven is set up according to this principle with the 24 elders. The New Jerusalem is the same way with 12 above and 12 below. My books *Hashamayim 1A* and *Hashamayim*

1B have to do with the lower 12 dimensions.

Pa'am is the mechanical structure that allows you to access time in this way. We do not use the clock for prayer anymore. Instead, we use it to time men's lives as a gateway for taking people's lives and paying salaries for them. That is what they do; they pay you for your life, but not what your life is worth. When you are working for someone, you are being paid for your life because your time is your life. Still, the best thing to do is to start your own business. The best thing still is to invent something or discover something. It may take you years longer, but if you succeed it gives you greater independence. Develop a model for what you are doing.

All of this takes practice and self-training. Remember Isaiah 40:31:

...but they who wait for the LORD shall renew their strength; they shall mount up with wings like eagles;

Sometimes God says, "Go do it yourself." Some Christians see God as their fairy godmother, mechanic, and toilet repairer. "Lord, my shoe is broken. Can you fix it please?" God the shoe cobbler! I am not trying to insult people, but I do not think you would treat a king or queen that way, would you? Why then do you do that with God? It is because you do not know the protocol of dealing with all God's servants, so you want God to get off His throne and come fix your toilet. How is that working for you?

Change the way you deal with God and things will be more effective in your life. I have seen this process come over from Judaism. I see Christians going through the same process, asking God to do what they themselves should do, or what angels or some saint from heaven should do. They do not believe in saints and they do not believe in angels, so they make the King of the universe come clean their toilet. I am being sarcastic, but it is true. They do not stop to think that treating God this way

> The dimension of mechanical time is one of the places where man gets himself in bondage.

247

PA'AM

does not make any sense. How can you ask the King of the universe to come and change your child's diaper? It does not mean the King does not like the child; it just means there are servants in the house who do that job. We do not deal with these issues in our lives or approach God the right way because we do not understand protocol. Christians must learn the proper protocol. There are angels who have been assigned to do what you are asking your Father to do. They are standing by while you are bypassing them and telling your Father to come and clean up your house.

I gave a testimony about an angel who repaired my car for me when I used to struggle financially. I talked about how many times I have had my car repaired while it was broken down without a mechanic. I did not go to the Father and say, "Repair my car." I just found out which angels deal with mechanical structures and I called them to come do the work. If I lose my key in my house, I do not say, "Oh God, please let me find my key." Instead, I say, "Okay, who are the angels around me? I need my key." After I have looked everywhere, I have had the key just appear in front of the chair. The angels do their job because they love me. The angels like me because I like them and I relate to them. If you relate to them, they will relate to you. Start acting out of protocol and they will work with you.

Many of your prayers are not answered because you have misdirected your prayer. You are asking the Lord of Lords to come and do something He has given you or the angels around you the power to do. Isn't that how it works in real life? You know how to do this. The problem is when you come to church you lose your sense of decorum and your sense of protocol goes away because now you are equal with God, too. It is true He is your Father, but He has created a structure where you reveal your divinity by learning how to relate to the servants of the house.

> Change the way you deal with God and things will be more effective in your life.

I love dealing with angels. I was talking to one of my friends, teaching him about angels, and he asked me why he needed angels. "I have Jesus. Isn't this what I have the name of Jesus for? Why do I have to talk to angels?"

I said, "Well, how is that working out for you in your industry?"

"Oh, they reject everything I bring out and get all these other guys who are in the occult."

I said, "What? Why doesn't Jesus go and do it for you? He did it the first time because you needed something, but why hasn't He opened another door for you? It is because that gave you the impression you do not need to actually do the work and talk to angels and engage all the other beings to get your work done. So those guys are engaging the angels wrongly, yet they are doing their work while you do not have anybody working for you."

It is the same thing in any business. We can talk about trading on Wall Street or we can talk about using angels to do what you want to do. So, you want to be in competition, and you think your intellect is going to get you there? Even Wall Street bankers have been initiated into something. You have been initiated as well, but you do not want to use what you have been given. It is important to learn this process yourself. Try it; it works. Try saying to the angels around you, "Okay, I don't know who you are, but I know you guys are around, so this is what I need to be done please." You must worship the Father and then ask his permission to deal with the angels. That is what Jews do. They say, "Oh, Master of the universe, Master of all legions, by the permission of the King of the universe, by the permission of the host of heaven, by the permission of the great assembly of saints I now engage the angels and ask them to do what I need them to do."

You get how it works now. You are not arrogant enough to act as though they are just your servants. They belong to a whole plethora of people, so when you ask permission, you release yourself from crossing boundaries.

Once I was traveling to Nigeria with a group of guys. I went on a mission

249

PA'AM

with a white guy and another Nigerian across the Enugu Road. The holes on this road were so bad, you would think a jeep would disappear and reappear on the other side! As if that were not enough, there were also bandits on the road. As we were driving, the car began to sputter. Then one of the guys starts shouting, "Oh God, Oh God, cause this car to get to where it's going, Lord!" I called my angel and I said, "I need you to do something about this car." I saw what happened, but they did not see what happened. The angel came. I told the angel to start the car after about 20 minutes. So, he started the car and we drove from Ore into Lagos, not even stopping for gas. The moment we got into Lagos, the car died completely.

The next time something like this happens, I must use my brain to figure out how to get where I am going. You might get frustrated because angels might help you along the way, but they may not take you all the way. That is why most of us do not get anything done because when we pray for a miracle, we do not expect to be part of the miracle. Angels do what they are supposed to do and we are meant to finish it as part of our training.

What is your place if God does everything? Where is your training as a god? You see, you are supposed to be trained as a god. If God does everything, where is your own training and practice? Most of the time we practice begging until God does it again. In reality, when God does something for you halfway, it is because He believes you have the power to finish it and it is your training to be like Him. It is not God denying you anything. In fact, it is the greatest experience.

I have learnt something from the Lord. When I started raising money for some land in Africa, God started providing the money just like that. It came to the point when we did not need much more money, but I forgot what God had taught me. So, I prayed for a miracle, but God refused to answer because He knew that I should know better. He said, "Use your head." I told Him I did not want to talk to people and He said, "Okay, don't talk to people, but use your head." Then I started praying for strategy to raise the money. Suddenly, just by talking to people and being strategic, people started making promises for the money we needed. But He raised the money. Somebody wrote a $30,000 check on the spot after just one announcement. Then I was in the miracle mode because I was excited.

You know, when God heals someone, you start singing, "Do it again, Lord! Do it again! Do it again, Lord!" But God says, "No you practice." Then we start going back and forth with Him about that. That is really the conversation going on between you and God. God tells you, "No, I want you to practice. If you fail, I will come in and we will do it again." No matter how smart you are, you get dumb with God. There I was in that situation and I wasted all that time praying for a miracle. When He told me to do it myself, I said, "Okay, I need a strategy." Then He told me what to do, I began to practice it, and money started coming in.

> ...what I have learned from God is to ask Him how He did what He did and then show me how I can do it too.

So then, what I have learned from God is to ask Him how He did what He did and then show me how I can do it too. You must get rid of the idea of God doing things for you all the time without you learning how to be a god. You are a growing god. You are a practicing god, an apprentice. That is really what you are. You are a divine novitiate. You are learning your Father's way. You cannot learn something if your Father does everything for you.

Jesus said to them, "Truly, truly, I say to you, the Son can do nothing of his own accord, but only what he sees the Father doing. For whatever the Father does, that the Son does likewise." (*John 5:19*)

Even Jesus said that, if God did something, He learned it, and He did it. He saw what the Father did and then He did the same thing.

The clock theme gives you a space to access the gateways of the day and their angels. Pa'am provides access to the 24 gateways of the day. It reflects the 24 elders in heaven who wear the crowns. Their crowns are the openings to the place of effulgence where the substance of God flows from the realm of nothingness and enters this realm.

251

PA'AM

חָרִישׁ

Charish

The gematria of *Shabbat* (שבת) is 702, which equals nine. It is
"restful time" or *"rejuvenation time."* It is also sacred time that is
impregnated by ordinary time or what we call ordinal time.

CHARISH:
PLOWING TIME IN REST

Remember how God operates when He deals with us regarding rest. The moment of rest is the moment of gestation where all the seeds that have been planted in the ground find a place of rest and get ready to spring forth for the next round. The Sabbath was supposed to be the day to brood on all the work that we did over the past week, and to bring forth the seeds we planted to call their future into this realm. Everything I do this week, every seed I plant, when I rest on *Shabbat*, I reach into the world to come and bring their fruit back into this realm. When you find that place of rest and sit on your seat of rest, every work you have done and every seed you have sown up to the moment of rest, gets a time to access its future.

We must do three things to deliver the harvest: change the process of harvest, bring things from the future into the present, and enter into a time of continuous productivity. For example, you may have a business and every March your business loses money. What will you do? You can start fasting and praying and wondering what is happening in this month. However, maybe one of the reasons that month is not producing is because you are supposed to be resting in it. Nonetheless, you cannot rest in it because you did not sow into its future. Now you keep repeating the same cycle. You pray about the times of your prosperity and do a lot of spiritual work, but you do not work towards that time because you know the pattern of your business already. Everyone intuitively knows how his or her business works. When this month approaches, a fear comes into you and you think, "Man, I am coming to that season again." But you should not think like that. Instead, you should spend time putting your spiritual energy into that season and bring the future into that time. Once you do that, the month will start to produce and you will notice that the cycle of your business will change.

Then you will no longer run into the same situation.

I did this with some friends of mine and with my students in South Africa. I told them to begin to use the angels that they were already dealing with during a prosperous time when things were flowing well. Then I instructed them to send those angels into that "bad" month. You see, you must sow your attention and your spiritual force into that month before you get there. Within a year that month changed for them and now is one of their most productive months. As a result, they are more relaxed in harvesting.

Shabbat is a time that allows you rest, but it is also very productive. It is not really a time of non-productivity. God created *Shabbat* to show you that you can still eat, even in times of famine. *Shabbat* is a key to God's abundance. You have to find this rest. This is not something that God is going to do for you; you have to find it for yourself. You have to learn how to rest and rest well.

In ten minutes you can access more by resting than you can by working, because you work all the time anyway. When do you allow the seed you have sown to actually rest in the ground and speak to its future? What is happening in your life when God does this? He is giving you the opportunity to speak to the future of what you have sown. When you actually do it effectively, you will notice you do not have the so-called "lean months." Things will begin to produce by themselves and repeat themselves. We tend to wait until the month comes and then start praying, "Lord, do something now." However, if we sow towards it ahead of time, if we set our intention towards that month and the people in that month with production, then by the time we get there, the month will give us what we have sown into it.

Most people who own a small business focus on praying only in the moment. When they have increase, they do not pray because they have plenty. Then they wait until the point of lack when they start crying to God. Lack is the result of what you refused to do while you had plenty. I do not say work yourself to death. I am saying that during that time when the business is easy, focus your energy on the time when you expect there is not going to be plenty and see what happens. Put angels to work. Once the cycle changes, it remains the same for a long time. It is rest and rejuvenation time. This is about rectifying your world. I am showing you the times and how you can use them.

It is the same thing with your family. You do not take the time to rest and all of a sudden one of you messes up. Most people mess up when they are tired. If you are tired, go get some rest. Sleep. Be like me and go to bed at 7 pm! There was a time I had to force myself to sleep until the morning. The first time I slept all night from 10 pm until 6 am was in my new house. I slept like a baby and I think it must be the house. But the house is number nine. Could the number nine be what we have discovered in *Shabbat*? Could the number nine itself be the principle by which time is transmuted and by which time itself changes? Could the number nine have something to do with that? How were the Egyptians able to understand space, Sirius, Pleiades, all those places? They had nine gods. The Greeks had nine gods and still do. The house of Odin and all the gods of the Nordic people total nine. All those nines! They discovered there is actually the capacity to transcend time at a certain level.

> The Sabbath is actually a gateway to participate in the life of the Messiah and in the life of the world to come.

God let Israel rest on the Sabbath as a way of allowing them to travel to other realms to trade in divine principles rather than just in the Earth. The *Shabbat* became a gateway, because the Sabbath, the seventh day, is the gateway to the eighth day, which is ultimately the first day. The Sabbath is actually a gateway to participate in the life of the Messiah and in the life of the world to come. One of the best ways to do this is to learn how to rest and how to operate from your seat of rest. God gave the Sabbath, but Israel must take the Sabbath. I am still worried about people who tell me I need to keep the Sabbath on Saturday. I asked them, when did the Gregorian calendar begin? How do you know that the Saturday that you are keeping is the exact Saturday that started from creation? Since the days have changed since that time, your Saturday is not the real Saturday, nor is your Sabbath the real

CHARISH

Sabbath. This is why the Jewish mystics will say, "One man chooses one day; another man chooses another day."

So, man can actually make the Sabbath. The Sabbath was made for man, not man for the Sabbath. Man can make the Sabbath and use it to glorify God. God said,

Remember the Sabbath day, to keep it holy.
(*Exodus 20:8*)

Yet, the Sabbath is more than that—God created the Sabbath for Adam to rest. God also created it for us so we would learn to create a space to rest. It is not just that God rested on the seventh day. Man also rested on the seventh day. God created it for men to rest because that was man's first day, just like a baby. A baby spends its first day of life sleeping because it is hard work to be born. It is hard work to be created, to get up from death, and to become conscious. Adam rested with God on the seventh day. His first day of work was the eighth day. Rest is important. Not just physical rest, but also rest for your soul. Jesus said, "You shall find rest for your souls" (Matthew 11:29). Sabbath time is physical rest that is connected to soul rest. For those who are operating in the spirit, rest allows the spirit to function at its best so it can brood over the body and the soul, over the environment where the work and physical labor occurs.

> Plowing time, charish, is creating a physical earthly space for productivity.

Let us go back to number nine. Your Bible uses different words for time. The problem is that it does not tell you what kind of time it is. *Charish* (חָרִישׁ) means "plowing time" in Hebrew. Its gematria is 518. You can see that $8 + 1 + 5 = 14$, and $1 + 4 = 5$. It is the multiplication principle. You can actually call it the season of intense work or the time for intense work. There are times in your life when you can work for hours and not get tired, and then there are times when you try to work but you just fall asleep or tire very quickly. The problem is, if you do not study your life and study how time affects you, then you will not realize when you are at the peak of your productivity and you will waste it.

I learnt not to pray the way I once did. I was praying to the point of frustrating myself, because I did not feel the Spirit of the Lord. I would have to spend ten hours with the Lord and finally, after ten hours, I would feel the Spirit. That process is living by frustration. Then I realized there are times when the Spirit of prayer just comes upon you. I figured that out and I could pray for twenty hours straight. Why then worry myself after I spent 24 hours in prayer that I did not pray for another two hours every day. I freed myself from that system. It is like trying to spend five hours praying in tongues. It is so tough the first time for people because they could not get themselves to pray in tongues for five hours. It is just so funny that an old man like me could pray for five hours straight and all these young people are falling down, getting sleepy, and behaving as if the world was ending. One thing I have learnt—you practice when you have the power and you figure out when you can actually do it. I can do that from that evening to the next morning until the afternoon nonstop. You can train yourself to do it as well. For instance, the Pentecostals typically pray every Friday night. What do you think they are doing? They understand why Sabbath nights are important and they have an intuitive understanding of peak times for praying.

Plowing time, *charish*, is creating a physical earthly space for productivity. *Charish* a kind of a time when energy just flows through you and it is easy to plow the ground. Many of us are in frustration, because we try to push ourselves when there is nothing left to push. The Bible says,

If the ax is dull, and one does not sharpen the edge,
then he must use more strength; but wisdom brings
success. (*Ecclesiastes 10:10* [NKJV])

So, if the axe is dull or blunt, you have to use the energy you have built up. But if the axe is sharp, what happens? Decide for yourself when you are sharp enough, when you can stay awake without frustrating yourself. If you cannot stay awake, then sleep. Train yourself to rest and then train yourself to stay awake when you cannot. But do not frustrate yourself because anxiety is still anxiety whether it is about God or about serving God. Just because you put God in it does not mean it is not anxiety. The Bible did not say, Be anxious for nothing ... except in serving God. It simply says, "Be anxious for nothing" (Philippians 4:6). When you create anxiety in your life, you actually close the door for your ability to get what you want. Jesus knew it and Paul knew it. Anxiety is one of the greatest debilitating and negative tools that a human being carries and it does not affect anyone but you. Once it gets you, it closes the door for people to be able to reach you. Then you get frustrated with people that they are not doing what you want them to do because you are anxious. Your anxiety has created fear and your fear has built a wall around you that nobody can break through. So obey Jesus and listen to the word that says, "Do not be anxious."

If you understand this, you know that times like these come and go in your life. Remember, there is a time when you are strong and there is a time when you are not. What would you do if the Spirit of the Lord lifts from you while you are doing spiritual things? You would keep forcing yourself to get it done. You try to force God to come back and do it. Before I learned this lesson, I would spend my frustrated spiritual energy, wasting everything that I had built up while I was having a good time with God. I would complain, "Oh God! Why?" I had forgotten I was just having a good time with God last month!

For example, on a recent trip, I had such a great time with God. That trip was so unique and God was so on me, I could feel His presence just by walking down the street. My whole being felt it and I was the one getting scared because God would come upon me and it would feel like I am about to go down under the presence. When I complained, the Lord would lift up and give me space to breathe. You think you actually want God the way you are asking so that He can press on you every day? You have no idea what you are asking for.

The presence was so heavy that I was almost going out of my mind. Now, if the greatness of God and the awe of God are upon a human being continuously, it can actually drive the person insane. I remember I had to say to the Father once, "You know I am a man. Can you please back off?" And He said, "Son, I know," and He backed off because the heaviness is serious. I know this may sound strange to you, but if the whole Kavod (כָּבוֹד) or glory of God landed on you, you would know what that means. I just had a glimpse and I felt like I was going to die. As great as I want to be, I want to be God's son and I know that is what I am. However, my body is not yet trained to handle that kind of presence. Why do you think the high priest went to the temple only once a year? You can handle some of it now because of the Holy Spirit, but you cannot endure all of it because your body still has not been trained to bear that kind of force. God has specific moments when He comes and floods you and this energy comes upon you, but you cannot sustain it. Even for people who go into His presence for five or six days need the Spirit to lift and give them a breathing space.

> If you use the time of your strength, you will have enough strength to continue in those times without anxiety.

So you have *charish* time, when this overflowing capacity comes upon you. Do not waste it. Do not worry about when it goes away. If you go for a month without feeling like praying, it does not mean that God is not with you. I have just committed the Pentecostal sin by telling you that you can go for two weeks without praying and God will still be with you. You will notice that if you do not force and fight it then it becomes easier for you to pray in those times. If you use the time of your strength, you will have enough strength to continue in those times without anxiety. In all that fighting and warfare, you really have only fought with yourself wondering why you cannot pray. "I feel so lost, God! Why have you left me?" He says, "Chill! I am around you. Get back to doing." The feeling is your issue. You think you need to get back to feeling nice. God allows times like these for teaching you not to depend upon your emotions for relationship with Him.

CHARISH

259

עֹלָם

Olam

Olam (עֹלָם) is the word for "eternity" and refers to limitless time. It is Ayin, Lamed, Mem or Final Mem.

You can calculate the gematria of olam as follows:

Mem or Final Mem	Lamed	Ayin
מ	ל	ע
40 or 600	30	70

$$600 \text{ (Final Mem)} + 30 + 70 = 700 = 7$$
$$\text{Or}$$
$$40 \text{ (Mem)} + 30 = 70; \; 70 + 70 = 140 = 5$$

Here you have an olam with a gematria of 700, which is also a Shabbat that opens up to double dimensions. Olam is a word used as "time," and it is used as "eternity" as well. Jewish philosophers call it "timeless time." They say that God created the Earth in timeless time, in a period of time that can be elongated back to eternity and to the future into eternity. Yet olam is a specific time.

The word olam can mean eternity, but it can also mean "worlds." The person with olam is operating in parallel times. If you left your body and found yourself in another time zone, you would be functioning in these parallel time zones at the same time. This is just an example. If I left my body when I am in my bed and decide to visit a friend in Japan, I have to bypass four other time zones to be there. I am present there and, if I really am operating with my various bodies, I should be able to leave my imprint in all the other zones. One of the gifts you were given when you were born from heaven is that eternal timeless time, which is the capacity to operate in parallel time zones. You can actually operate in different places at once. If I left my body and went to Kenya spiritually, I will still be here while I am operating over there. So I will operate in two different time zones on Earth.

Every planetary system in the universe has its own particular mode of time. On Earth, it is 24 hours. On Mars, it is 36 hours.

If you are here on Earth and you are also in heaven, how many worlds are you in? By virtue of the gift that was given you in your birth, which is the gift of eternity, when you activate that and are able to truly leave your body, your body can function fully in all kinds of time zones on Earth. Not many of us can actually take our physical body

> The person with olam is operating in parallel times.

with us when we go. I have gone, but I have not been conscious of going with my body, even though I have come back with marks on my body proving I was there.

Thus, the idea of olam is your access to divine time. In other words, the gift of the divine time gives you access to worlds and their time zones so that you can actually operate in parallel universes. Now we know this concept has not been taught in the church, but Jesus said it very easily:

> **... I will come again and will take you to myself, that where I am you may be also. (*John 14:3*)**

If I am where Christ is, then I am already in another time within the context of eternity. I can do only that because I have received the gift of eternity. Eternity is not just in my heart—my very life and salvation are a gift of eternal life. This gift of Eternal Life gives you the capacity to live in multiple worlds at the same time.

In this way, olam becomes one with the word for God. God is called Adonai ha'olam which means "God of all time zones" or "God of all worlds." This is what we become when we are saved. We can use this gift by training ourselves to go from here to there. When I say you can leave your body, I am not doing that because I want you to be somebody who says: "I left my body yesterday and I went in the air and I was looking down on the city." That is not what I am trying to do.

What I am trying to do is to have you actually experience the worlds that you came through as you were born into the earth. As you were born again, because you came through the ages, you came through eternity and passed through worlds to become a born-again believer. You actually came from the realm of God and through the universe to get here. The reason you did that was God released you from inside the throne room. From inside His own being, He let you come through the structures of creation so that all creation can feel your vibration as you are being born again. When you are born again, there is an affirmation of the sound that you carry throughout the entire universe.

It is not as if you just came from heaven and plopped on Earth. You actually went from infinity to time. You were born in eternity and you were transported into time, which means you carry the gift of eternity by virtue of being born. Eternity is already in your heart as one who is a human being created by God. That means that you have now a double witness. You have eternity in your heart as a human being and eternity is a gift to your being because you came from eternity. This sound leaves a mark on your DNA, which replicates the frequency of your being in all of creation. You came from the edge or the margin of creation, also known as the event horizon. In fact, you came from beyond the event horizon and through the event horizon. As you come through the corona of creation itself, you leave your mark on the edge of the universe. Your resonance is there and comes through it all the way to this moment. Whatever you do now as a child of God, the resonance and the frequency of your identity vibrates throughout the universe.

Because you came through that dimension, they must remember your frequency as it continues to expand. Everything that comes out from there carries your frequency. There is nothing God will ever create or that His creation will ever produce that does not know who you are. God took eternity and encapsulated it in me when I was born from above. The first gift that God gave me was the gift of eternity, which is the gift of Himself. This means that my new soul has a record and a sound that the universe can understand. That is what changes in you as a believer, that capacity where Satan does not know your name anymore. The resonance is different. This is why you can talk about the fact that you are a stranger in this current world (not a stranger to the

OLAM

world but a stranger in it because your sound is different).

Until the sound becomes a reality on Earth, your sound is a strange sound in the earth. Your sound is re-creating the earth. You do not realize how much the sound of a believer causes the people who are in control to keep changing their plans and strategies. "The sun shall not smite you by day nor the moon by night," (Psalm 121:6) because the frequency of your being has to pass through all of these dimensions to get here.

Remember, we started this book by talking about if Christ is what He is, then there is nothing in the universe that does not know who He is. If you are who you are in Him and your will is connected to Him, then there is nothing in the universe that does not know who you are. There is nothing in the universe you cannot overcome.

> When you are born again, there is an affirmation of the sound that you carry throughout the entire universe.

To push it further, you come from the very center of who Christ is. The resonance of His being is in everything. When you come through the matrix of creation and pass through all the galaxies and worlds to come here, the very sound of Christ Himself is upon you. Therefore, creation knows who you are because it is no longer the sound of Adam; it is olam.

זֶרַע
Zera

The word zera is Zayin, Resh, Ayin (זֶרַע). It is the word for seed or offspring in Hebrew, and is used for time as well.

ZERA:
THE ALCHEMY OF TRANSMUTATION

Every seed encapsulates time. It draws the future into the present. Zera is a very important concept. The way it is used in scripture is always called "sowing time," but it is translated as just time. So time is a seed in itself.

The use of time or zera is the alchemy for transmuting time. This is different from time itself. It is the use of time, yet it is connected to time. If you take time and use it in a particular way, it changes the structure of the time. How do you structure your life so that you can use time to change things?

I have a revelation of building this mechanical structure using the name of God, His four faces, and the four elements. Think of the structure as a four-sided pyramid that you build from the ground up using the vibration and frequency of your voice. Look at the following diagram as if you are looking down on a four-sided pyramid. You stand inside the pyramid at the center. The Shin is at the top of the pyramid.

You can use this pyramid to do meditative exercises to train your body, soul and brain to engage God and the structures He has created. It is an effective understanding and practice for unlocking powers of times and divinity. Here are some exercises for you. You won't be able to do them all at first, but that is not a problem. It is about continual engagement and change.

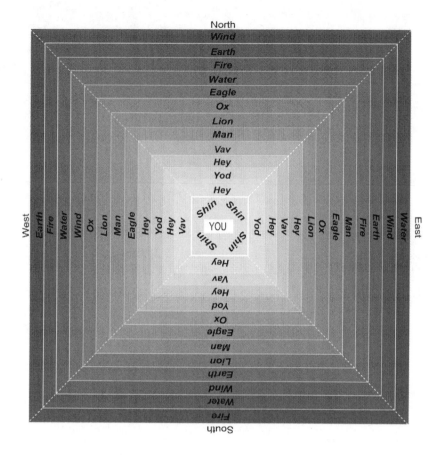

You can start by facing the East and speaking / chanting "Yod," rotate to the right, "Hey," rotate to the right, "Vav," rotate to the right, "Hey," and so on, according to what it shows you as the first four layers of the pyramid. The letters are all around you. The "Yod Hey Vav Hey" is in front of you, the "Hey Vav Hey Yod" is on your right, the "Vav Hey Yod Hey" is behind you, and the "Hey Yod Hey Vav" is on your left. The key is for you to try to see them simultaneously without having to read them. If you can get close to that, you are now beginning to see sixteen dimensions at once. You force yourself to see all of them and where they are.

You must practice this process. Once you set them up around you, try to see them completely. You can use the English (YHVH instead of the Hebrew letters) and do the same thing. Any way you do it, the key is for you to be able to close your eyes and see all of them at once, which means you do not need to use your eyes. If I tell you see to something in the spirit, you start pushing your eye forward to try to look at it, which means you are not seeing. You are still trying to use your physical mode to see what is spiritual. If I told you in English to take VHYH and put it behind you on the ground as a structure like Lego, can you see it? Do you need your eyes to see it? If you placed it there, is it not there? One of the keys to seeing is that the things are there simply because they are there. You do not need your eyes to create them, yet they are present.

Put YHVH in front of you. Try not to see it with your eyes, just perceive it. As you are saying the YHVH and the VHYH, look at them simultaneously without having to shift your mind back and forth. It is doing something to your brain. Now take the HVHY on your right. Now look at the three of them. Push yourself to see them. You notice that your left brain is really quiet, but both your frontal and back lobes and your right brain are busy. Now take that perceived image and add the HYHV on the side. Then, without moving, focus on all four sides, all sixteen structures, at once. The goal is not that you can actually see them immediately. The goal is what is happening to your brain and mind. At a certain point, after you have been working at this for a while, your mind will be frustrated. But you have to keep working at it. You have to be willing to bend your mind.

Now let us add another twenty dimensions on top, by adding YHSVH. You have to see the twenty dimensions above and, at the same time, see the sixteen below. To push yourself, move to the Man, Lion, Ox, and Eagle, and look at them in the four dimensions around you. Now you are looking through the Lion, through the name of Yeshua and the name of Yahweh at the bottom. In that case, you are looking at 52 structures. What if I say to you, now look from above, and add the elements Fire, Earth, Wind and Water, which add another sixteen

The use of time or zera is the alchemy for transmuting time.

269

ZERA

dimensions. You are now looking at 68 dimensions simultaneously. Adding the name of God makes it 70 dimensions. If I tell you to add Malchut (the name of the structure itself) and Uriel (its Cherubic angel) to the center, you would have 72 dimensions. Then try to grasp all 72 at once. If you say you can do it, then that is not true. This practice is not meant for you to be able to do it; it is meant to push your mind beyond its limitation.

> At a certain point after you have been working at this for a while, your mind will be frustrated. But you have to keep working at it. You have to be willing to bend your mind.

Can you actually perceive the 72 at once? Not really. Your mind, body, and spirit know it, but it is hard for you to bring it into the focus of your mind. It is just one practice. Close your eyes and move the letters like you are moving the squares on a Rubik's cube. Shift the YHVH to the right, HVHY to the back, the VHYH to the left, and the HYHV to the front. Every time you shift them, see them in a different position.

Keep shifting the letters until you bring the YHVH back in front of you and keep looking at it. Each time you stop, look at the letters in a different position. Shift the YHSVH to the left while you shift the other one to the right. Shift one clockwise and shift the other one counter-clockwise. You can do that because your mind is much more complex and capable than you actually realize. Start doing the same thing with the Lion, the Ox, and the Eagle. Shift their positions from left to right and clockwise. With the fire above your head, move it around, and then move it left. You are now moving two things clockwise and the other two things counter-clockwise. Now speed them up. Speed it up as fast as your mind can. Breathe.

I want you to put Yod in front of you and push it as far away from you as you can in your mind's eye. Push the Yod far away to the ends of the universe. Just keep pushing it until it comes to the end of wherever your consciousness can take you. Now pull back the Yod until it comes back to your chest. Go to your right, take the Hey, and bring it close to your ear. Now push it away from your ear towards the right, keep going until you get to the end of where your consciousness can take you. Now bring it back all the way to your ear. Go to your back, put the Vav right behind your neck by your pineal gland, and push it away from your back. Keep pushing. Now bring it back and let it just touch your back. Take the Hey on your left, get it close to your ears, look at the Hey at your left, and now push it away from yourself. Focus on that side and push that Hey far away. How far can you go? Now bring it back. Breathe. Open your eyes.

Now to look at the inside of the back of your head where there is nothing. Do not try to figure out anything. Stop every part of your thinking process. Do not think or hear anything else. Simply focus on inside the back of your head and see nothing but darkness. Do not try to conjure light because that is your temptation and you are trying to see angels. I do not want you to see anything because this exercise is the key to the revelations in your life. Even if you can do that for one minute, you will have a greater breakthrough when you come out than you will by exerting unnecessary energy to do other things. Find that place in the back of your head and just stay where there is nothing because, as we know, creation comes out of nothing.

You now have an amazing introduction to governing time, with powerful insights and understandings and exercises. Remember, God wants this for you even more than you want it for you. It was His idea. So be at rest and, in relationship with God and all of heaven, begin your journey of unlocking the powers of times and Divinity!

271

ZERA

יהשוה

Yeshua

NAMES OF GOD

Therefore God has highly exalted him and bestowed on him the name that is above every name, so that at the name of Jesus every knee should bow, in heaven and on earth and under the earth, and every tongue confess that Jesus Christ is Lord, to the glory of God the Father. (Philippians 2:9-11)

...the one who sows to the Spirit will from the Spirit reap eternal life. And let us not grow weary of doing good, for in due season we will reap, if we do not give up. (*Galatians 6:8b-9*)

Names of God		
Hebrew	**Transliteration**	**Meaning**
אֶהְיֶה אֲשֶׁר אֶהְיֶה	Ehyeh-Asher-Ehyeh	I Am that I Am
יהוה	Yehovah	The Name of God
יְהֹשֻׁעַ	Yeshua	Jesus
ישוע המשיח	Yeshua HaMashiach	Jesus the Messiah
אֱלֹהִים	Elohim	God
אֵל שַׁדַּי	El Shaddai	God Almighty
יהוה אֵל עֶלְיוֹן	Yahweh El Elyon	God Most High
יהוה יראה	Yahweh Yir'eh	God Provides
אֵל הַכָּבוֹד	El HaKevod	God of Glory
אֵל הקדוש	El HaKadosh	Holy God
אֵל עולם	El Olam	Everlasting God
אֵל הַשָּׁמַיִם	El HaShamayim	God of Heavens
אלוהי צבאות	Elohei Tz'vaot	God of Hosts
אֵל אֱמֶת	El Emet	True God
יהוה שמה	Yahweh Shamah	God is there
יהוה נִסִּי	Yahweh Nissi	God is my banner

ZERA

ABOUT THE AUTHOR

Adonijah Okechukwu Ogbonnaya (BA, MATS, MA, Ph.D) is the founder of AACTEV8 International, an Apostolic and Kingdom Ministry which works with the Body of Christ across the globe for Soul Winning, Discipleship, Training, and Equipping the saints in Kingdom mysteries and Kingdom living. Located in Venice, California, Dr. Ogbonnaya (also known as A. Okechukwu or "Dr. O") began preaching the Word of God in the 1970s in his teenage years. He has served as a missionary, church planter, pastor, and professor. Dr. Ogbonnaya has traveled and ministered in over 25 nations in Asia, Africa, Europe, and North and South America with the message of the Gospel of Jesus Christ. He has seen God perform various signs and wonders as He promised in Mark 16:1–17 - the blind receive sight, the deaf hear, the lame walk, the dead are raised, the barren receive the fruit of the womb, lives are transformed and minds renewed. He has focused on helping believers engage the spiritual realities which have been opened up for them in the person of the Lord Jesus Christ. He is a Hebrew-born native of Nigeria, West Africa. He earned his Ph.D and Master's degree in theology and personality and his Master's in religion from Claremont School of Theology. He completed his M.A. in theological studies at Western Evangelical Seminary and his B.A. in religion at Hillcrest Christian College in Canada. He also holds a Ph.D in business publishing.

He is also the presenter of numerous teachings found at: www.aactev8.com.

Dr. Ogbonnaya is married to Pastor Benedicta and is blessed with four wonderful children and grandchildren.

SeraphCreative

Heaven's Heart for Earth

Seraph Creative is a collective of artists, writers, theologians & illustrators who desire to see the body of Christ grow into full maturity, walking in their inheritance as Sons Of God on the Earth.

Sign up to our newsletter to know about the release of the next book in the series, as well as other exciting releases.

Visit our website :
www.seraphcreative.org

Made in the USA
Las Vegas, NV
18 September 2022

55532774R10155